MEANING AND PURPOSE IN THE INTACT BRAIN

MEANING AND PURPOSE IN THE INTACT BRAIN

A philosophical, psychological, and biological account of conscious processes

ROBERT MILLER

CLARENDON PRESS · OXFORD
1981

Oxford University Press, Walton Street, Oxford OX2 6DP

LONDON GLASGOW NEW YORK TORONTO
DELHI BOMBAY CALCUTTA MADRAS KARACHI
KUALA LUMPUR SINGAPORE HONG KONG TOKYO
NAIROBI DAR ES SALAAM CAPE TOWN
MELBOURNE AUCKLAND

Published in the United States by
Oxford University Press, New York

British Library Cataloguing in Publication Data

Miller, Robert
Meaning and purpose in the intact brain.
1. Consciousness
I. Title
153 BF311
ISBN 0–19–857579–3

Filmset in Monophoto Times
by Latimer Trend & Company Ltd, Plymouth
Printed in Great Britain
at the University Press, Oxford
by Eric Buckley
Printer to the University

Preface

This book has evolved slowly over a period of five or six years. Most of the writing has taken place in the last three years, and has formed, until recently, a number of independent small articles, none of which were publishable by themselves. Only in the last six months have I seen the possibility of linking them all together in the form of a monograph, thanks to the Oxford University Press and their advisers.

Some comments are needed on my use of the literature. Biologists in general, and with good reason, distrust long chains of reasoning, unsupported by experimental evidence. I have therefore tried, as far as possible, to cite research findings which support theoretical postulates, even though this does not generally amount to proof of that postulate. I never cease to be amazed at how much information is actually available in a university library, and I find that almost any question which I, as a non-specialist, can ask, has been investigated by others. I have therefore tended to use the library as my laboratory—first framing my own questions, then investigating the experimental literature, to see which hypotheses were most viable. In doing so, I hope I have not been totally unaware of pitfalls of particular experimental techniques, or of the dangers of extrapolating too easily from animal brains to the human brain. The literature which could be cited in a book like this is vast, and I have tried to limit this to allow easier reading. In general I have attempted to cite review articles, or references that are sufficiently recent to allow easy access to other literature on the particular point at issue, though sometimes a particular matter requires an older reference for support.

An essay like the present book rests on a vast amount of experimental work performed in many laboratories in many countries. I would therefore like to acknowledge my enormous debt to all these dedicated scientists whose work has influenced my thinking. Only a proportion of these are actually cited in the reference list, and only a handful of them have I actually met. I feel I should also acknowledge, in rather an Irish fashion, the smaller number of people who have influenced me by their provocative remarks at one time or another. In fact the foundations of this book were laid during the periods when I was forced to work out why I had found their remarks so provocative. Apart from these influences, I also trace some of the ideas presented here to chance comments by friends and acquaintances, which served as pointers for me, when I was unsure in which direction the argument should move.

In particular I wish to thank Bill Trotter for having established such a congenial environment in the Department of Anatomy, in which to undertake a work of this nature. I am most grateful to Charles Phillips, whose continuing interest and support of this work was instrumental in its appearance in monograph form. I thank George Gordon and Peter Usherwood, who in different ways, have given me vital support in the years before I came to Otago; and I thank Dick Laverty and Richard Faull for a number of specific pieces of advice on matters where I was out of my depth. I am indebted to Chris Heath, and Robin Harvey on whom I could always rely for constructive criticism of the manuscript in preparation; and I am grateful to Margaret Ogilvie for her design and preparation of the diagrams. Finally, I would like to thank my wife Mary; without her help it would certainly have been more difficult.

Otago RM
August 1980

Can all the sky,
Can all the World, Within my Brain-pan ly?

Thomas Traherne (*c*. 1636–74)

Contents

Introduction

A GLANCE at any list of titles of academic journals in the biomedical area will give an indication of the large amount of space within university libraries devoted to the neurosciences. For instance, in any edition of *Current Contents* (*Life Sciences*) approximately 10 per cent of journals listed relate solely to the neurosciences; about a further 15 per cent of less specialized journals contain a varying proportion of articles dealing with the nervous system. Journal titles also indicate another feature of contemporary neurosciences besides the sheer volume of literature in this field, namely, the tendency for the neurosciences to be divided into a large number of subdisciplines—neuroanatomy, neurophysiology, neuro- and psychopharmacology, neurochemistry, psychology (itself subdivided into several different approaches)—and also several clinical disciplines—neurology, psychiatry and neuropathology. Perhaps the most fundamental division here is between the various biological approaches and the rather different approaches adopted by psychologists.

These observations are an easy measure of the large amount of scientific effort which has been devoted, especially in recent years, to the study of nervous systems in man and animals. It is also surely an indication that a considerable foundation of knowledge has been laid down. If, however, we ask, 'What is the long-term aim (if any) of this large-scale endeavour?' the picture becomes rather less clear.

Ask an 'intelligent layman' what he thinks is, or should be, the goal of brain research, and he or she will probably say, 'to understand the nature of consciousness' or some similar phrase. From such a general statement we could derive a number of more precise goals: 'to understand the whole intact brain and its role in behaviour and experience'; 'to define psychological concepts in biological terms'; 'to bring within the scope of rational medicine the various neurological and psychiatric disturbances whose effect is mainly shown at the level of the whole person'.

If we put any such questions to the average practising neuroscientist it is more than likely that he will dodge the questions in one way or another. In particular he may say that we lack sufficient basic information even to think of tackling such large-scale questions. The common belief among neuroscientists appears to be that the only way forward is by step-by-step advance, each step made certain by rigorous experiment. Any synthesis in the neurosciences, giving a picture of the whole, if it is ever to be achieved, will come about at some indefinite time in the unforeseeable future. However, the present book has, as its main driving force, a rather different set of beliefs: (i) a logical approach to all of the above questions is possible, but not until satisfactory solutions have been found to certain theoretical and/or philosophical problems; (ii) we are not making sufficient use of the wealth of knowledge in the neurosciences which already exists. This book is thus an attempt at analysis of some of these theoretical problems, which may help lay a foundation upon which synthesis in the brain sciences can be built.

Consider the claim that we need more basic information in the neurosciences before attempting any synthesis. Certainly there are many areas of research where the experimental approach can be expected to bring forth much new knowledge, some of it undoubtedly of enormous significance. But there are also many signs that the problem of synthesis is not soluble using this approach alone.

First, and most obvious, is the universal complaint that there is now so much current literature relating to any one topic that it is scarcely possible to keep abreast of it. To keep up with current research findings in the neurosciences as a whole is now *quite* impossible—even if one completely abandoned any ambitions of producing original experimental findings oneself. Hand-in-hand with this overwhelming problem is the fact that to actually survive in academic life it is almost universally necessary to specialize upon a tiny area of knowledge, so that a narrow-minded approach to the large questions is positively encouraged. Sometimes this shows itself when scientists adopt postures of territorial defensiveness of their own subspeciality, coupled with dismissal of many other equally important subspecialities, though this may reflect a hidden wish to avoid the enormous task of assimilating the vast amount of information produced by alternative approaches.

A third attitude, which is sometimes noticeable amongst scientists with an international reputation in the neurosciences, is the unwillingness to answer (or even to voice tentative opinions on) questions which lie outside their own subdiscipline, but which, in terms of biological or medical ideas, are in fact closely related to their own sphere of interest. No doubt this is a realistic attitude on their part, since it is a formidable enough task to become master of the techniques and achievements in one subdiscipline, let alone to be able to relate the different subdisciplines to one another.

At a lower level, discussion amongst neuroscientists is much more commonly concerned with the technical details of an experimental approach rather than with the biological ideas to which a piece of work relates. This is also evident in the vast majority of research papers, which seldom explore in much depth the significance of new findings with respect to ideas of brain function. Often, research papers are regarded in a hypercritical manner because in themselves they are in some way technically incomplete, and have significance only when considered in the context of a large body of other literature, much of which itself may be similarly incomplete. The occasional brave soul, who, in an attempt to define useful new ideas with respect to brain function, tackles a bigger problem than his (or anyone else's) experimental methods can analyse, usually meets with a scornful reception from his colleagues.

What inferences can be drawn? To some extent these attitudes reflect the different reactions people have to a situation in which there is not enough time to come to terms with the enormous expansion of neuroscience literature. But they are also an indication that the acquisition of new information in the neurosciences is now such a highly technical business that it is becoming increasingly difficult to be competent technically and at the same time to be very deeply concerned with the fundamental ideas which are at stake in current neuroscience research. Consequently, the major subdivisions within the neurosciences relate to the type of experimental technique used, rather than to the biological ideas which are under investigation. Communication is easy between those who use similar techniques. Comparison of the concepts which are the driving force in the different subdisciplines is very difficult. Thus, the development of ideas which attempt to unify the different subdisciplines is greatly hindered.

No doubt the situation I describe is true in many branches of science at present, but in the neurosciences it is particularly undesirable. The brain is perhaps the most complicated entity which scientists will ever study. Although it is generally convenient to study it as a set of parts, as in the single nerve cell approach of the electrophysiologist, or the particulate fractions which the neurochemist obtains by differential centrifugation, nevertheless, the interrelationships of these parts to one another are exceedingly rich and complex, in all respects in which we can study them—anatomical, electrical, chemical or functional. It is a truism to suggest that the most important aspects of the operation of the brain are a property of the intact organ, and cannot be deduced from a study of the separated parts of the brain. If we are ever going to be able to understand these aspects of brain function, relating to the structure as a whole, it will require consideration of all or of several subdisciplines simultaneously, so that ideas can be formulated which are consistent with data derived from all branches of the neurosciences. It will also be necessary to take more seriously the large number of papers which are not self-contained and complete. Clearly it will be difficult to move in this direction unless different subdisciplines can communicate with each other and can compare and contrast their different ideas about brain function.

This weakness of contemporary neurosciences applies not only to the strictly academic aspects of the subject, but also to its practical clinical aspects. Neurological and psychiatric disorders are amongst the most incomprehensible and frightening of human ailments. They often seem to reflect disturbances at a level so fundamental that all aspects of the mind and personality may become disorganized in consequence. If these disorders are to be placed within the framework of rational medicine a global understanding of brain function will be necessary. The traditional approach of correlating anatomical lesions with functional deficits will not be adequate for an understanding of disturbances which affect the atom-like unity of the mind.

It may be objected here that any sort of global scientific understanding of the human brain is basically beyond the capacity of the human mind. Certainly it is likely that there are theoretical limits to what scientific man can understand when he is dealing with something of the same order of complexity as himself. However, the implication of this is that it is impossible for an individual scientist to understand another human individual in the scientific sense. When considering the *general* principles governing the functioning of the mammalian (including human) brain, one is studying something at a lower level of complexity than the unique individual. It is by no means clear that there are theoretical limits to the understanding of such principles.

Viewed in historical perspective, science consists of a fruitful interaction between experiment and theory, between observation and idea. Often it can be seen that fields of enquiry pass through successive phases—an experimental phase in which large amounts of information are gathered either by direct description or by experiments designed to test small-scale theories—followed by a phase of synthesis in which such information is worked into a much larger coherent theoretical whole. Viewed in closer perspective, however, the relationship of theoretical to experimental science at any one time has often been far from harmonious. Radically new theories—such as Galileo's idea that the earth moved around the sun, or Darwin's theory of the origin of species—arouse consternation and resistance, not usually because the observations on which they are based are in question but because of their reinterpretation in novel or otherwise unacceptable theoretical contexts. Other examples have been given by Polanyi (1958, p. 150). The creative interplay between experiment and theory is most firmly established in physics, though there have been periods of strong resistance to theoretical physics, particularly in Germany during the 1930s (Beyerchen 1977).

It is not surprising that experimental and theoretical disciplines should frequently have mistrusted one another. Formulating a theory and investigating one are quite different mental activities, and use logic in different ways. The experimentalist is concerned with testing hypotheses. In this the primary form of logic used is deductive, for deriving testable particular predictions from a general statement. The theoretician, on the other hand, uses primarily inductive logic for arriving at a general statement which is compatible with a number of particular items of evidence. Admittedly he may present his theory as a deduced statement—such as a chain of mathematical reasoning—and in such a form the experimentalist is naturally likely to find it more acceptable. But the actual process of deriving the theoretical statement (which does not concern the experimenter unless he is versatile enough to have a foot in both camps) must involve some form of inductive inference. For instance, the realization that a number of particular steps in an argument (be it verbal or mathematical) can be combined together to produce a far more important argument, has a vital inductive component. (It should be pointed out here that this distinction between deductive and inductive inference forms an important theme later in this book, though for quite different reasons from those outlined above.)

At the turn of the twentieth century all branches of the neurosciences were contained within one discipline. Attempts to create unifying ideas were limited by the inadequate groundwork of basic information, but not by communication difficulties. In the last 40 years the neurosciences have been through a phase of massive accumulation of data. I believe that an imbalance now exists between experimental evidence and theoretical constructs, and that some of the most exciting advances to be made in the next 40 years will be theoretical in nature. In particular, it is hoped that these will centre around the deepest rift in the neurosciences—that between psychology and biology. At present the psychologists have almost all of the theory, some of it potentially very fruitful, and very little solid evidence which can be accepted unambiguously without also having to accept many theoretical assumptions. In contrast, the biological neuroscientists possess most of the solid factual information, but very little of the theory. Until these two can interact at a fundamental level, global approaches to brain function cannot have many successes; nor can psychological theories be formulated in biological terms, and unambiguously resolved by experiment. Only if this interaction can be brought about will we be using existing knowledge to its best advantage. In short, I am suggesting that it is high time that a theoretical subdivision of the neurosciences should emerge, *complementary* to the various experimental disciplines.

What should theoretical brain research consist of? A variety of talents are required. (i) Most important is the intellectual skill involved in formulating new concepts. This includes powers of analysis of existing concepts, and an imaginative approach in recombining published items of information in novel ways, always striving for the greatest economy in any reformulation. Occam's razor—the rule that unproven postulates should be kept to the absolute minimum—is thus the keystone of a theoretical discipline. (ii) In addition any theoretician should have a wide knowledge of the neurosciences literature, and probably first-hand knowledge of a variety of experimental approaches to the study of the nervous system. Thus, in interpreting the literature the limitations of methods can be appreciated, the general nature of experimental work will be understood, and suggestions for future lines of experimentation can bear in mind those factors which determine the feasibility of an experiment. (iii) Skill in the use of library facilities and of information handling techniques would be an advantage, so that large amounts of literature can be studied and systematized in such a way as to permit easy access to all kinds of detailed information, as and when it becomes relevant. (iv) Scientific theories are often formulated in mathematical terms. Undoubtedly mathematical and computing skills have an important part to play in theoretical neuroscience. (v) Some of the more complex theories are formulated, at least initially, in non-mathematical form, especially when the number of interacting variables is very great. The classic example is Darwin's theory. Many theories in the neurosciences may be of this nature, and may have to be formulated using verbal rather than mathematical logic. For this a training in philosophy would seem to be a valuable qualification, especially since there is a large area of common ground between the fundamental issues of philosophy and the theoretical approach to whole brain function.

1. Philosophical background

1.1. Introduction

THE title of this monograph—'Meaning and purpose in the intact brain'—was chosen with deliberation. It turns out that the most characteristic end-product of conscious processes, those processes served by the intact brain, are the apprehension of meanings and the formulation of purposes.

The two words 'meaning' and 'purpose' can be used naïvely and we may think we understand, but when we enquire more deeply they become problematical. For a start these two words can be used at a variety of levels. One may speak of the meaning of a simple word, or some other sign, and one may speak of the purpose of a simple action. Such usages of the words merge into larger scale notions of meaning when considering a complex concept or complex phenomenon, and the purpose of complex strategies or philosophies of action. The same words are also used for posing universal questions about the 'meaning' and 'purpose' of our existence. It is not proposed to give any particular answer to these latter questions, merely to note that in so far as many of us want to ask such questions, it is an extension of fundamental faculties which all of us use continually in other contexts.

Apart from the wide range of phenomena which are included under these terms we have, however, the difficult problem of understanding what general class of phenomena these words refer to. These words can be taken in two rather different senses. On the one hand, we might point to observable pieces of behaviour which indicate the apprehension of meaning, or the formulation of a purpose: Archimedes jumping from his bath at the moment of comprehension, or some complex piece of skilled behaviour which obviously fulfils a predetermined goal. On the other hand, we all know that we can apprehend a particular meaning, or formulate a new purpose *without* showing any overt outward sign that we do so. In this case these processes seem to be internal, subjective happenings. They are not to be *observed* but rather to be *experienced*. With this statement we are plunged into age-old metaphysical questions about what phenomena we should consider to be real, and what are the relative merits of observation and experience as methods of discovering reality. The primary aim of this initial chapter is to present a brief discussion of these issues, and express some personal opinions on them. These opinions are hardly likely to be universally acceptable, and indeed it seems improbable that unambiguous resolution of these metaphysical issues will ever come about. It is, however, quite necessary to make explicit the general conceptual framework in which consciousness—in the rest of this book—is to be discussed. In this process we will also touch upon a number of other philosophical issues, some of which come to have important significance again towards the end of the book.

Ideas about the nature of reality are the most fundamental of all ideas. Hence, it is impossible to derive them by logical appeal to yet more fundamental ideas. It is impossible, therefore, to obtain a definite, logically secure decision when two proponents put forward opposing views on the nature of reality. The most that philosophy can hope to achieve in this is to present each position in the most consistent form possible, so that the implications of each position are displayed with optimum clarity.

Even before we begin discussing metaphysical issues an awkward problem is evident. One of the stated aims of this book is to enquire into the process of apprehension of meaning. Throughout this book it will be necessary to use words to refer to abstract ideas. Yet it is a virtually impossible task to give precise definition to the meaning of an abstract word. Indeed, at the present stage of the argument the nature of meaning itself is still very hazy. Should one conclude from this that meaningful communication between humans about abstract ideas is simply not possible? I believe not.

In fact this paradox is but an example of a much larger paradox, which happens to be one of the most important themes in this book. This concerns the validity or otherwise of inductive inference. Inductive and deductive inference are commonly contrasted with one another: the former is argument from particular statements to a general statement; the latter from a general statement to a particular one. Deductive inference apparently presents no problems, because if the premises of an argument are true the conclusions must also be true. In the case of inductive inference, the truth of the conclusions cannot be guaranteed but only suspected with a varying degree of certitude. Later in this chapter many examples of this will be given. Here it is appropriate to refer to David Hume, the philosopher who most pointedly drew attention to the fallibility of inductive inference—as in the following quotation:

> 'Tis evident that Adam with all his science, would never have been able to demonstrate that the course of nature must continue uniformly the same, and that the future must be conformable to the past. . . . This, therefore, is a point which can admit of no proof at all, and which we take for granted without any proof. . . . 'Tis not therefore reason which is the guide of life but custom. That alone determines the mind in all instances to suppose the future conformable to the past. However easy this step may seem, reason would never, to all eternity, be able to make it.* (Hume 1740)

This hardly seems a satisfactory state of affairs: to live in the world we continually have to trust to conclusions derived from inductive inference, yet to a critical mind all such conclusions are clearly 'not proven'.

*The words 'reason' and 'custom' are used here in much the same sense as deductive and inductive inference, respectively.

The solution to this paradox, in my view, lies in the realization that inductive inference (and with it the capacity for apprehension of meaning and formulation of purpose) is a faculty in which human beings to a greater or lesser extent excel – a faculty displayed to a lower degree by other mammalian species. The products of this faculty are delivered directly to consciousness, and as such determine not so much what we *know* objectively or can *publicly* prove, but rather what we *believe* and will *trust*. The fact that we have great difficulty in analysing this faculty is because it is so utterly fundamental to our psychological nature. In the main, therefore, we should accept this faculty of ours for what it is and seek to refine our own use of it, and only secondarily to understand and evaluate it.

This may seem a tall order for the sceptical scientist. However, I entreat any such readers to stay a while longer, for the substance of this book is mainly concerned with presenting a theory of a cerebral mechanism by whose operation inductive inference can be possible, and ultimately to consideration of why such a mechanism might have evolved. The whole argument is in some respects a circular one, with paradoxes revealed at the beginning of the journey being resolved at the end, rather than where they first arise. In the first instance, therefore, the theory which is developed must be regarded as a mental construction rather than a rigorous inference from evidence, arrived at using step-by-step deductive tactics. Nevertheless, a good deal of empirical evidence will be cited at various stages to support the theory.

In the section that follows it is hoped to use words meaningfully, but no attempt will be made to provide a self-supporting 'mathematically rigorous' set of definitions. One can never define something into existence starting with nothing definite. Definitions will be used here to a limited extent when they seem helpful. But just as important as this, it is hoped that the meaning of the more problematical words will become evident from the particular contexts in which they appear. Likewise it is hoped that complex words initially used in a rather naïve fashion, can be handled with increasing sophistication as the argument proceeds. This strategy arises from the belief expressed in the previous paragraphs, that we have a faculty to apprehend meanings of words, when they are used consistently, by processes of inductive inference. In just the same way a child learns the meaning of words, without their ever being explicitly defined.

As long as there have been philosophers, the relative statuses of the subjective and the objective have been debated. In discussing this topic MacKay (1978) gave as a definition of reality '[that which] is there to be reckoned with'. This is a useful starting point because it does not presuppose answers to the metaphysical questions at issue: reckoning could be either a subjective mental process, or an objective process occurring in a man-made device. Starting from this definition it is proposed to expound a well-known, though perhaps unfashionable metaphysical position – that of psychophysical parallelism. Various versions of this position exist, but underlying them all are two premises, to be called here *the dualism premise* and *the causality premise*. These will be dealt with in the following two subsections.

1.2. The dualism premise

We must reckon with two utterly different types of reality. This duality may be expressed in various ways. We may talk of the duality between external 'things', and the 'some-thing' we are aware of internally (our 'mind' or 'consciousness'). We may talk of the duality of two processes – 'observation' and 'experience', which we should always try to separate. We may talk, alternatively, of the duality of information – 'objective' information (such as the sentences in a book, or the sequence of nucleotides in a gene) and 'subjective' information (inner experience having a distinct, though abstract form). In any of these cases, the dualist premise will influence the definitions we give to key words, such as 'thing', 'process', and 'information', all of which will have to be defined in a way which embodies dualism.

To the scientific mind there is little need to stress the objective side of this dualism. However, it is appropriate to give examples of subjective phenomena with which we all must reckon. When I go to a doctor and say, 'Doctor, I'm feeling terrible this morning', he may decide to conduct various scientific tests on me, in an attempt to establish a diagnosis. However, even if they are all negative, he will, if he is a competent doctor, usually take me seriously in my complaint. He therefore assumes that I have access to inner sources of information which may not be revealed by objective tests. Similarly, when a witness is questioned in a court of law, it is assumed that the witness knows something of value. If this knowledge was objective information, there would be no need to *question* the witness, asking him to divulge his inner knowledge. It should be possible to observe the information by some sophisticated test. The same argument applies to the methods of the psychophysicist or experimental psychologist who enquires from a human subject what he can detect or distinguish. In all these examples, and many more (in fact whenever we use the word 'subject' to describe the responding participant) it is assumed by one or both participants that the person answering questions has access to inner sources of subjective information, which under favourable circumstances he may choose to reveal. By extension one might add that statements such as 'I know' or 'I see' or even 'I am' indicate that the subject who makes such a statement has access to internal information about the state of knowing, seeing or being. All these examples can be included in the process called *introspection*.

Bunge (1977) has written: 'Hunches got by introspection must be regarded not as self-evident, but as hypotheses to be subjected to objective test.' It is true that statements based on introspection are not one hundred per cent reliable: they may be in error due to deliberate attempts at confusion (humour, sarcasm, lying) or, in the case of difficult subjective judgements, they may simply be mistaken. It is therefore, indeed, often necessary to find ways to make objective, statements which are based on introspection. But to regard every statement based on introspection as merely an hypothesis leads to ridiculous conclusions. If this were so it would be necessary for every scientist reading a dial to have a so-called 'objective' supervisor peering over his shoulder to check that he was being objective.

Subjective descriptions are individual assessments, whilst objective descriptions are collective assessments about which different subjects should agree. What is the relationship of these two types of assessment? All objective observations depend on the existence of an observing subject and his capacity to form subjective impressions. Moreover, the capacity to make an objective assessment is not an *a priori* faculty of the human mind: it is learned, and this learning process is in part a collective activity. Piaget and his school (see Piaget and Inhelder 1969) have studied human psychological development in considerable detail. At a very early stage an infant is apparently unaware of the distinction between 'self' and 'outside world'. At definite times after this stage an infant comes to appreciate the various fundamental concepts by which the external world is to be described and manipulated: the 'permanent object'; 'constancy of form and size'; concepts of 'space', 'time', and 'causality'; etc. Thus one may imagine our subject, at a very early age, 'to be shut up in a solipsistic world, ignorant of everything except his own mental states and their relations' (Russell 1946). Gradually, with increasing experience, this subject would come to realize that an important part of the succession of mental states varies independently of any other mental states, and when he initiates actions he finds that he can influence these components of experience in consistent though complex patterns. The subject thus comes to believe he is part of a larger external world, though initially this world has a somewhat secondary status compared with the world of primary sense impressions, since it is to a degree hypothetical, a mental construct, dependent on prior existence of a mind. The critical testing and validation of this mental construct comes when the child develops the capacity to communicate, for then the child must reckon with the fact that there are other subjects who have their own views of the situation, that must be reconciled with his own. When this happens, a child realizes that many of the impressions which reach him from the external world have a broadly similar significance for subjects other than himself. In so far as different subjects agree about impressions from the external world, thus far has an objective description been established, and the subject thus becomes to this extent an observer. Here we echo the words of Schrödinger (1959):

> No single man can make a distinction between the realm of his perceptions and the realm of things that cause it, since however detailed the knowledge he may have acquired about the whole story, the story is occurring only once, not twice. The

> duplication is an allegory, suggested mainly by communication with other human beings and even with animals, which shows that their perceptions in the same situation seem to be very similar to his own apart from insignificant differences. This objective world remains a hypothesis, however natural. If we do adopt it, is it not by far the most natural thing to ascribe to the external world, and not to ourselves all the characteristics that our sense perceptions find in it?

The process of making things objective is exploited to its fullest extent in the natural sciences. However, objective descriptions are no more to be considered as accounts of 'ultimate reality' than are subjective descriptions, as the history of science repeatedly shows. They are fallible, collective accounts, just as subjective descriptions are fallible, individual accounts of reality. Here we can quote MacMurray (1935):

> Thus science is endlessly referred from one thing to another and chases objectivity over the infinite cosmos, like Noah's dove, no place on which the sole of its foot may rest. For science reality is always round the next corner.

Our quest for ultimate reality involves both subjective and objective assessments as sequential processes. In the development of our awareness of reality, the *objective world comes to have a status equal to the subjective world by which it was discovered; but it cannot lay claim to a status higher than that of the subjective world*.

Certain parts of human subjective experience do not correspond to any outer observable reality. For instance, experiences associated with vital functions such as sex appear to be generated to a large extent internally. Artistic vision to a major degree arises internally with links to the external world often being very indirect. Experiences comprising mental illness may have no correspondence with the outer objective world as seen by other observers (though we may hypothesize, and sometimes even prove, a correspondence with observable brain processes). If the world of objective reality were supreme over subjective reality, these manifestations would have no status at all. If, however, the reality of subjective phenomena is granted, then such experiences can often be made objective in the same way as are impressions from the external world—namely by communication with other subjects about them, in order to establish common features. In the case of psychotic delusions and similar phenomena, such a process is of considerable practical importance not only as a part of therapy, but also in order to help establish objective criteria for diagnosis.

When we consider some of the highest of human mental functions (particularly our attitude towards novel concurrences of information) many more examples are provided of the initial primacy of subjective experience, even though during an individual's development the status of the objective world largely comes to equal that of the subjective world. (i) When we are given a complex new pattern of visual information to describe (a fitting example is provided by the task of describing the cytoarchitecture of a region of brain tissue under the light microscope) in no sense can our description be called objective. Description of complex patterns must be selective, so we must make a subjective decision about what is most significant in the new pattern, and therefore what is most worth including in the description. The fact that we now have access to computerized methods of microscopy which can provide an objective assessment of, say, the location of a cytoarchitectural boundary in the cerebral cortex, is no grounds for dismissing the earlier assessments on the grounds that they were subjective: after all many of these assessments, though subjective, are still regarded as correct. (ii) When we attempt to assess correlations between separate occurrences we can certainly make objective (i.e. operationally defined) measurements, and we can perform precise statistical tests to assess the probability of these measurements having occurred by chance; but, in the end, the decision to accept a probability of less than 0·05, rather than one of less than 0·0001 as a criterion of significance is not objective. Presumably it depends on inbuilt subjective intuitions about probability, made objective to a small degree by consensus amongst many people. (iii) Classification of a series of complex objects can never be objective unless one starts from *a priori* assumptions about what features are most significant for the purposes of classification. For instance, Linnaeus's concentration on reproductive organs in botanical classification depended on his own personal subjective intuition, which as it happens, was shown to be wise when the significance of biological classification for evolutionary theory became apparent. (iv) Formulations of scientific hypotheses, elaboration of new concepts, creations of hunches and opinions (all in some respect valid processes) cannot be made systematic or objective. They are functions of human mentality which cannot be mimicked by man-made devices. (It should be noted here that all the examples cited above are, in one form or another, cases where inductive inference is essentially involved.)

However far the process of making judgements objective may go, its roots are in subjective assessments, and there must always be a crucial subjective judgement in deciding the significance of a result, simply because part of the essence of science is that it is a mental activity. We can quote Schrödinger again here:

> The observer is never entirely replaced by instruments; for if he were he could obviously obtain no knowledge whatsoever. . . . Many helpful devices can facilitate this work, for instance photometric recording . . . on which the position of the lines can be easily read. But they must be read! The observer's senses have to step in eventually. The most careful record, when not inspected, tells us nothing.

He goes on to quote Democritus who, in the fifth century BC, clearly was aware of the line of argument presented in the above pages. In all these matters, where we have to make subjective judgements (even if it is a judgement as simple as the position of a line), we find ourselves taken back to childhood, once again adopting a rather solipsistic stance, to greater or lesser degree, depending on how independent we are from the intuitions of our peer group. (See Polanyi (1958) for an extended presentation of the arguments of the above paragraphs.)

In many instances, including most of those cited in this section, the distinction between experiences originating internally (available only to introspection), and those impressed on us from outside (which we therefore claim we observe) is clear enough for us to formulate the notion of two forms of reality—the internal and the external—and thus to adopt a dualist philosophy. But this clear distinction is not always evident. Often the picture we build of external reality is dependent upon impressions from our sense organs in only a very indirect way, a host of internal thought operations being also required. In conducting personal relationships it is particularly difficult to know whether an occurrence within our own mind has originated there or has been influenced from outside by the person to whom we relate. Likewise it is common for psychologically disturbed people to attribute to the external world significances which no-one else can recognize—and which probably are a reflection of internal realities. Here again the distinction between external and internal reality is not made. To maintain our dualist philosophy with consistency we must regard these as such complex situations that the mind's powers of reckoning with reality are taxed to their limit. The primary data on which the dualism premise is based are simpler, and (we assume) more fundamental.

In conclusion it may be observed that dismissal of, or equivocation about subjective reality is closely related to a similar attitude to the process of inductive inference, for, as noted earlier, the conclusions of inductive inference arise primarily as subjective impressions.

1.3. The causality premise

No attempt at full analysis of the concept of causality will be made here. In particular no consideration will be given to causality as understood by physicists. They have a more mature understanding of this concept than biologists, with the triple interaction of experiment, theory, and philosophy well established in their discipline. With this proviso I venture to assume, at least, that a causal relationship is a relation between *observable* features of reality. According to this premise the relationship between the world of internal experience and the observable world can never be one of causality. Historically this premise was crucial to the beginning of natural science. In the time of the ancient Greeks there was no clear distinction between a natural law and a law imposed by a conscious human or quasi-human agency. Natural phenomena such as the winds were considered to be initiated and controlled by quasi-human deities. Natural science could not begin until a distinction was made between relationships amongst observable entities on the one hand, and the relationship which exists between human volition (basically a subjective experience) and the observable performance of a corresponding act, on the other.

For students of the physical sciences, and for most biologists there is little need to elaborate on this second premise. For neuroscientists however, this premise has the implication—astonishing perhaps—that the human experience of volition is not the cause of objective happenings, even if it be the volition of one such as Alexander the Great or Genghis Khan. However, this implication has very definite advantages when we attempt to understand the brain scientifically. Two examples can be given here, one rather esoteric, the other directly relevant to the explanations experimental scientists give to a widely reported observation.

The first example concerns the disputed phenomena of parapsychology. These include telepathy (transmission of information from one mind to another without intervention of normal sensory mechanisms, or perhaps even without intervention of any energy-dependent signal), and psychokinesis (initiation of movement in inanimate objects by, or during, the exercise of the mind without participation of normal mechanisms of 'voluntary' control of the environment). Clearly, if either of these phenomena really does occur, it is capable of influencing the objective world and therefore demands a causal explanation as much as any other phenomenon in the external world. However, in discussions of parapsychology it is often unclear whether the causation is supposed to be a relationship between observables, or a relationship between an unobservable inner reality and an observable outer reality. Nevertheless, it is clear that no scientific investigation of these phenomena is possible if investigators adhere to the latter notion of causation. Unless internal realities are given objective expression, any experimental finding whatsoever can be explained in terms of hypothetical internal realities. All the rest of experimental science would then become questionable. Inner feelings of expectation which an experimenter might have about an experiment in progress might, in fact, influence the result of the experiment by some sort of psychokinesis, and in psychology in particular, every subject's report might be biassed by telepathic interference. On the other hand, if experimental parameters are limited to publicly demonstrable information it may be possible to demarcate precisely the circumstances in which these phenomena occur. This is not to deny the subjective reality of paranormal experiences, merely to point out that any such experience in itself leads to a hypothesis about existence of parapsychological processes, rather than to a demonstration of its veracity.

The second example concerns the widely-studied phenomenon of intracranial self-stimulation: a conscious animal, with electrodes implanted in the appropriate regions of brain will repeatedly perform operant responses to stimulate its own brain. Isaacson (1974) describes such animals in the following terms, apparently in an attempt to provide a causal explanation of this phenomenon:

> The goal of their efforts was most easily described in terms of obtaining pleasurable experience. Thus, the experiences of the organism had to become a factor in describing or explaining behaviour.

Is this an adequate statement of the strategy to be employed in explaining this well-known behavioural finding? Does it suggest any obvious experimental approaches? The answers to these questions must surely be 'no', because, in this quotation reference is made to a relationship between an inner reality, intangible to the experimental scientist, and an observable item of behaviour. The passage quoted above is no more than tautology, since the only possible way in which the word 'pleasurable' could be defined for a scientist is 'that which an animal will strive to experience again', which the experimenter already knows. If a truly causal explanation of self-stimulation is to be provided it would be better to seek it in processes of synaptic modulation, or any other objective process which might be invoked to account for the objective fact of operant learning. In fact, a hypothesis of this sort is discussed in Chapters 5 and 6.

If the word 'causality' is to be used, as suggested here, to refer only to a relationship between *observable* events, this will place constraints on the usage of this word in a scientific context. In a lengthy treatise advocating the possibility of causal interaction between the mental and the physical, Popper writes: 'Take a simple example, like looking at a tree and opening and closing your eyes. The causal effect of nervous changes upon your experience is obvious' (Popper and Eccles 1977). Certainly causal processes are involved here, but it is questionable whether the final step by which physical processes in the brain are related to experiences are best described as 'causal'. In fact, it is maintained here that for the natural sciences, including the neurosciences, this is not the most coherent way of using the word 'causal'. Such a usage, if it became more widespread amongst scientists, could severely undermine attempts to unravel the principles or orderliness of natural phenomena. It would be easy to cite further examples from this work (some of them more complex than that quoted above) in which this crucial aspect of the concept of causality for science is ignored.

Before closing this section it should be clearly acknowledged that the notion of causality explained above is still beset with the fundamental paradox mentioned earlier, concerning the validity of inductive inference. Despite all our observations we have no grounds for supposing that there is such a general principle of causality, which dictates the regularities we observe, unless we can accept inferences based on inductive logic. We will return to this paradox in the final chapter.

1.4. Psychophysical parallelism

What consequences does all this have for ideas about relationships between mind and brain? If we think we can speak of reality at all, we have a right to speak of both subjective reality (an individual view) and objective reality (a collective view). These two views are of course closely related, although a complex transformation may sometimes be needed to display the relationship. It is when we turn our gaze to the human brain that the two viewpoints are juxtaposed most starkly: for at once we must reckon not only with the objective facts of structure and causal relationship in the brain we are observing as experimenters, but also the subjective fact of inner experience in our own brain. It is at this point that our philosophy crystallizes. Somehow we must be able to reckon with the relationship between these two facets of our nature, so that it becomes valid to seek features in the anatomy or physiology of the brain which match with subjective descriptions. In this process, the logic we employ will not be like that used in explaining causal relationships. What we observe in the brain is so utterly different from what we experience with the brain that any suggestion of causal interaction between the two would destroy our concept of causality. However, we may use a more abstract form of logic, a *logical transformation* without causal implications. The most obvious analogy of this transformation is the process by which geographical landmarks have their correspondence with features on a map of the same area. Not surprisingly this view of the relationship of subjective to objective reality is often called psychophysical parallelism—a name which has perhaps the simple-minded implication that corresponding information in the subjective and objective realms are to be matched together as easily as are two parallel lines. Originally such simple matching was described using the analogy of two perfectly accurate clocks, which always told the same time, though not on account of any causal interaction between the two. Both Leibniz and Geulincx (one of Descartes' intellectual descendants) used this analogy. The term 'parallelism' is used here in a much more flexible sense than this, to imply the sort of mapping of a 'field' of information that might be possible in a multidimensional space.

In more recent times, this position has been advocated by Hughlings Jackson, and concisely stated in the following quotation:

> States of consciousness (or synonymously states of mind) are utterly different from nervous states of the highest centres; the two things occur together, for every mental state there being a correlative nervous state. Although the two things occur together in parallelism there is no interference of one with the other. . . . Hence we do not say that physical states are functions of the brain (highest centres) but simply that they occur during the functioning of the brain. Thus, in the case of visual perception there is an unbroken physical circuit, complete reflex action from sensory periphery ultimately through the highest centres back to the muscular periphery. The visual image, a purely mental state, occurs in parallelism with—*arises during* (*not from*)—the

> activities of the two highest links of this purely physical chain (sensorimotor elements of the highest centres)—so to speak it 'stands outside these links'. (See Brain 1957).

Schrödinger (1959) is very eloquent on this subject:

> [but let us assume you observed] several efferent bundles of pulsating current, which issue from the brain and through long cellular protrusions (motor nerve fibres) are conducted to certain muscles of the arm, which as a consequence, tends a hesitating, trembling hand to you to bid you farewell for a long heart-rending separation; at the same time you may find that some other pulsating bundles produce a certain glandular secretion so as to veil the poor sad eye with a crape of tears. But nowhere along this way from the eye through the central organ to the arm muscles and the tear glands—nowhere you may be sure, however far physiology advances, will you ever meet the personality, will you ever meet the dire pain, the bewildered worry within this soul, though their reality is to you so certain as though you suffered them yourself—as in actual fact you do!

As a modern-day expression of the parallelist position the phrase used by MacKay (1978) that brain processes 'embody' subjective experience also has much to recommend it. Apart from slight differences of semantic emphasis his formulation comes to much the same as that which is advocated here.

In closing this section it is interesting to enquire why the debate on this subject brings to light such bitter and deep divisions, with so little mutual understanding. A tentative explanation is offered in which a correlation is suggested between the psychological characteristics of the various proponents, and the philosophical positions they propose. The typical materialist is a person who takes observation much more seriously than introspection. He may be an experimental scientist, perhaps highly trained in techniques of objective observation, and he will tend to think of objective reality as much more reliable than subjective reality. The typical idealist (literally, one who believes in the primary reality of ideas) on the other hand, is one who takes introspection far more seriously than observation. He may be a creative artist who is continually trying to crystallize into tangible form a vivid but elusive inner vision—which may be as complex, sharply focussed, and demand as much direct attention as the topic under scrutiny of a highly trained scientist. The typical dualist, on the other hand, shares some of the attributes of both the other two, recognizing the importance of both observation and introspection. If he is also a neuroscientist, he will probably find it necessary to believe in parallel forms of reality. It is pointless to debate which of these three has a more complete philosophy. There are particular strengths and weaknesses in all the positions, and which one we choose depends on our personal predelictions more than on the strictly logical merits of each case. I would, however, contend that the position adopted here is useful for the particular purpose with which this book is concerned, namely the consideration of a mysterious, but nevertheless widely recognized concept—consciousness.

Differences on philosophical issues are important in the neurosciences. In particular it is important that each student in the neurosciences should openly declare his philosophical assumptions, though he cannot convince all others of their truth. However, these differences are not so important as to bar communication between the adherents of different positions. But it is a sad fact of present day neuroscience that unspoken philosophical differences are often used to set up barriers between the different subdivisions of the subject.

2. Psychological issues: the agenda

2.1. The unity of the parts and the whole of consciousness

THE previous chapter has outlined the philosophical framework within which the concept of consciousness is to be discussed. In this chapter an outline of the principal issues to be discussed within this framework will be given. The chapter will thus be a statement of the agenda, for more detailed discussion in subsequent chapters. In this first section the most overwhelming and pervasive of these issues will be spelt out—an issue which, in conjunction with the problem of inductive inference is one of the central themes of this book.

The problem is this: subjectively consciousness is a unity, or integrated whole. This fact is attested to every time we use a personal pronoun—'I', 'you', 'he', etc.—for these words specifically refer to the fact that in a whole person, a vast range of subsidiary processes, and portions of information are subjectively perceived as part of the person, the central *ego*. The thesis of psychophysical parallelism therefore provokes us to ask: *What is there in the objective properties of the brain which can match with this subjective fact of unity and form a substrate for a unified consciousness?* Schrödinger (1959) was well aware of this issue. He writes:

> I find it utterly impossible to form an idea about either how, for example, my own conscious mind (that I feel to be *one*) should have originated by integration of the consciousness of the cells (or some of them) that form my body, or how it should at every moment of my life be, as it were, their resultant. One would think that such a 'commonwealth of cells' as each of us is, would be the occasion *par excellence* for mind to exhibit plurality if it were at all able to do so.

At an abstract level it is indeed far from obvious how anything can be a unified whole, if in fact it consists of separable portions; but it certainly is true that consciousness is not a homogeneous, uniform entity, though its subjectively distinct parts *are* somehow welded into a whole.

This statement is true at more than one level. In overall terms we are aware of major psychological functions—perception, volition, motivation, memory—which are logically separable, but nevertheless part of a unified whole. In finer detail each of these functions itself can deal with myriad different portions of information, all of which will register on the much larger and well-knit whole which is consciousness. To put this another way, any subjective impression of which I am aware contains, besides all the details of a perceptual, volitional or mnemonic picture, a further signal which signifies *this picture is part of me* (*or part of my mind*). Put this way it is so simple as to be almost tautologous. Yet this phrase refers to a quite definite and undeniable property of consciousness. If subjective information has its objective counterpart in the brain, then this additional signal which binds to every other portion of information in our consciousness must itself correspond to an objective process or scheme of organization within the brain. Speculations about the nature of this process are fundamentally concerned with the mechanism by which items of experience are integrated into consciousness. If an account of this integrative process can be suggested, considerable constraints will be placed on our notions of the functioning of the major structures of forebrain and midbrain which (presumably) underlie the phenomenon of consciousness.

At this point a slight qualification is perhaps appropriate, because there are times when the integrity of consciousness referred to above is clearly less than perfect. Often, people have a real difficulty in incorporating certain information presented to them into the rest of their consciousness. Some topics are particularly liable to give rise to a hiatus of this sort, so that many people find it particularly difficult to deal with subjects such as sex or death in the well integrated manner they would adopt to any other subject. It would be wiser, therefore, to regard 'the unity of consciousness' not so much as an everyday reality, but as an ideal to which many people approximate, and which is a convenient simplification for some important aspects of the following discussion. Physical scientists often make similar simplifications to aid clarity of thought, when making theoretical formulations of various sorts, for instance when a physicist refers to a 'frictionless surface' or to 'inelastic spheres'. Whether the 'unity of consciousness' is an everyday reality or an idealized concept, we still have a massive theoretical problem in accounting for its biological substrate. This problem is more easily tackled if we start from the 'ideal' simple situation.

Before proceeding it is appropriate to point out here that we have now referred to the two major issues which distinguish psychology from lower level, 'biological' approaches to central nervous mechanisms. Firstly, when attempting to understand the brain, it is only in psychology that we receive any help from the process of introspection (either 'casual' introspection, or more sophisticated objective versions of the same which have been 'made objective'). Secondly, in the strictly biological approaches one can often avoid reckoning with what is in many ways an obvious fact—that the brain and its mind function in their most characteristic fashion *as a whole*, that is when they are in all senses intact. In the psychological approach one never can do this, because integration is an underlying assumption of all psychological questions.

2.2. Cognitive functions: consciousness, meaning, and memory for knowledge

In the previous section reference was made to the idea that there is unity within and amongst the various major components from which consciousness is built. In the next three sections of this chapter an attempt will be made to define major modes of operation of consciousness—modes which are logically separate, though nevertheless working together simultaneously in harmony. The first of these three modes will be called the *cognitive mode*—the process whereby we acquire knowledge of things which at one time or another have impinged on us via our sense organs.

In the process of acquiring such knowledge, a memory trace cannot be laid down in a form readily accessible for retrieval into consciousness unless the information so encoded has at some previous time impinged upon consciousness. It is thus a contradiction in terms to be 'able to remember' some portion of information, but to be unaware that it was once a new item of experience. *There is thus a close relationship between cognitive memory and consciousness.*

It is not intended to imply here that we can instantaneously recall anything of which we have ever been conscious: the gradual process of forgetting may remove many memories beyond recall, except perhaps in response to a fairly specific triggering stimulus. Moreover, all phenomena included under the term 'acquisition of memory' need not be accompanied by conscious awareness of the process. For instance, subliminally-presented information can be shown to have registered in memory (e.g. Somekh 1976). In such a case, however, the person concerned would not say 'he could remember it', or to rephrase, he would not have properly integrated this information with all the other information which is freely available to consciousness. Similarly for many situations involving learning, occurring very early in our lives, we would not say 'we could remember': such patterns of cognition laid down during this early phase of learning are not really accessible to consciousness, but are retrieved automatically. For instance, none of us remembers learning the grammar of our native language, and consequently when we are interpreting language in our adult life we do not consciously have to consider grammatical structure (Moskowitz 1978). Perhaps the patterns of integration which underlie consciousness have not themselves developed properly at such an early stage. Bearing in mind these qualifications we may say, in a strict sense, that the relation between consciousness and memory is such that *memories which can be retrieved into consciousness, must have been acquired during a state of consciousness.*

Given this, it nevertheless seems inconceivable that the processes of 'acquisition' and 'retrieval' of cognitive memories are comparable with the workings of a tape recorder, in which there are no prior comparisons with previous records, with an accompanying process of selection. Were this to happen there could be no distinction in our minds between the background jumble of irrelevant information, and the contrasting 'events' or 'objects' on which our attention comes to rest. There must therefore be processes occurring during, or prior to formation of cognitive memory, which determine whether new memory traces need to be formed. Marr (1970) has pointed out that the world is, in information terms, full of considerable redundancy, and can, in large part, be represented by *groupings* or *classes*, each of which is defined by clusters of properties displaying tight statistical association. It seems likely, as Marr assumes, that the mechanism of coding memory is closely related to the existence of these *classes*, *patterns* and *meanings* within the sensory input. Efficiency of the memory mechanism would thus be improved by interposing, at an early stage in the formation of memory, a step in which statistical significance of associations within these patterns is assessed, so that representations of these associations (rather than the jumble of other incoming information containing no such associations) can be made. Indeed Marr assumes that the cerebral cortex is specialized, at the level of single neurones, for detection of these associations and encoding them as memories. (It should be pointed out that statistical significance of immediate associations is not the only sort of significance with which the brain might be concerned: higher level significances are considered in Section 2.4.)

It thus seems likely that a close relationship exists between three concepts—consciousness, memory, and meaning. What is true for one may therefore have implications for the others. This statement may seem of trivial importance if these concepts are regarded solely as *psychological* or *philosophical* in nature—the relationships may be dismissed as purely semantic. However, each of these concepts has undertones rooted in the *biology* of higher nervous functions; hence, if valid suggestions can be made about the biological basis of any of these concepts it will have implications for the biological nature of the other two.

2.3. Operant functions: consciousness, purpose, and memory for the effect of actions

The information within reach of consciousness is not limited to cognitive records, nor is the brain merely a 'library' in which significant aspects of sensory input are stored. Executive processes also exist (in both subjective and objective forms) by means of which a large variety of patterns of behaviour are generated. With the insight derived from human subjective intuitions, such behaviour would be called 'voluntary'—a word with curious connotations, at least to the scientific mind. When apparently similar behaviour occurs in animals, it is labelled 'operant' or 'instrumental' behaviour. In either case, it is not a stereotyped response to an immediate stimulus as in the case of reflex action. Often, particularly in a child or young animal, such behaviour may have no particular aim in mind, but appears to be an expression of an innate, non-specific purpose merely to engage in movement. However, with advancing maturity, an increasing proportion of this stream of 'voluntary' actions become quite accurately matched to the sensory situations in which they occur in order to fulfil some necessary motive or goal of a more restricted character. *Any account of the conscious processes presumed to be a function of the forebrain must explain both these aspects of voluntary (or operant) behaviour: first, it must explain the origin of spontaneous behaviour, and, more important, it must account for the gradual acquisition of intelligent, purposive, or goal-seeking behaviour.* In the latter case, the explanation must studiously avoid teleological reasoning otherwise one would be employing as assumptions those very features of voluntary behaviour which one is attempting to explain.

The problem of goal-directed behaviour may in fact be divided into two subsidiary issues. The first concerns the concept of motivation itself. We are all familiar with the subjective side of various motives—hunger, for instance. What could be its objective biological counterpart, and where do motives come from? Presumably, since they involve essential goals, necessary for the self-preservation or self-expression of an organism, one may conclude that they have evolved by a process of natural selection, and thus, in an individual animal are determined by the genome rather than the environment. In some way therefore, hard-wiring of connections, or some other stable feature of neural organization may underlie motivation, as is usually also assumed for reflex actions; but the biological substrate of motivation must reside in the structure of the brain in a deeper and more abstract sense than does that of reflex action, since in the case of motivation neither the sensory stimulus, nor the motor response are defined in any precise way, other than that a particular goal must be fulfilled. In the rest of this book it is not intended to inquire further into the generation of these patterns of hard-wiring, apart from this general statement. Their existence in some form is thus to be taken as an assumption underlying some of the arguments.

The second question about goal directed behaviour asks how spontaneous, random, voluntary behaviour can actually become linked to the motivational systems, so that voluntary behaviour may seek goals in an intelligent fashion. Here we come to a crucial distinction between cognitive and operant functions: *whereas in the former, acquisition of memory entails registration of associations entirely within the sensory input, in the latter it involves detecting and recording the associations between spontaneous behavioural acts and their subsequent effects with respect to motivational systems.* (This statement is expanded in Chapter 4, p. 77.)

In the previous section a close relationship between consciousness, meaning, and memory for cognitive information was suggested. For information about operant processes, a similar relationship seems to hold true. *Whenever, in an adult animal, a voluntary motor act is called upon in order to fulfil a certain goal, the relationship of the act to the goal fulfilment must initially have been detected during a state of consciousness.* Spontaneous voluntary actions, motivational states, and rewarding (or punishing) changes in these states can all be registered upon consciousness. Hence their interlinkage to form purposive voluntary actions must also initially be a process involving consciousness. The logical status of motivation, as a concept is thus as follows:

motives are a focus towards which subsequent learning is directed, and learning of adult strategies of operant behaviour could not occur without a motivational focus of this sort. (These statements do not apply, without qualification, to some aspects of the behaviour of higher primates, especially of man. In these species, behaviour may come to be controlled by deductive processes, rather than by the more primitive, genetically in-built motivational systems, which are widespread and more characteristic of mammalian intelligence in general.)

In later chapters of this book biological ideas will be put forward which, it is hoped, form a counterpart to logical statements such as those made above, about the relationships of consciousness, motivation and the acquisition of purposive behaviour. Any proposal of this nature, if successful, can be expected to avoid the curious connotations of the word 'voluntary'—namely that some internal agent is acting as if freed from the constraints of physical laws. It should suggest an alternative view of operant behaviour which is less mystical.

In so far as such behaviour is a response of the whole animal, fulfilling a motive of the whole animal, it has the same inherent unity as has just been attributed to the cognitive aspects of consciousness. An explanation of this unity must therefore be sought, although such an explanation may not be identical with that which applies to cognitive processes.

2.4. Higher-order functions: novelty detection, curiosity, and contexts

In Sections 2.2 and 2.3 a clear distinction was made between cognitive functions, in which learning depends on sensory input alone, without the involvement of motivational systems or behavioural acts, and operant functions, in which patterns of action of an organism are modified and focussed towards an inbuilt motive, or goal. In the intact behaving mammal it is, however, highly debatable whether learning can occur independently of either actions or motivation, as in the first of these two modes. It must be admitted that there are a few unusual situations in which cognitive learning can occur independent of any actions. For instance, surgical patients at operation who are under the influence of muscle relaxants may temporarily recover from anaesthesia sufficiently to be aware of, and hence subsequently to be able to recall their surroundings, though at the time they were incapable of voluntary action. However, it is much more difficult to maintain that learning can occur without any motivation, if one includes phenomena such as curiosity and attentiveness amongst the list of motives.

To make quite clear the sense in which this distinction is to be made, it is necessary to mention here a third major mode of operation of conscious processes. This is interlinked with, and in some ways a controller of the other two modes. In part it is concerned with detection of novelty or discrepancy in the information available to consciousness. It will not receive such detailed attention in this book as the other two modes, but has importance in overcoming some of the weaknesses inevitably present in the model to be proposed for these other two.

It should be added that, as the argument progresses, the inter-relationships between these first two modes will be discussed to an increasing extent. Thus, the clear separation of the two modes, made at this stage, will be seen as a necessary step in describing how these two fit together in harmonious union.

Commonplace observations suggest that we are particularly sensitive to novelty (or discrepancy with previous experience) in our environment. If I discover an object in my living room whose presence there I cannot account for, it will attract a great deal of my attention, while no time will be devoted to other familiar objects in the room. People living near the Niagara Falls are said to be so distracted by the silence which reigns when the waterfall freezes, that they cannot sleep. It seems that novelty and familiarity can arouse distinctive experiences quite apart from the other subjective information with which they are also usually associated. The widely reported and rather unnerving *déjà vu* phenomenon appears to be an example of these experiences occurring in isolation—the feeling that one has been in a particular situation before, without any recollection of when or where this could have been. Occasionally it has been possible to elicit such isolated experiences of 'familiarity' or 'strangeness' by electrical stimulation of particular brain regions during neurosurgical operation (Penfield and Perot 1963).

What significance can we attach to the related notions of 'familiarity' and 'strangeness' referred to above? The obvious initial answer to this is that objects 'we know' are familiar, those 'we do not know' are strange; if this is so we are dealing merely with examples of the cognitive processes discussed in Section 2.2. However, another example will show that there may be more to these concepts than is initially apparent. When one is in a room crowded with many people, all engaged in different conversations, one may be able to pick up some fragments of conversation without giving them much attention, but there may also be occasions when one recognizes a particular voice, or a particular word (e.g. one's own name), and it stands out in one's mind above all the rest, and commands all one's attention. On the other hand voices and words which, in themselves are equally recognizable may arouse no such attention, or may even induce loss of attention ('boredom'). What is the difference between these two types of stimulus, which in straight cognitive terms are equally recognizable? The answer must be that in the former instance, although the stimulus is recognizable, one is simultaneously aware of shortcomings in one's knowledge about it. One does not know all the important associations of the stimulus. Succinctly, although one knows the stimulus, one does not know 'all about it', that is, the *context* in which it appears is in some respect, unknown. To put it another way, when a stimulus is presented, one's subjective experience depends not only on the stimulus itself, but on whether or not new learning connected with the stimulus is possible. In this example, and in the two given above (i.e. the familiar but slightly altered room, and the frozen Niagara Falls) the process that occurs, to detect whether new learning is possible, must be a higher-order process than that which merely mediates recognition of individual objects, since it depends on assessment of sensory input in a large scale manner, scanning the environment more widely than is necessary to recognize individual features considered separately. The importance of large scale representations of contexts is also clear when one considers the processes that occur in recognition of familiarity. For instance, as a simple mental exercise we would have great difficulty in recalling the features of a particular street we have travelled a few times. However, when we are actually on location in that street, the information we receive from being in that particular context will remind us of things, as yet invisible, around the next corner of the street.

Thus, cognitive learning, as defined in Section 2.2 is simply concerned with immediate statistical significance of associations within the sensory input, and the new meanings acquired by such processes have only this limited importance. On the other hand, this third mode of conscious information processing deals in significance in a much broader sense, involving comparison with information acquired over long periods of time and in a much wider context. It will also be argued that information relevant to life-promoting motives also comes to have this larger-scale significance of a *context*. The third mode is probably also concerned with operant functions as well as with cognitive ones, since we naturally become increasingly attentive to the consequences of our actions when trying out a new strategy of behaviour.

A function of consciousness which can detect whether relevant new information can be acquired either in the cognitive or the operant mode must have considerable potential significance for the total operation of conscious processes of learning. It can influence learning in either of the other two modes. On the one hand, when deficiencies in knowledge are detected, behavioural responses may be initiated, so that the organism explores, focussing his attention particularly on the features where he has most to learn. This is the psychological function of curiosity, a prominent feature of many mammalian species. On the other hand, a second, purely internal process may be initiated which by some means allows learning to occur more efficiently. This is the psychological function variously referred to as attention or arousal. For both these two manifestations of the novelty-detecting mode, when all that can be learned in a particular context has been learned, then curiosity and attentiveness will tend to decline, the organism will explore less, and will be less responsive to most stimuli.

In the earlier years of this century (see Hilgard and Marquis 1964, p. 411) learning theorists have argued at great length whether learning can occur without a motive and without corresponding internal 'rewards' and 'punishments'. The initial account of cognitive learning given in Section 2.2 suggested that this was possible. We are now in a position to qualify this simple notion, and thus move closer to a realistic account of learning in mammals. In operant learning, motivational systems control internal rewards and punishments which in turn determine *what is learnt*. Curiosity is also in many ways like the motives controlling operant behaviour, since it specifies a goal which behaviour must fulfil. In similar fashion the function of attentiveness also specifies a goal for cognitive learning. If this is so then cognitive learning as well as operant learning is dependent upon a motive. However, if curiosity and attentiveness are to be regarded as motives, they are very special motives compared with any others, since they determine not precisely what message is learnt, but *whether and to what extent learning as such occurs*. In other words the goal fulfilled by the motives of curiosity and attentiveness is learning itself.

Three modes of operation of consciousness have now been discussed. In each the close relation of learning to consciousness was evident. In the brief but profound book by the physicist Schrödinger, to which reference has already been made, the same relationship was emphasized: 'Metaphorically' he writes, 'consciousness is the tutor who supervises the education of the living substance but leaves his pupil alone to deal with all those tasks for which he is already sufficiently trained.' Learning is thus to be regarded as perhaps the central process occurring within consciousness.

It is also interesting here to refer to an item of linguistic usage which underlines the close relationship of learning to consciousness. The word 'experience' originally had the meaning 'to try out' or to 'put to the test'. Over the last few centuries, however, it has been possible to use it (in the noun form) to refer either to 'inner subjective awareness' as such (the sense in which it was generally used in Section 1), or to the gradual process of acquiring memories (see *Oxford English Dictionary*). This ambiguity can hardly be coincidence, but is rather an indication of close relation between the two concepts.

2.5. Temporal aspects of consciousness: parallelism between subjective and objective time

A most important aspect of the concept of consciousness is the sense of passage of time which it includes. No sense organ apparently exists for perception of this fundamental measure, and it seems likely that apprehension of information about time is more intimately bound up with the very essence of consciousness than is apprehension of information from the external world via the sense organs. In so far as consciousness is a temporal stream of subjective impressions, so time must be an omnipresent fundamental variable in psychology.

For the physicist, time is described as an infinite number of sequentially arranged instants, each of infinitesimal duration, arranged like the points on a line, with the additional property that the line has an arrow indicating that time can only 'flow' in one direction. The philosophy of psychophysical parallelism prompts one to ask what might be the relationship between time as defined by the physicist, and subjective time as experienced by consciousness. As early as the 1890s it was pointed out by James (1890) that subjective time cannot possibly correspond exactly with physical time, otherwise consciousness would consist of a sequence of instantaneous and unrelatable 'snapshots' of the world, each of infinitesimal duration. If this were so, any consciousness of the surrounding world would be an impossibility, because any scanning device, however fast, could not build up representations of extended objects, or observe change (for this implies integration of information from different instants), let alone store information in memory. In other words, for consciousness to exist, the 'psychological moment' must be of finite, though perhaps brief, duration and events within this duration must be integrated to yield even the most transitory subjective impressions.

Using casual introspection alone, it is very difficult to obtain any idea of the scheme by which physical time is translated into subjective time, perhaps because the latter is such a fundamental part of consciousness. However, a considerable amount of work by experimental psychologists (ultimately dependent of course on the powers of introspection of the experimental subjects), amplified by a number of everyday examples of the temporal limitations of various sorts which pertain to conscious processes, has led to a general picture of this parallelism. Some of this work has recently been reviewed by Blumenthal (1977), with particular reference to work on humans, and the framework presented by this author will be used here. Basically the transformations of physical time required to match subjective time are, according to this framework, of three kinds:

(i) The *psychological moment*—that is the smallest unit of physical time which can be separated experimentally in the stream of subjective time—appears to be a short interval variously estimated at 50–250 ms (usually around 100 ms). Within intervals of this magnitude immediate experience is integrated, so that 'temporally separate events included in one integration are fused in experience to form unitary impressions. . . . When these events are structurally different or incompatible, some may be omitted rather than fused' (Blumenthal). The process of integration occurring during these brief intervals is an active one, and does not disregard temporal relationships within the integration interval, though the process yields to consciousness impressions in which these relationships are not perceived as temporal ones. For instance, when viewing motion pictures, two nearly identical pictures presented within the integration interval give rise not to an impression of two separate images, or to an impression of one image in an intermediate position, but to a single image, one of whose properties is the impression of movement. Likewise the details of the first vibrations of a musical note (the 'attack') do not register as temporal sequences, but they are nevertheless crucial for recognition of one musical instrument from another (Taylor 1969). It seems that these 'rapid attentional integrations' (Blumenthal's phrase) cannot be explained by the properties of the peripheral parts of the sensory systems. Moreover the same central integration process seems to occur whether the information being processed reaches consciousness via visual, auditory or tactile senses, or if voluntary responses are to be consciously generated (as in reaction time tests) or indeed, if information is retrieved to consciousness from internal memory stores. This central integrative process creates the impressions which form the stream of immediate experience, but associated with it are two kinds of temporal delay which make the subjective representation of physical time more complex.

(ii) Firstly, there are *pre-attentive delays*. These delays can 'hold' the incoming flood of information for periods of 1 s or slightly less, while awaiting the attention of the rapid integrative process (which has a limited capacity). An everyday example of these delays (called 'buffer' delays by Blumenthal) is found when reading aloud. The eye can take in written words up to approximately 1 s ahead of the spoken word. Perception of musical rhythms (which is not possible for intervals much longer than 1 s) probably also depends on these buffer delays. Whereas the rapid integrations unify sensory information, and ignore what cannot be unified (or is beyond the limited capacity of the integration process), during the preceding buffer delay many separate items of the information may persist independently. Thus much of the information held in the buffer storage may decay before it is integrated, and may never reach consciousness.

(iii) The second type of delay is a *post-attentive delay*, otherwise known as 'short-term memory'. After an impression has been integrated, and thus delivered to consciousness, the impression will decay over a period variously estimated at 5–20 s (usually about 10 s). Only if the impression is repeated within that interval by further stimulus presentations, or some internal process of 'rehearsal', is it likely that the impressions of the 'psychological moment' will become laid down as permanent memory. It should be added that during these repetitions, whether by recurrence of environmental events, or by internal rehearsal, a further integrative step occurs, which can record common features in somewhat variable patterns of information. The permanent memory is thus laid down in a highly organized form. As a result of these processes the transformation of objective time within consciousness will be complete, because these memories can now potentially be recalled at any subsequent occasion, regardless of the temporal sequencing which accompanied their initial acquisition. At any rate this is the idealized situation which seems to be implicit in the simplest usage of the word 'consciousness' (or perhaps one should refer to 'total consciousness'). In fact of course, as has been pointed out in Section 2.1, unity of consciousness, whether thought of as a spatial attribute (if referring to simultaneously occurring information) or as a temporal one, is a phenomenon to which real conscious processes can only approximate. Whether real or ideal, the unification of temporally diverse experiences is a most important phenomenon to be explained in any analysis of consciousness. The above three processes will form a useful framework for discussion of this subject in later chapters.

2.6. Control of consciousness

One obvious property of consciousness for which an explanation must be sought is the *fluctuation of the level of consciousness*, varying from the various stages of sleep through 'normal' wakefulness to the 'heightened' levels of consciousness which occur in situations of extreme motivation, or under the influence of drugs and other agents. In most physiological accounts of consciousness, the occurrence of these different levels is given undue prominence, at the expense of the other more philosophical aspects of the concept of consciousness. In this account an attempt will be made to incorporate an account of the varying levels of consciousness into these other more general considerations. If it is accepted that learning is the most important of conscious processes, control of the varying levels of consciousness is very closely related to the control of the learning process. Part of the control process has already been mentioned—that whereby the higher-order aspects of the learning process influence the functioning of the lower order processes. There are undoubtedly other control operations, which can influence the novelty-detection mode as well as the cognitive and operant modes. Overall control of this sort is necessary to determine sleep and wakefulness, and changes of mood during wakefulness.

2.7. The problem of introspection

An important aspect of the dualist position which was expounded in Chapter 1 was that it acknowledged and gave validity to the process of introspection. Indeed, introspection is regarded here as important because it gives insight into integrated brain function in a way which no other method is capable of. The questions raised in earlier sections of the present chapter all derive some of their force from our capacity for introspection. In the first instance, therefore, introspection is an *a priori* faculty which we accept without too much enquiry. However, when we come to consideration of the highest of mental faculties, the problem of introspection becomes a scientific conundrum in its own right.

Consider some specific examples of statements based on introspection. In various appropriate circumstances I might say 'I am confused', or 'I am drunk', or 'I am exhilarated'. That my statements are not totally empty can be proved by the fact that I make them generally in appropriate circumstances. My statements of this nature are usually taken at face value even when the circumstances are not known by a listener. Apparently, therefore, each of us has a direct access to some internal reality. As pointed out earlier statements such as 'I know', or 'I see' or even 'I am' also indicate direct access to an internal source of information.

When I say 'I see a tree', my subjective impression of the tree is paralleled by objective neural events, consequent on activation of certain visual receptors. Since these receptors are influenced by external events, I can also say that I observe the tree, rather than merely 'experience' it. On the other hand, the subjective impression of 'knowing that I see (something)' is not related to sense organs or to the outside world. It is, therefore, an item of experience, but not an observation. Such an item of experience, according to the thesis of psychophysical parallelism should also have its counterpart, and this should be some internal state of the brain, unrelated to sense organs.

If the conclusions of Sections 2.2, 2.3, and 2.4 are accepted—namely that learning is one of the most important of conscious processes—we must conclude that introspection involves learning about some internal state. While we are learning to distinguish these states, our utterances about these states can be regarded as hypothetical, in the sense implied by Bunge (1977) (see p. 10). Later, however, they can be thought of as referring to validated hypotheses. Most of our statements based on introspection are in the latter category, and should therefore usually be taken at face value.

It is possible to modify experimentally the internal state of an animal or human brain. It is also possible to assess what an experimental subject can distinguish. The process of introspection thus becomes accessible to experimental investigation. We may therefore attempt to define empirically which internal states are potentially available to introspection. In addition to this wholly empirical matter however, there is an associated theoretical problem: how can introspection be possible? It seems a formidable enigma. But if it is noted that only a limited range of internal states can be the subject of direct introspection then the question becomes slightly more accessible. Towards the end of this book the question will be raised again.

It might be suggested that to regard introspection as a scientifically investigable attribute of brains, rather than a somewhat mystical *a priori* faculty, is admitting a premise which undermines the philosophical basis advanced in Chapter 1. There is certainly an element of truth in this argument. It will be considered in the final chapter.

2.8. Special attributes of higher primates

The higher primates are distinct amongst mammalian species because of the sophistication of some of their mental processes. The emergence of human intelligence is commonly regarded as the culmination of evolutionary processes in this regard. At this point it is appropriate merely to list some of these distinctive faculties, leaving discussion of them until Chapter 7. Those to be considered are: the capacity for construction of a sensorimotor model of the environment prior to any action (i.e. the faculty of 'thought'); the capacity to imitate; and the linguistic ability, which has had such a powerful influence on the development of the human species.

This résumé of the various problems to be dealt with in defining consciousness is by no means exhaustive. However within the limits of the above psychological ideas, it is hoped to show that the tangled network of apparently indefinable concepts to which the word 'consciousness' may apply, may, by careful analysis, be reduced to a rather more manageable system of ideas.

3. Anatomical substrates of conscious processes and the representation of meaning within the cerebrum

3.1. Cerebral localization of function, and the holistic approach—a compromise

3.1.1. ALTERNATIVE NOTIONS OF LOCALIZATION OF FUNCTION

IN the first chapter of this book a conceptual framework was presented in which the information which is subjectively available to consciousness is supposed to have its counterpart in parallel objective processes within the brain. The most obvious way in which such parallelism might exist is in terms of spatial mapping of information. It is the aim of this chapter to consider further such a notion of mapping.

Before beginning this task, a possible source of misunderstanding should be clarified. What is being mapped is information *in abstract*—subjectively apprehended information, that is. This information, being abstract, has no spatial location, though its objective parallel certainly does have. As Schrödinger (1959) put it:

> Mind has erected the objective outside world of the natural philosopher out of its own stuff. . . . While the stuff from which our world picture is built . . . is, and always remains a construct of the mind, and cannot be proved to have any other existence, yet the conscious mind itself remains a stranger within the construct, it has no living space in it, you can spot it nowhere in space.

Thus, we should not say that a portion of experience is *located* in a certain region of the brain, though the abstract structures of experience are paralleled by spatial relationships of objective brain structures. It is in this sense that the concept of cerebral localization of function assumes its considerable significance.

A debate of very long standing has existed between the localizationist approach to cerebral function and the holistic approach, which appears to conflict with it. The former asserts that different memories, and different perceptual, motivational, and volitional processes are spatially localized in different parts of the cerebral cortex, or of other cerebral structures. The latter asserts that these psychological functions are more or less uniformly spread throughout large volumes of cerebral tissue.

As a further caution against a simplistic view of cerebral localization of function, the words of Hebb (1958) can be quoted:

> No psychological function can exist within a segment of cortex by itself. We commonly say that vision is localized in the visual area, a part of the occipital lobe; but this does not mean that the whole process of seeing (or even visual imagery) can occur in the visual lobe. What it means is that an essential part of the process occurs there, and only there.

However, even with Hebb's qualification in mind, considerable uncertainty exists concerning the range of applicability of the localizationist approach to cerebral function. To what degree of spatial resolution can valid correlations be drawn between pathophysiological signs, and localized disturbance of cerebral tissue? Is such localization really an indication of the principles of normal function, or is it merely a consequence of some aspects of anatomical connectivity, while *functional* localization is in fact more flexible and variable? Does cerebral localization refer to mechanisms of *processing* information or to the mode of *storage* of information? Does the concept of localization of function apply at all to some regions of the cerebral hemisphere, or to some identifiable psychological functions? Or are there other conceptual approaches which can form a better basis for unifying existing evidence? The localizationist framework fits most easily into the traditions of clinical neurology, because localizing signs are of clear importance in diagnosis. Recent approaches to study of the central nervous system by means of single unit electrophysiological methods also inevitably encourage ideas of punctate localization. However the holistic approach also has its roots in older neurological data and ideas, for instance, in the writings of Flourens (see Young 1970), and in recent times it implicitly underlies much neurochemical and neuropharmacological work, where the influence of drugs or transmitters on whole brain performance is under consideration. There is certainly strong evidence to point each way in this debate (Lashley 1950; Walshe 1965; Geschwind 1965*a*, *b*; Phillips 1973), and one of the aims of the present chapter is to reconcile some of this conflicting evidence.

In one sense of course, cerebral localization of function is a well established fact. This fact rests partly on a large body of information relating the nature of a functional deficit with the site of the cerebral lesion, in sensory, motor, or association cortex, which causes it (Geschwind 1965*a*, *b*; Phillips 1973); it also rests on descriptions of a variety of motor manifestations (Phillips 1973) or subjective experiences (Penfield and Perot 1963; Brindley 1973) which are brought about when abnormal electrical activity originates in these various cortical sites as a result of electrical stimulation or seizure discharge. The fact of cerebral localization of function can hardly be questioned, though its significance for the functioning of the whole brain is a subject for debate. Suffice it here to point out that the localization of function revealed by this evidence is at a relatively gross level, commonly on the scale of the different cytoarchitectural fields rather than that of the basic building blocks of nervous tissue: the neurone, the axon, and the synapse.

Moreover, the deficits which follow many cortical lesions, whether they be motor or sensory deficits, or the various disconnection syndromes typical of lesions in areas of association cortex, are disturbances of whole channels of information flow rather than deficits which apply only to discrete 'units of information'.

Since techniques for studying the electrical activity of single neurones became available, much information has been obtained about the response properties of cerebral cortical neurones, particularly in areas of primary sensory cortex. The most important principle to emerge from such work is that neurones in primary sensory cortex function as 'feature detectors'—that is they respond selectively to certain simple spatial and/or temporal features in the information detected by sensory receptors (Whitfield 1969; Brooks and Jung 1973; Werner and Whitsel 1973; Imig and Adrian 1977). For instance, neurones in the visual cortex, which has been most extensively studied, may respond specifically to straight lines in the visual field orientated in a specific direction, or moving in a specific direction, or subtending a specific angle at the retina. Visual stimuli which do not contain the appropriate features for a particular neurone will not excite it (Brooks and Jung 1973). Neurones with related properties tend to be segregated in discrete bands or columns of the cortex (Mountcastle 1978). Moreover, the development of the selectivity of these feature-detecting neurones depends on the sensory environment to which an animal is exposed in the early post-natal period (Hirsch and Spinelli 1970; Blakemore and Mitchell 1973; Spinelli and Jensen 1979; Rauschecker and Singer 1979).

The precise relevance of feature-detecting neurones for psychological processes such as perception is uncertain. However, one hypothesis suggests that feature detectors which have so far been observed represent the lower end of an extensive hierarchy of feature detectors. Neurones in primary sensory cortex send projections to other areas of cortex (Jones and Powell 1969; Pandya and Kuypers 1969; Kawamura 1973), and by virtue of the convergence of these projections on neurones in these other areas, it is supposed that more complex features can be detected by neurones in non-primary sensory cortex. This hypothesis can also incorporate convergence from different primary sensory regions on to single neurones in association cortex, as a mechanism for polymodal feature-detection. The logical extension of this hypothesis is that single neurones exist in some regions of association cortex, which require such a complex combination of features as an adequate stimulus, that they are, in effect, specific to a single 'unitary percept'. Given that the functional connections required for such a mechanism can be modified in order to specify a new combination of features in the neurone on which they converge, this hypothesis also proposes that single neurones encode specific, individual 'units of memory'. This hypothesis has been referred to as the doctrine of the 'pontifical cell' (Sherrington 1940), and the individual neurones in such a scheme have been named by Konorski (1967), 'gnostic units':

> Having at our disposal the recent data derived from Hubel and Wiesel's experiments we can extrapolate their findings and explain the origin of perceptions according to the same principles, which were found to operate on the lower levels of the afferent systems. In other words, we can assume that perceptions experienced in humans' and animals' lives are represented not by *assemblies* of units, but by *single* units in the highest levels of particular analysers. We shall call these levels *gnostic areas*, and the units responsible for particular perceptions *gnostic units*. . . . According to this hypothesis, there is an essential difference between the role played by gnostic areas and that played by transit areas. Whereas the role of the transit units consists in integrating the elements of perceptions into more and more complex patterns, constituting the raw material for the gnostic units, the latter units represent the biologically-meaningful stimulus patterns which are used in associative processes and behaviour of the organisms. . . . The more developed the given analyser and the more complex the stimulus patterns represented in its gnostic units, the higher the ladder of transit fields mediating the final result.

The above hypothesis has also been colloquially termed 'the grandmother hypothesis' implying that somewhere in the cortex a single neurone exists, possessing all the connections required to recognize 'my grandmother'. The idea that a single neurone can encode the combination of information required to define a single complex class or pattern is also embodied in a recent theoretical approach to neocortical function by Marr (1970), who refers to 'diagnosis by a single cell' of a class or concept.

To clarify the direction of the following pages it should be confessed that the 'grandmother' hypothesis is an 'Aunt Sally'; her real function will have been served when she has effectively been demolished. Thus an extreme and highly explicit statement of the hypothesis has been given, not because it is given wide credence, but in order to clarify the arguments surrounding it. It clearly gives the concept of localization of function an entirely different meaning from that summarized earlier. Whether it is compatible with the neurological evidence on which the idea of cerebral localization of function, at the gross level, rests, is not immediately obvious. In the following sections the experimental evidence relating to this hypothesis will be discussed under three main headings, and subsequently theoretical arguments will be presented suggesting that, while this hypothesis might be superficially compatible with the philosophical principle of psychophysical parallelism (Section 1), it cannot give an answer to the central question which this principle allows us to ask, concerning the biological substrate of the subjective unity of consciousness (Section 2.1).

3.1.2. EVIDENCE CONCERNING CEREBRAL LOCALIZATION OF FUNCTION

3.1.2(a). Single unit approaches. The most direct kind of evidence which might substantiate the extreme localizationist viewpoint (the 'grandmother' hypothesis) should derive from the single neurone electrophysiological approach which actually led to the birth of the hypothesis. For rigorous validation of this hypothesis it would be necessary to show that electrical stimulation confined to a single neurone, presumably in some region of the human association cortex, was reliably associated with a 'single' sensory experience, which in itself should be atomic, but should nevertheless represent a complex stimulus. No evidence of this nature, which would presumably involve intracellular stimulation, is available. A less stringent criterion to be fulfilled, if this hypothesis were true, is that single neurones would give a response if, and only if, a highly complex and meaningful polysensory stimulus combination were presented to an animal. Such unique polysensory feature detectors certainly have not been found (see, for instance, Mountcastle, Lynch, Georgopoulos, Sakata, and Acuna 1975). However this cannot be regarded as conclusive evidence against the 'grandmother' hypothesis: it can easily be argued that failure to detect the unique 'grandmother-type' neurone may reflect purely the experimental difficulty of discovering the right appropriate stimulus out of an almost infinite array of other complex stimuli to which a neurone might alternatively be responsive Moreover, a small amount of evidence does exist, albeit restricted to a single sensory modality, that fairly complex feature detecting neurones do exist (Gross, Rocha-Miranda, and Bender 1972). In summary, single neurone studies do not provide positive evidence either for, or against the 'grandmother' hypothesis.

3.1.2(b). Experiences and other effects associated with gross electrical stimulation of brain tissue in conscious humans and in animals. Another approach to evaluation of the concept of cerebral localization of function derives from the procedures sometimes carried out during neurosurgical operations for relief of epilepsy, in which a variety of experiences are reported, and other motor responses are produced within the conscious patient by electrical stimulation of different regions of cerebral tissue. Similar procedures have been carried out more extensively in animals, though the information obtained is necessarily limited to motor manifestations rather than sensory experiences.

It is well known that stimulation of the primary motor cortex in such circumstances can give rise to highly circumscribed motor movements (Phillips 1973). In this case, cortical localization of function clearly applies on a much smaller scale than the individual cytoarchitectural areas which constitute the motor cortex. After stimulating areas of primary sensory cortex in conscious patients, sensory experiences are reported, corresponding in type to the region of sensory cortex stimulated (Penfield 1958). Such experiences may contain spatial information of some precision, so that the relative position of two simultaneously-evoked phosphenes can be described reliably and consistently (Brindley 1973). Here again, it is clear that cortical localization of function applies at a much smaller scale than that of the cytoarchitectural field. In both cases however there is some dispute about the precise nature of localization—that is, whether it is an 'abrupt and discrete mosaic', or a series of 'minute but overlapping fields'. In general much of the evidence derived from stimulation of areas of primary sensory and motor cortex in conscious man and animals is compatible with the idea of punctate localization, even at the single cell level. However, it certainly does not rule out other hypotheses where localization of function applies at a somewhat larger level than the single neurone, since minimal electrical stimulation of brain tissue excites a great many nerve cells simultaneously.

In contrast to this evidence, stimulation of other regions of cortex—most of the extensive regions of association cortex—produces no comparable coherent or precise subjective experience or motor effect, though vague and confused experiences may be reported and functions occurring at the time (such as speech) may be abolished during the period of stimulation (Penfield 1958; Penfield and Perot 1963). The existence of these large regions of 'silent' cortex would seem to argue against the 'grandmother' hypothesis in these regions. This conclusion requires further comment however since stimulation of association cortex in the temporal lobe, and of the underlying hippocampus to which it sends many projections can be associated with very vivid experiences, amounting in some cases to coherent reruns of past experiences. Such results might be taken to indicate that some key to the retrieval of distant memories is spatially localized with some precision in these cortical regions. However, Penfield and Perot warn against ideas of such a punctate localization of the memory trace:

> It is clear that there must be in the cortex a most important mechanism of inhibition associated with, and protecting the activation and facilitation. The electrode applied to the cortex must bring electric current into contact with many possibly responsive neurone circuits. But the result is only the activation of *one* previous strip of experience, not two or three or more, which would result in confusion. Subsequent stimulation at approximately the same point may produce a different scene in a different time, but again only one, not two.

To summarize, stimulation of exposed cortex in conscious humans and animals has provided evidence for small scale localization of function, not necessarily at the cellular level, in primary sensory and motor regions. However, it has also provided some clear evidence that other principles underlie the organization of large areas of association cortex.

3.1.2(c). Functional deficits after cortical lesions. When the functional deficits resulting from limited lesions of cortical tissue are considered, a contrast is seen, similar to that noted above, between primary sensory and motor cortex, on the one hand, and the bulk of association cortex on the other. Small lesions in primary motor or sensory cortex can produce highly restricted, but quite definite functional deficits—such as sharply demarcated areas of blindness, or paralysis and spasticity confined to single limbs or parts of limbs. Damage to areas of association cortex also produces functional deficits which may amount to deficient discriminative ability (in association areas related to a single sensory channel) or to various types of disconnection syndrome (in association areas which integrate information from more than one sensory channel). Here, however, in contrast to the primary sensory areas, 'there is little evidence to suggest that very discrete lesions of association cortex . . . have major behavioural effects' (Geschwind 1965*a*). Increase in the size of a lesion of association cortex will increase the severity of the global deficit in the associative function concerned (Luria 1973), but there is no evidence that individual items of associated information are selectively lost following small-scale destruction of association cortex. Thus, the more complex discriminative and associative tasks are more easily disrupted than the simple ones. Admittedly the central nervous system has an extraordinary capacity to 'cover up' its own deficits (Gazzaniga 1978) so that subtle deficits resulting from small-scale lesions might be very difficult to detect. Nevertheless, at first sight, these findings suggest that different loci in any individual region of association cortex are more or less equipotential, in contrast to the primary projection areas, and that the neuronal connections which encode any identifiable acquired association are not localized, but are more or less uniformly distributed throughout the region.

The concept of equipotentiality has perhaps been most strongly stated by Lashley (1950) who, on the basis of extensive experiments on animals concluded that there was no localization of the memory trace at all: he did not obtain evidence of specific disconnection syndromes on damaging different parts of the association cortex. These conclusions have been questioned on the grounds that rather complex situations were used, so that animals probably used a variety of cues. Some of the findings may have relied on preservation of intact subcortical pathways (since the extensiveness of cortical projections to the basal ganglia was not recognized at the time Lashley was working). Other findings may have relied on use of animals in which the high degree of cerebralization found in higher primates does not apply. Nevertheless, other evidence does indicate some degree of flexibility of cortical tissue. Although under normal circumstances certain areas of cortex are most efficiently able to acquire their corresponding categories of information, nevertheless under abnormal circumstances other cortical areas may assume the same function. This has been shown by comparing the behavioural effects of single stage cortical lesions with those of equivalent lesions made in more than one step. Recovery of function can be more complete in the case of serial lesions, especially if rehearsal of the task, or non-specific enrichment of the environment occurs in the inter-operative period (Ades and Raab 1949; Orbach and Fantz 1958; Dru and Walker 1976). From such experiments it seems that Lashley's concept of equipotentiality is still useful, subject only to the qualification that different cortical areas are quantitatively different in potentiality, though qualitatively more or less equipotential. This conclusion seems applicable despite evidence that neurones in neighbouring cytoarchitectural regions have different response properties: the differences between adjacent regions are usually described as shifts in the proportions of cells having a particular response pattern, rather than as abrupt all or none qualitative changes (e.g. Sakata, Takaoka, Kawarasaki, and Shibutani 1973; Mountcastle *et al.* 1975).

The notion of equipotentiality seems directly opposed to the extreme localizationist position, in which it is supposed that individual memories are encoded in individual neurones. However, at this point in the argument, the advocate of the 'grandmother' hypothesis might parry with the suggestion that there are several unique feature detector neurones for each unitary percept. Both Konorski and Marr make use of this idea. The latter writes: 'If, as seems likely, there do exist several representations of any given concept, they are probably independent' (Marr 1970). Thus if these several representations are situated in different loci in the cortex, detection of deficits following lesions might be very difficult. The general conclusion to be drawn from lesion experiments seems, despite this qualification, to give stronger support to some form of holistic mechanism of memory coding than it does to the ultra-localizationist interpretation.

3.1.2(d). A comparison between association cortex and corpus striatum. At this point in the discussion of the concept of cerebral localization of function, it is appropriate to point out certain features of similarity between the extensive areas of association cortex, each of which appears to be an 'equipotential' surface of grey matter, and those very large blocks of subcortical grey matter—the caudate and the putamen (collectively 'the striatum'). These nuclei, despite their large size, have no gross order or system in their layout. They seem, in many ways, to approximate a random network of interconnecting cells, so that considerable divergence and convergence is possible in passage of information from cortical to striatal tissue.

The three types of evidence used to evaluate the concept of localization of function in the cortex indicate important similarities between association cortex and caudate–putamen. Thus, studies of the responses of single neurones in caudate–putamen have not revealed a topographical relationship between the location of an active neurone and the location of concomitant motor movement: the behaviour of neurones in these nuclei seems to reflect other aspects of motor function (Niki, Sakai, and Kubota 1972; Soltysik, Hull, Buchwald, and Fekete 1975). Electrical stimulation of caudate–putamen has been carried out in animals and has been reported to produce inhibitory effects on concomitant motor movements with low frequency stimulation (Akert and Anderson 1951; Buchwald, Wyers, Lauprecht, and Heuser 1961), or activation of movement if stimulation frequency is high (Forman and Ward 1952). These effects are global in character, affecting many aspects of movement and posture simultaneously, and although differences in emphasis and aim of these complex changes have been observed, it seems improbable that a detailed motor map, such as that in the motor cortex, still awaits discovery. This evidence suggests that important aspects of the motor function of the striatum cannot be discerned by studies at the neuronal level, or the level of limited foci of nervous tissue, but must be discovered from observing the operation of large structural entities as integral wholes. This view is confirmed when one considers evidence about anatomical lesions in these structures. In monkeys, no significant motor impairment can be observed if lesions are less than 3 mm across (Mettler and Mettler 1942). In man, substantial lesions to the corpus striatum resulting from haemorrhagic episodes (Jung and Hassler 1960) or neurosurgical intervention for Parkinson's disease (Meyers 1951) may have neglible effects. Larger-scale damage may affect tone and gait contralaterally (Liddell and Phillips 1940), or cause disorders akin to choreoathetosis, in chimpanzees (Kennard 1944), and if damage is bilateral, animals will automatically walk straight ahead, regardless of obstacles (Mettler and Mettler 1942). These effects, however, represent global damage to the motor mechanisms in the brain rather than discrete limited functional deficits, and there is little evidence of localization of separate functions in different parts of the caudate–putamen. In this respect, these disorders are similar to the various motor disorders of the basal ganglia which can be clearly attributed to neurochemical or cellular pathological processes affecting all regions of the striatum fairly uniformly (Bernheimer, Birkmayer, Hornykiewicz, Jellinger, and Seitelberger 1973; Bird, MacKay, Rayner, and Iversen 1973).

In qualification of the previous paragraph it is worth adding that although there appears to be no topographic motor map in the striatum, this does not mean there are no functional gradients of any sort in this region. A number of examples have been found in which complex behavioural functions (often goal-directed behaviour) are disturbed to differing extents by lesions in dorsal and ventral striatum (Neill and Grossman 1970; Morgan and Routtenberg 1977; Neill and Herndon 1978). The significance of these various observations is uncertain, but they must eventually be reconciled with a concept of the striatum in which motor movements are represented diffusely rather than in an orderly map.

3.1.2(e). Conclusion. The conclusion of this section takes the form of a compromise, which recognizes two fairly distinct types of organization within cerebral structures. On the one hand, the primary receiving areas of cortex show localization of function on a quite small scale. This will be referred to as 'punctate' localization, a term which deliberately leaves open the question of whether the single neurone itself is the fundamental functional unit in which information is stored. On the other hand, many of the various cytoarchitectural divisions of association cortex, and also the caudate–putamen appear to operate as larger functional units, where the single neurone does not, by itself, display responses of strong functional significance for the animal as a whole.

In terms of the overall organization of the brain, the latter two parts of the cerebral hemispheres have an important feature in common: they both comprise the intermediate bridge between primary inflows to the hemisphere via the sensory pathways, and the primary motor outflows via the pyramidal system or the limbic outflow pathways. This statement is readily acceptable as it applies to association cortex. Its application to the striatum needs some justification however, since the basal ganglia are traditionally regarded as a subcortical centre from which a major descending system arises, independent of the pyramidal tract—the so-called extrapyramidal system. A consideration of the efferent pathways from the striatum must indeed mention—besides a large projection to the thalamus—descending pathways supplying structures such as the substantia nigra, subthalamus, zona incerta, hypothalamus, red nucleus, and midbrain reticular formation. However, from these structures the descending pathway becomes obscure. Moreover, many of the structures mentioned (such as substantia nigra and subthalamus) have ascending pathways as their major outflow, projecting to the caudate–putamen itself, to the globus pallidus or directly to the thalamus. It thus seems likely that the principal structure to which nervous activity in the striatum is channelled is, directly or indirectly, the thalamus, especially nuclei ventralis lateralis and ventralis anterior (Brodal 1969; Poirier, Filion, Langelier, and Larochelle 1975; Faull and Mehler 1978). From here, activity returns once more to the cortex, especially the motor cortex and regions in front of it. In qualification one should add that there is recent evidence that the substantia nigra (pars reticulata) projects to the tectum, a region of origin of a direct pathway to the spinal cord (Faull and Mehler 1978; Beckstead, Domesick, and Nauta 1979). Nevertheless the recurrent pathway from striatum to cortex should still be regarded as the major route of outflow from the striatum. Clinical evidence confirms this view: abnormal motor movement associated with disorders of the basal ganglia can be decreased or abolished by lesions in the pathways from the corpus striatum, via thalamus, motor cortex, and pyramidal tract (Bucy and Case 1937; Putnam 1940; Meyers, Sweeney, and Schwidde 1950).

Since the caudate–putamen receives an important input converging on it from most regions of cortical grey matter, and its efferent activity is directed mainly back to the cortex, it seems justified to consider it, along with the association cortex, as part of the unknown territory lying between the relatively well-charted regions concerned with sensory inflow and motor outflow. It seems that unusual principles of organization underlie the function of this *terra incognita* which make it difficult to comprehend if one is closely wedded to the concept of punctate localization of function as it applies to primary receiving areas of cortex (and to many other parts of the nervous system). It appears, by contrast, that any definite portion of information is distributed diffusely in these regions, in a manner akin to holographic devices, though the principles of organization of the 'cerebral holograph' will surely be very different from any man-made device. Furthermore, it will be argued that essential properties of consciousness (and by extension, of many other psychological concepts) may find some form of explanation by referring to the principles of organization of these central regions which form the elusive frontier between 'the way in' and 'the way out' of the cerebral hemisphere.

3.2. Anatomical substrates of conscious processes

3.2.1. THE UNITY OF CONSCIOUSNESS AND THE HOLISTIC APPROACH

In Chapters 1 and 2 the concept of consciousness was analysed (though not rigorously defined) in terms of a variety of premises, some philosophical or metaphysical in nature, others of more definite psychological significance. Cerebral localization of function, at the small scale (including that of the single neurone)—that is punctate localization—is readily compatible with the basic philosophy of psychophysical parallelism put forward in Chapter 1: portions of information apprehended in subjective form within consciousness are paralleled by combinations of electrical activity within the many individual loci of which the primary receiving areas are made up. However, the most important of the psychological premises, concerning the subjective unity of consciousness (Section 2.1) cannot be accounted for simply by a punctate relationship between structure and function in the brain. An hypothetical cortical surface, entirely composed of many loci, independent except in so far as they have overlapping sensory inputs or supply overlapping motor groups, cannot account for the existence of the central 'I' to which all portions of information are subjectively available.

Is it possible to amend our idea of punctate localization, so that it can incorporate this premise? This could be attempted in two ways: (i) All the different punctate loci of the cerebral cortex could radiate axonal projections inwards to a supremely central focus where 'the person' is to be found. This possibility corresponds to the notion, succinctly expressed by John (1967) 'that the cortical mantle is a screen on to which pictures are flashed, to be viewed by a popcorn-munching homunculus'. (ii) Alternatively this functionally central focus might radiate axonal projections outwards to each separate cortical locus. In either case, the electrical activity in the converging or diverging radiations must be imagined to generate the signal, which adheres to every other portion of information in the mind/brain, and signifies 'this picture is part of me'.

Consider alternative (i). At the sites in the central focus where the inwardly-directed projections meet, the signals carried in the converging pathways may either merge, or remain discrete. For instance the *former* would inevitably happen if the converging signals relied entirely on currently-known electrophysiological mechanisms, since by these mechanisms a neurone has no way of registering which synaptic inputs, out of a large number of possible inputs, actually contribute to the firing of the neurone. In this case, the combination of inputs from the cortex would not specify the picture contained within the cortex. No message equivalent to 'this picture is part of me' can be generated because the picture is not available to the central focus. The *latter* possibility, in which converging signals remain discrete could not be accomplished by known electrophysiological mechanisms. However, hypothetical biochemical codes have been proposed which would allow a neurone to record which of its synapses contributed to its firing (Ungar 1968). Nevertheless, such small scale (perhaps intracellular) processes have in no way explained the unity of consciousness. They have merely transferred the philosophical problem from the large scale of the cerebral hemisphere, to the small scale of the central focus, or central neurone: the hypothetical biochemical code is equivalent to the principle of punctate localization, with all its attendant problems. Unless some other principle of organization can be suggested, the above argument leads only to an infinite inward spiral, a veritable *reductio ad absurdum*.

Consideration of alternative (ii) leads to comparable snags. At the sites where the diverging projections meet with the various cortical loci, the signals radiating from the central focus, supposedly giving rise to mental unity, may either merge with or remain separate from the signals related to the outer environment in each cortical locus. The alternative electrophysiological or biochemical mechanisms by which signals respectively merge with, or remain separate from each other, would be the same as mentioned in the previous paragraph. If the signals merge, it remains unexplained how mental unity has been created, since the signal representing mental unity could not be distinguished from other inputs which contribute to neuronal firing. If the signals remain discrete, no solution to the problem is provided either, short of something totally mystical. The system would seem to be capable of functioning unchanged without the central focus.

The above arguments may seem abstrusely theoretical. However, it is necessary to consider and reject these possibilities in order to clarify the paradox inherent in the belief that punctate localization of function can give an account of conscious processes. Unless some other principle of organization can be suggested, it is impossible to explain the curious complexity of consciousness: many patterns of information exist in the mind, but a further omnipresent pattern of information co-exists with them, ensuring that they are all experienced as part of a tight subjective unity.

Consider an analogy. If a group of people want to form an association for some reason, their coming-together may be initiated either if they all write a letter to one of their number ('the secretary'), or if the secretary writes a letter to each one of them. But an association formed in either of these ways will not function as a cohesive integral whole until all persons concerned have the *possibility of communicating with all others*. If this potentiality is present, the overall functioning of the group will be radically changed.

When a portion of information passes through consciousness, and we can say of it 'this is part of me', what do we mean? Can this loose description of experience be translated into more abstract terms, in which the essentials of the interaction of information to which this expression refers can be identified. A suggested clarification of the phrase 'this picture is part of me' is as follows: 'This portion of information is part of a whole, because it has the *potentiality* of interacting with any other portion of information comprised within the whole'. This statement implies that, as long as consciousness is preserved, there is no theoretical limit to the associations which can be made between apparently unrelated portions of information held within the mind. This does not mean that *all* possible statistically significant associations are, of necessity, detected by any conscious being. Some associations are more obvious, because they are statistically more significant, or are more concrete, or less dispersed in time. Often, one person can detect an association which his peers have not noticed, though they may then recognize the association when it has been pointed out. Nevertheless, the enormous potentiality for interaction between initially separate portions of information does seem to be a definite property of consciousness. Without it, in an hypothetical mind where all groups of information remain quite separate, one could scarcely use the word 'consciousness'.

By what mechanism can this interpretation of the notion of consciousness be represented at the objective level? The simplest parallel of the interpretation given above is in anatomical terms: consciousness exists because of the existence of a structure (or structures) in which, by virtue of the structure's internal organization, all parts (neurones) are in potential synaptic contact with every other part. In such a network the existence of connections at the microanatomical level does not mean that the association of any grouping of related inputs will *of necessity* be detected by the network, but it does mean that the *potentiality* exists that it can be detected. In such a structure, every incoming portion of information would be spread more or less evenly through the whole network, so the structure would show the type of equipotential relationship between locality in the brain tissue and information storage, to which reference has already been made. In this hypothetical network it is not necessary that every neurone should be literally in synaptic connection with every other: polysynaptic connections could ensure the rapid spread of a signal to all parts of the structure. Thus, although any one neurone may have sufficient synaptic outputs to influence, at most, a few thousand other neurones monosynaptically, nevertheless, the neurone could influence thousands of millions of neurones trisynaptically ($2000^3 = 8 \times 10^9$, the latter number being comparable to the neurone numbers in the human forebrain.) The essential anatomical feature is that there should be no parcellation or separation of channels of information flow. Rather, there should be the possibility, at the anatomical level of thorough intermingling of all inputs. Such a structure will henceforth be referred to as an *omniconnected structure*.

If mechanisms existed for forming a lasting imprint of each portion of information, all such coded portions would be potentially capable of interaction (and correlation) with any other. Learnt information would thus be stored in a holographic fashion, without a punctate relation between information and locality of storage. It might be suggested that such an omniconnected network would have an information capacity much less than one in which independent neurones encoded discrete portions of information. This point cannot be given a satisfactory answer until the omniconnection principle can be described in mathematical terms; but it should be pointed out that in the scheme proposed here (in contrast to the 'grandmother' type of information map) a variety of independent associations can be represented in any one neurone and its synapses. An actual example of this is provided by the experiments of Ramos, Schwartz, and John (1976) in which cats were trained to respond differently to slightly different visual stimuli, and were then presented with an intermediate, ambiguous stimulus. Single cortical neurones gave consistently different patterns of response to the one stimulus according to the way the cats interpreted it (as shown by their subsequent behavioural response). An interesting corollary of the multiple coding functions of a single neurone appears in Chapter 5 (p. 106).

It may also be objected here that if the brain is to be able to recognize portions of information in such an omniconnected network, there must be some sort of 'homunculus' which 'takes note' of the various combinations of connections which represent each portion of information. In one sense this is true. However, a homunculus defined in this way would be an elusive and ghostly beast, with no restricted anatomical localization in the cerebrum. It would be defined purely in physiological terms and it would be particularly concerned with the physiological processes involved in acquiring memory. No self-respecting homunculus would be satisfied to have a physiology without an anatomy. The previous paragraph has in fact described the substrate of anatomical organization which can permit conscious processes such as memory to occur within itself, in a self-sufficient manner, demanding no external independent 'homunculus' as 'observer' and 'learner'. The mode of physiological operation of this type will be dealt with in subsequent chapters.

It should be pointed out that the internal relationships envisaged within omniconnected structures underlying consciousness are entirely those of synaptic connections. The synaptic relationships supposed to operate in these holographic structures would be an intricate and specific web, as opposed to some models of the function of massed nerve cells in which the postulate of a random neuronal network is taken to imply the ordered transmission of simple linear or planar waves of excitation through blocks of brain tissue (Beurle 1956). Furthermore, 'field effects' are not involved here though they have sometimes been postulated in discussions of holistic function of the brain (John 1967). I do not want to adopt a dogmatic attitude to this important issue of 'connectionism' and its possible limitations. Indeed, in later sections of this work psychological functions are considered which challenge the connectionist premise and seem to require diffuse quasi-hormonal action of neurotransmitters. However, as yet I see no sure reason for also invoking electrical field effects as carriers of biologically-significant information. In stating this, evidence should nevertheless be mentioned that field effects can significantly influence both electroencephalographic rhythms and some behavioural functions (Gavalas, Walter, Hamer, and Adey 1970; Bawin, Gavalas-Medici, and Adey 1973). Ultimately it may be necessary to include field effects in an account of the essential biological organization of the brain.

The argument presented in the preceding paragraphs has brought forward the tentative suggestion that the essential anatomical substrate of consciousness is a structure where there is no punctate localization, simply because all the neuronal units within it are capable of influencing all others in the structure. This concept stemmed from an analysis of the idea of Section 2.1 concerning consciousness *as an integrity*. However, an exactly analogous argument can be provided concerning some of the subjective *subdivisions* of consciousness. Thus, just as we may say (of a portion of information of which we are, in general terms, *aware*) 'this picture is part of me', so we would say (of a picture which, in a more specific sense, we *see*) 'this picture is part of my visual world'. We *know* it is part of our visual world, rather than that of some other sensory channel, without any possibility of denial (unless we are under the influence of hallucinogens, when, according to some descriptions, stimuli in one sensory channel may influence perceptions in another). Thus, any portion of information in our visual world is impregnated by the additional message contained in this phrase, thus ensuring the subjective unity of our visual world. This subjective fact must be explained by arguments similar to those already presented, namely by postulating an omniconnected structure. The same arguments of course apply to other sensory modalities in so far as they are subjectively separate and recognizable. It is also possible that volitional processes in humans can be subdivided into 'verbal' and 'non-verbal' volitions, which are subjectively separable, and therefore correspond to separate omniconnected structures. It is not the purpose of this section to identify all the partially independent subjective entities within our consciousness which have a separate representation in different areas of the brain. However, it is fairly clear that the different cerebral regions which each display some form of equipotentiality, do correspond to different subjective unities within the overall structure of consciousness. Indeed, it might not overstretch the concept of 'omniconnection' to apply it to those primary receiving areas where some form of punctate localization of function is evident: the individual loci therein, whether 'abrupt and discrete' or 'minute but overlapping' might themselves be very small holographic structures, rather than collections of functionally independent neurones.

Thus, consciousness consists of parts, and has its own complex structure. But all these parts must be welded into a whole, if our concept of consciousness is to be preserved. To put this in a developmental context one could quote Piaget and Inhelder (1969), concerning the inner representation of the environment: 'In the beginning there exists no single space. There are rather several heterogeneous spaces, all centred on the child's own body—buccal, tactile, visual, auditory, and postural space. . . . The different spaces are then gradually co-ordinated.' We must therefore postulate that the subdivisions of consciousness are *relatively* separate from each other because, *within* the representation of each subdivision, interconnections are richer than *between* subdivisions. Just as Lashley's concept of equipotentiality must allow that different regions may be *quantitatively* different in importance for a particular function, so the concept of omniconnectedness is qualitatively true but not true in strict quantitative terms.

3.2.2. GESTALT PSYCHOLOGY AND THE HOLISTIC APPROACH

Before leaving this discussion of the unity of consciousness, there is another important strand to be unravelled in this psychological and philosophical analysis, which introduces the question of the nature of meaning. Many times in the preceding pages the phrase 'portion of information' has been used, leaving open the question whether these portions are amorphous or have their individual structure. When we say of a portion of information which impinges on consciousness, 'This picture is part of me', what significance should be given to the word 'picture'? Is it a unit of information; or a number of units of information, whose most important characteristic is the *quantity* of such units; or is there more to it than that? It is suggested here that any portion of information which is subjectively recognizable contains, in essence, not only a number of individual items of information but also a much larger number of interrelationships between the different items. The intricacies of these profuse interrelationships are crucial for recognition: without them we could not, for instance, distinguish between a horse, and a 'horse' in which nose and tail had changed place. In brief, for any recognizable pattern or picture the *whole is greater than the sum of the parts*. This definition is relatively easy to grasp, and forms the basis of a series of loosely connected ideas, united under the term 'Gestalt psychology' (Gestalt = form or shape).

The basic idea, applied most easily to perception, particularly (as above) visual perception, has in fact a considerably wider range of applicability. It applies to any recognizable entity within our other senses (except for 'pure' primary sensations, closely linked to function of individual sensory receptors, such as primary colours or primary tastes). Any relatively separate portion of information stored within our memory also has the character of a Gestalt, namely a set of parts whose essence and unity is defined by the structure of a large number of relationships between the parts. Any idea in our minds is in the form of a complex constellation of interrelated subsidiary concepts and memories, although the separateness of the individual words with which we label our ideas may give a false impression of simplicity of any idea. What is more, any relatively separate motor skill or learned routine, verbal or non-verbal, is defined in part by the interrelationships between its components as well as by the significance of the components in themselves. In the most general terms, anything to which a conscious person attaches *meaning* at the subjective level, is a complex structure, a network of bits of information in which prolific inter-relationships are the essence.

The Gestalt idea has been defined as follows: 'When spatial, visual, auditory and intellectual processes are such as to display properties other than could be derived from the parts of summation, they may be regarded as unities illustrating what we mean by the word "Gestalten" ' (Kohler 1938). In a Gestalt the whole is more than the sum of the parts simply because the parts can be related in many ways other than by summation. To put it another way, if information is to be meaningful, it is not merely a quantity—though it may often be convenient to quantify it, for other purposes. In fact the meaningfulness of information may have little to do with its quantitative aspects. It must be admitted, however, that a mathematical account of meaningfulness might be derivable in rather more complex terms than that of simple quantity—for instance as some rational comparison between the number of components and the number of linkages between these components necessary to define a particular concept.

Usually we are not much aware of the complexity of structure of familiar meanings, though if we develop a high degree of skill in some direction our capacity for analysis and resynthesis of the meanings with which we are specially concerned will increase. In pathological circumstances (lesions of secondary sensory, or of association cortex) the disruption of the mental faculty for instantaneous assemblage of the components of a Gestalt may be clinically obvious (see examples quoted by Luria 1973, pp. 121–5).

A Gestalt is not a random association of items, otherwise we might without a moment's pause for thought, consider that an arbitrary grouping consisting of, say, 'penicillin', 'Paganini', 'baked beans', and 'scissors' was a meaningful unit, rather than a random collection of naming words. The multitude of Gestalts which fill our consciousness are clusters of associations grouped mainly in the same way as are statistically significant associations filling the environment. Furthermore, some of these statistically significant relationships represent negative correlations of features in the external world. In elucidating the organizational substrate which underlies our appreciation of 'meaning' (in its most general sense) we have, therefore, to explain how a Gestalt can find representation within the brain tissue, and moreover, how clusters of significant negative and positive correlations can be imprinted, in lasting form, into the memory trace.

A point of clarification is needed here. In one of the above paragraphs meaningful patterns were described as '*relatively* separate Gestalts'. In fact, strict separation of blocks of meaning does not occur; all Gestalts may be to some extent interlinked within the overall structure of consciousness. This is easily overlooked by those for whom meaning is too closely linked to verbal nomenclature. Thus, for instance, in discussing the 'grandmother' hypothesis, a basic fallacy has so far been overlooked. The single word 'grandmother' in fact means rather different things according to the context in which it is used. It might bring to mind any of the following associations: 'grandmother's appearance', 'the sound of her voice', 'grandmother's house', 'grandmother's childhood memories', and so on. Here we have a basic flaw in the notion previously described in which there is a punctate representation of subjective phenomena, such as 'individual memories': such phenomena cannot be dissected into units without their essence being destroyed. There is a sense in which it is incorrect to speak of individual memories. It would be more correct to speak of 'memory' as such, since memory is to a considerable extent a faculty to be considered as a whole, in which all the complex correlations found in the external world are encoded in a fashion which preserves their manifold inter-relationships—spatial, temporal, statistical, logical, causal, and so on. The weakness of the 'grandmother' hypothesis is that it allows classification in representation of information in the brain, but it does not allow multiple cross-classifications.

By what kind of anatomical structure can the interlinked clusters of information which have just been described, be represented? Certainly not by a punctate relation between structure and 'bits' of memoranda, since with punctate localization no way can be found to map the *network* of interrelated parts, which are the essence of meaning. Although for certain restricted types of meaning the internal relationships may be of a rather specialized nature, nevertheless, meaning *in general* demands a very versatile and unspecialized medium for its representation. Just as there is no theoretical limit to the possible associations *between* Gestalts, there is also no limit to the associations *within* Gestalts, which consciousness may be called upon to make. So we must conclude that the anatomical substrate for representation of meaning is, once again, a structure, or structures, in which all units (neurones) are in potential relationship with every other. Further, since negative correlates are part of the information structure of many Gestalts, the web of connections by which a Gestalt finds its representation must include many inhibitory connections as well as excitatory ones. These may be likened to 'inhibitory surrounds' at a lower level of the nervous system with the difference that a complex network of interconnected cells, rather than a single cell, has an inhibitory surround. Subjective phenomena suggestive of inhibitory surrounds are to be found in the difficulty we commonly experience in attending to more than one complex Gestalt (such as two conversations), simultaneously.

From the large and random network of excitatory and inhibitory connections an unlimited variety of much smaller network configurations can then be selected to represent the various meanings which are to be held within the network. The actual mechanism by which the anatomical (i.e. potential) connections in the overall network are selected and turned into the physiologically active (i.e. actual functional) connections, which represent meaning will be dealt with in subsequent chapters.

3.2.3. EVIDENCE ON CORTICAL AND STRIATAL CONNECTIVITY

It should by now be clear that the omniconnection principle as initially stated is intended to be no more than a first approximation to the situation which exists in real brain structures. It will not be surprising to find elements of omniconnectedness co-existing with discontinuities and heterogeneities in the network, and this in turn implies that linkages of many regions may be indirect (multisynaptic). In practical terms the real significance of the omniconnection principle is that it serves to focus attention upon diffusely organized pathways, whereas commonly the pathways displaying the most precise topographical organization are regarded as most interesting. At many levels of the nervous system there is evidence of diffuse organization of connections, alongside the more precisely distributed pathways. In the cerebellum for instance, there is a striking contrast between the precision of the climbing fibre terminations, and the diffuseness of the mossy fibre/parallel fibre sequence of inputs (Llinás 1970). The present book is, however, more particularly concerned with the forebrain, especially the neocortex and neostriatum.

In the neocortex, all regions contain a network of *short* association fibres (1–3 mm in length) which do not leave the grey matter, and which link adjacent areas uniformly, without regard for cytoarchitectural boundaries (Cajal 1911; Jones and Powell 1969; Colonnier and Sas 1978; Jones, Coulter, and Hendry 1978; Murray and Heath 1978). Szentágothai (1978*b*) has drawn particular attention to the diffuseness of distribution of recurrent collaterals of cortical pyramidal cells. Such components could provide the web of connections required for integrating cortical function on a small scale.

In addition, a great many long association pathways have been described, linking more distant regions of cortex (e.g. Jones and Powell 1969; Pandya and Kuypers 1969; Kawamura 1973). Recently, much evidence has been presented to suggest that some of these long pathways in the cortex are very precisely wired, with regions of origin or termination of a pathway lying in discrete columns or bands (see Mountcastle 1978). This evidence applies to thalamo–cortical, cortico–cortical and commissural pathways.

A great deal of this evidence refers to primary or secondary sensory cortex, or to motor cortex, that is to regions not primarily involved in the omniconnection principle postulated here. For some of these regions it has been shown that the earliest pattern of connections, present shortly after birth, is diffusely organized, and becomes discretely banded later (LeVay, Stryker, and Shatz 1978). Moreover, early environmental stimuli can play a role in determining the distribution of connections in the adult (Lund, Mitchell, and Henry 1978; Innocenti and Frost 1979). In the primary sensory and motor regions, where information patterns are still sufficiently closely related to the outside world to be regarded as spatial, or quasi-spatial representations, meanings are likely to be of a restricted type, with relationships largely limited to those possible in a two- (or three-) dimensional matrix. It is not surprising that the pattern of connections which come to form the adult structure of such regions is more highly ordered, and therefore less versatile than in other cortical regions.

In the association cortex, the usual pattern of distribution of cortico–cortical fibres is a more or less diffuse one, with waxing and waning density of connections within the regions of termination rather than systematic patterns of banding (e.g. Künzle and Akert 1977; Kaas, Lin, and Wagor 1977; Beckstead 1979). These regions are generally limited in extent to one or a few gyri rather than the whole cortex. This limitation of distribution is, however, counterbalanced by the large number of independent sets of connections which may pass from one cortical region to others. Mountcastle (1978) mentions some regions possessing known linkages with 10 or 20 other regions of cortex. Goldman and Nauta (1977) have presented some evidence of columnar distribution of connections within association cortex. Such evidence was, however, obtained from very young animals, and became less obvious in more mature brains. This study may thus relate to a developmental stage in the growth of genetically-wired connections, rather than to columnar distribution in the same sense as in primary areas of cortex. In conclusion, the association cortex has a very complex set of connections, but not a homogeneous uniform one. The relative separation of some components of consciousness thus finds an explanation. In any event the adult cerebral cortex appears to contain a sufficiency of diffusely converging and diverging connections, both long and short, to approximate the type of network postulated as a substrate for consciousness in the adult.

The striatum receives a major input of long axons from cortical structures, which are to some degree organized topographically (i.e. on an area to area basis) (Webster 1965; Kemp 1968; Kemp and Powell 1970; Blake 1974). However, both neuroanatomical (Kemp 1968; Kemp and Powell 1970) and 'electroanatomical' (Blake, Zarzecki, and Somjen 1976) studies indicate the existence of extensive overlap within the striatum of projections from separate cortical regions, so that considerable divergence and convergence is possible in passage of information from cortical to striatal tissue. In adult monkeys

Jones, Coulter, Burton, and Porter (1977) have produced evidence of discrete pockets of termination of cortical projections within the striatum. Likewise, Royce (1978) has shown patchy distribution of fibres from the centromedian nucleus of the thalamus terminating within the caudate nucleus. In addition, examples of histochemical heterogeneity in the striatum have been reported (Olson, Seiger, and Fuxe 1972; Graybiel and Ragsdale 1978). Nevertheless, Jones *et al.* (1977) make it quite clear that there is still extensive overlapping of projections, and it seems highly likely that an essential part of the organization of the striatum is a very diffusely wired input from the cortex.

It has recently been argued by Mountcastle (1978) that columns of cortical tissue are the fundamental unit for processing of information throughout the cortex, and also that reciprocal 'pericolumnar inhibition' is an important aspect of this processing throughout the cortex. These postulates are part of a wider scheme for functional organization of the brain, in which small groups of nerve cells (modules) are repeated a great many times in each of the major entities of which the brain is composed. Mountcastle argues in favour of a distribution of any functional system widely through the brain; but this is a different concept from that proposed here, since it depends on specific wiring of cortical columns to precisely related small groups of cells in other large entities of the nervous system (basal ganglia, thalamus, etc.) rather than on diffuse connections within any one entity. Implicit in these ideas is the notion that columns of cells throughout the cortex are concerned with extraction of features from the information impinging on the cortical region, in the same way as is known to occur in primary areas of cortex, and that pericolumnar inhibition is responsible for 'isolation' of neighbouring functional groups so that information represented in any active column is not confused. These proposals seem to be a modern version of punctate localization of function (albeit not at the single cell level) to be applied throughout the cortex. The evidence on which these proposals is based is largely the various electrophysiological studies which indicate columnar organization of neurones with similar functional properties in the cortex. These include not only studies of visual, auditory, somatic sensory and motor cortex but also studies of association areas 5 and 7 (Hyvärinen and Poranen 1974; Mountcastle *et al.* 1975).

Disregarding the fact that evidence of similar columnar organization is not available in other areas of association cortex, Mountcastle's formulation and particularly the evidence about areas 5 and 7 is not immediately reconciled with the arguments put forward here on theoretical/philosophical grounds. Two possibilities of reconciliation can be suggested, however. *Firstly*, it may be suggested that the columnar organization of areas 5 and 7 as a *physiological* finding is not reflected in the *anatomy* of the actual connections of these regions, which may be more diffuse than might be assumed from the physiological results. Underlying this suggestion is the idea that physiological columniation has been acquired either during earlier experience of the animals, or in the pre-experimental training period, by modification of the efficacy of synaptic connections, without apparent anatomical changes of the actual connections. The next few chapters consider in detail the rules which might govern such changes, and their macroscopic consequences. Legendy (1978) has in fact presented a theory to explain, by assuming such rules to operate, how alternating columns of cortical tissue with contrasting functional properties might develop from a uniform pattern of connections, on exposure to a varied sensory input. This sort of mechanism could underlie Mountcastle's findings without implying inflexible hard-wired columniation in the association cortex. It is relevant to refer here also to evidence in the visual cortex (Hubel and Wiesel 1962) in which both diffuse and punctate localization appear to co-exist in the same region of cortex: neurones with 'simple' receptive fields are related to discrete areas of retina, but those with 'complex' receptive fields have their selective responsiveness 'generalized over a considerable retinal area'. If physiological columns in association cortex are acquired in the manner just suggested, it does not of itself explain how complex Gestalts can be represented, since this would involve more complex interrelationships than are possible on the basis of spatial adjacency in the two (or three) dimensions of cortical tissue. However, since the interpretation preserves the idea of a diffuse network of connections, it is possible for the more complex and widely distributed Gestalt representations to co-exist with the simpler (and more easily detected) representations which happen to be mapped in discrete columns of cells.

The *second* way of reconciling columnar organization with the omniconnection principle depends on the assumption that omniconnection applies hierarchically both within a small group of cells (a column) and between the large number of such groups that exist within the cortex as a whole. Szentágothai (1978*a*, *b*) has emphasized that the diversity of neocortical structure can be simplified by regarding it as a large number of columnar modules, whose cellular arrangement differs little from one area to another in the cortex. He also recognizes diffuse connectivity, both within and between such modules. Braitenberg (1978) has presented calculations based on numerical estimates of neuronal and axonal distribution in mouse and human cortex, showing that an hierarchical version of the omniconnection principle—based on a 'modular' construction—is quite plausible. His basic concept is that of the 'square-root compartment'—the unit of cortical structure which contains sufficient efferent neurones connecting with other units, that all such units could be informed about all others. Such a scheme of organization might co-exist with omniconnection within each column, the consequence then being that by a hierarchy of short and long connections any neurone can influence any other, though not usually monosynaptically. If this concept of cortical organization is true, it would imply that the contrast in gross localization of function between primary areas and association areas, discussed earlier, is not reflected in the basic architecture of the cortex, which would have an underlying unity of cellular arrangement. Such a unity is in fact suggested by evidence of Sloper, Hiorns, and Powell (1979) that cortical areas with very different microscopic appearance (namely areas 4 and 3b) nevertheless show striking quantitative similarities.

Both these schemes permit omniconnection to co-exist with columnar organization. One issue remains problematical, however: the pericolumnar inhibition, which Mountcastle proposes as an important feature throughout the cortex. If this type of reciprocal inhibition were the only type existing in the cortex, there could be no way of 'isolating', or heightening the contrast between neural representations, except in so far as they are in spatially adjacent columns of the cortex. An essential part of the theory being developed here, however, is that such reciprocal inhibitory interactions could exist, or could develop to isolate or distinguish extended groupings of interlinked neurones scattered throughout the larger diffuse network.

3.2.4. CONNECTIONS AND TEMPORAL INTEGRATION

In the above paragraphs it is easiest to assume that the interconnections between neurones by which any Gestalt is represented in the brain would result in *simultaneous*, or almost simultaneous activation of the appropriate group of neurones when a stimulus is presented. Consequently, convergence at a single neurone, which constitutes the basic linkage in the network configuration corresponding to each Gestalt, would involve *simultaneous* arrival of signals along various axonal channels. Such a mechanism can readily account for the representation of simultaneous associations—that is the 'spatial' aspects of a Gestalt. However, many Gestalts, particularly those in the auditory mode, such as speech, are complex patterns in the *temporal* dimension. To explain the representation of Gestalts which are extended in time, the assumption of simultaneous activation of convergent synapses is not sufficient. However, with the help of this assumption it is possible to make use of other data about the substrate of anatomical connections in the forebrain, and thus to show how a Gestalt can be mapped in a manner which preserves real-time relationships within itself. In passing, it should be pointed out that the significance of simultaneous activation of convergent inputs cannot be fully appreciated until the discussion in Chapters 4 and 5.

Perception of temporal relationships undoubtedly involves a variety of mechanisms, depending on the magnitude of the time intervals involved. However, for relatively short time intervals it is possible to explain mapping of temporal relationships in connectionist terms analagous to those put forward for 'spatial' relationships. For this it is necessary to consider some functional details of the axonal connections within the cerebral hemisphere. In a recent study (Miller 1975) of cortical and subcortical regions in the cat, antidromic stimulation techniques were used to estimate conduction velocities of axonal projections from single neurones which connected one cortical region with another, or connected cortex and basal ganglia. A proportion of these projections were rapidly conducting so that latency between excitation of a neuronal soma and subsequent activation of its synaptic terminals would be only a small number of milliseconds. Such intervals represent virtual simultaneity as far as conscious processes are concerned, and so such axonal connections would be involved solely in mapping 'spatial' Gestalts. However, in the above study, some of the axonal projections were much slower-conducting, having latencies (for a conduction distance of about 1 cm) of up to 50 ms. For technical reasons, it is likely that the proportion of such slow-conducting axons whose responses were actually recorded was an underestimate of the true proportion of such axons: (i) Microelectrodes record more easily from large neurones than from small ones, thus biassing latency histograms in favour of the more rapidly conducting axons (Towe and Harding 1970). (ii) In such antidromic stimulation experiments it is unlikely that many of the responses were evoked by stimulation at the most remote parts of a neurone's axonal arborization. Latencies would thus be an underestimate of the true conduction time between soma and synapse, particularly since the slowest-conducting part of a neurone's axonal tree is the terminal arborization. Electron microscopical evidence confirms that a large proportion of intracerebral axonal connections would be very slow conducting: 50 per cent or more of axons in the corpus callosum in cat and rat are under 1 μm in diameter (Naito, Miyakawa, and Ito 1971; Seggie and Berry 1972). Furthermore, in the higher primates, particularly in man, the latency between soma and synapse is likely to be much greater than in cat, since the dimensions of the forebrain, and the lengths of intracerebral axons are likely to be four or five times greater than in the cat (see Swadlow, Geschwind, and Waxman 1979). It seems probable that a proportion of intracerebral axonal connections might have conduction times as large as 250 ms, though judging from latency histograms for single unit recording in animal brains, there would probably be a wide dispersion of conduction times ranging from a few milliseconds, right up to this much larger figure.

Axonal conduction constitutes a very precise measure of time compared with most biological processes. It could thus form a basis for encoding temporal information, and for perception of temporal patterns, at least for short time intervals. If two stimuli were separated in time by 250 ms they could nevertheless converge simultaneously on neurones within an omni-connected structure, provided the first of the two stimuli was carried along slowly conducting axons which imposed a delay of 250 ms on the corresponding neural signals. Such convergence would then represent not only the fact of the association of the two stimuli, but would also encode their temporal separation in real time. Moreover, if polysynaptic pathways were involved, resulting in accumulated delays from several different axons, it would be possible to encode temporal patterns lasting even longer than 250 ms, perhaps up to 1 or 2 s in the human brain. It should, however, be emphasized that the major signal delays which represent temporal information are those of axonal conduction, rather than of synaptic transmission (as is often assumed by electrophysiologists). Indeed, if too many sequential synapses were involved in a linkage, variables of convergence and divergence at each step in the linkage would limit the validity of the connection as a time-labelled stable connection.

This notion of perception of temporal pattern is related to the earlier discussion of the omniconnection principle. Just in so far as latency histograms for cerebral axonal connections show a fairly even spread from short to very long, so it is possible that the omniconnection principle applies (over a limited range of short time intervals) to the temporal dimension as well as to the spatial one. In formulating hypotheses about brain function, both types of omniconnection have the virtue of economy: in both cases an apparently sophisticated mental process is explained merely by postulating a random process—either random distribution of connections spatially, or random distribution of axonal diameters (reflected in random spread of conduction velocities).

A question which has emerged a number of times in the past few pages is whether polysynaptic linkages in an omniconnected network are valid connections in the sense demanded by present arguments. The significance of the overall connections would surely become ambiguous, because of the possibilities of convergence and divergence at the intervening synapses. In particular it might be argued that the omniconnection idea becomes less plausible if it is demanded that every neurone is connected with every other, not only spatially, but also by a whole range of axons each with its own distinctive conduction velocity. Despite the vast number of connections present within the cerebral hemisphere the force of this argument is recognized. Two comments can be made on this topic. Firstly, some of the limitations that have been discovered relating to cerebral mechanisms of learning and memory can be explained by reference to the potential ambiguities involved with polysynaptic linkages. In particular, mention will be made of the limited capacity of a neural network during acquisition of information (see p. 75), and the dependency of the neural network during retrieval of a memory, upon the overall patterning of electrical activity (i.e. the 'context' of activity in which items of information are represented) (see p. 75). Secondly, as will be discussed in Chapter 7, it is possible that one of the structures of the forebrain, namely the hippocampus, has a function which in a sense tends to overcome the shortcomings of the neocortical network compared with an 'ideal' omniconnected network (see p. 151). In any case it must be admitted that a more precise formulation of the omniconnection principle might be possible in mathematical terms, and this may expose inherent weaknesses in the principle.

3.3. Summary and comment

René Descartes gave as one of four maxims for the direction of his thinking 'to divide each problem . . . into as many parts as was feasible, and as was requisite for its better solution' (*Discours de la Méthode*, first published 1637). Definition of the concept of consciousness is made difficult because two distinct issues must be dealt with simultaneously. On the one hand, there is the *general* relationship of subjective and objective phenomena. On the other hand there is the problem of the structure of consciousness and the nature of the relationships of the parts to the unified whole. Separation of these two issues is perhaps not an obvious strategy. Indeed, a clear separation of this second issue depends critically on the type of answer that is given to the more general first issue. Proponents of some metaphysical positions would have great difficulty in even formulating the question about the unity of consciousness. However, assuming that our view of reality allows us to ask this second question, it is the belief of this author that the second question is not basically a metaphysical one, but one in which a definite answer can be derived logically from more basic information. This answer, it is believed, provides an essential link between the biological approach to brain function, and psychological concepts used to describe the behaviour of whole organisms.

The strategy adopted here, therefore, is to make a clear separation of those topics which are essentially metaphysical, and therefore probably eternally mysterious, from those on which some logical analysis and empirical investigation might be fruitful. On the one hand we therefore have psychophysical parallelism, an *a priori* assumption whose nature is ultimately quite mysterious. On the other hand we have the unity of consciousness, whose anatomical substrate has been the topic of the present chapter. Two alternative strategies might have been adopted. (i) We might try to down-play the status of subjective reality, in which case the problem of the unity of consciousness fades into the background, we lose the concept of *the self*, though we preserve the concept of *causality*. (ii) We might believe that the world of subjective experience is quite comparable with the objective world in terms of causal efficacy, in which case both the concepts of *the self* and *causality* become blurred, and therefore logically unmanageable.

It has been argued in this chapter, that the structure of consciousness, the overall channel for subjective awareness, and that of its component subsidiary channels, implies an omniconnected anatomical structure in which all parts have the possibility of influencing all others, leading to a diffuse distribution of the representation of any definable portion of information, in the manner of man-made holographic devices. The same conclusion has also been reached from a consideration of the nature of meaning: such a vast variety of internal relationships may exist in any portion of information which is meaningful, that such information can be represented only in a structure where there are no constraining principles of connectivity between the component parts. In other words, there must be a random network, in which all parts are in potential functional contact with all others. Representation of temporal relationships within meaningful signals is also explained by a form of omniconnection principle: every axonal connection in the network has its own characteristic latency, which is a simple function of diameter and length of the axon involved. In a large population of neurones there would be a wide and randomly distributed range of latencies. Thus, any neurone would have the potentiality of being influenced by other neurones with a wide range of intervening delays. Hence, within the range of intervals over which such a principle applies, any temporal pattern can find a representation in neural connections. Selection of the appropriate connections for representation of associations, either in the spatial or the temporal dimension, is to be dealt with in Chapters 4 and 5.

It should be mentioned here that the omniconnection principle, was in fact implicit in the writing of D. O. Hebb:

> The best analogy to the sort of structure which would be set up or 'assembled' is a closed solid cage work, or three dimensional lattice, with no regular structure, and with connections possible from any one intersection to any other. . . . It must appear to the reader . . . that there was something unlikely about it being arranged . . . to have such neat connections exactly where they were most needed. . . . The answer of course is statistical . . . given a large enough population of connecting fibres distributed at random, the improbable connection must become quite frequent in absolute numbers. (Hebb 1949)

Thus, in general terms at least, it is postulated that major psychological attributes of the brain are a function of its most striking anatomical feature— the prodigious number of connections it contains.

One further matter of a topological nature is worthy of mention. It has been suggested that part of the biological basis of memory involves coding of information within macromolecules, in terms of sequences of either amino acids or nucleotides (Hydén 1960; John 1967; Ungar 1968). The account of psycho–biological organization outlined above is scarcely compatible with such a chemical hypothesis. The principal interrelationships evident in these macromolecules are those between adjacent bases in a sequence, with occasional cross-links (in proteins) between different chains of amino acids. The paucity of interrelationships possible in such essentially one-dimensional information networks, makes it unlikely that such chemical coding could underlie the psychological processes involved in representation of meaning, in which the internal complexity of a great many interlocking Gestalts must somehow be mapped. Even if a mechanism could be suggested which would satisfactorily explain the translation of information coded in terms of nervous impulses into a hypothetical biochemical code, the representation of the complex structure of meaning would be in exceedingly inefficient form.

However, although it is unlikely that chemical coding can explain memory *as a conscious process*, it is certain that biochemistry of macromolecules plays a crucial part in many other aspects of the operation of memory processes.

A general objection that might be raised about the omniconnection principle is that it is such a strong assumption that it can explain any possible behavioural finding, and can be falsified by none. There is an element of truth in this, inevitable perhaps when one is attempting to analyse a property as complex and as magically versatile as consciousness. However, even in its most idealized form, the omniconnection principle is not a licence to assume connections between a neurone and every other in the whole of the brain. In particular this principle is supposed to apply individually to a number of separate structures in the brain—notably to the neocortex and striatum—but not between them.

The debate about localization of function versus holism has been long and heated. It is still very much a live issue, though there are signs of reconciliation in recent publications (Mountcastle 1978; Edelman 1978; Thatcher and John 1978) with proponents on each side showing greater willingness to concede some of the counter-arguments. The 'grandmother' hypothesis—the Aunt Sally of this chapter—is no longer a serious contender in theories of forebrain function. At the other extreme the equipotentiality of Lashley is recognized to be far too simple a hypothesis. The concept of the cell assembly put forward thirty years ago by Hebb has taken on a rather different significance from that originally intended, in the accounts of Mountcastle (1978) and Edelman (1978), in which columns or some other non-random neuronal groupings are seen as the substrate in which meanings are to be represented. Somehow the anatomical and physiological evidence must be presented in a way consistent with Hebb's theory, in which a cell assembly is just one of many small networks embedded in a much larger network.

The concept of an omniconnected structure is thus of considerable significance in giving a biological account of the unity of consciousness, and of the representation of meaning in the cerebrum. However, it also constitutes an important premise in Chapters 4 and 5, concerning the biological basis of learning. A substantial body of theory exists exploring the logical processes that must occur during acquisition of memory, i.e. learning theory. This theory is entirely at the psychological level, rather than the biological level. However, armed with the omniconnection concept a preliminary account of some types of learning can be given, which integrates psychological theory with biological fact.

4. A possible connectionist basis for cognitive and operant learning processes

4.1. Introduction

CHAPTER 3 brought forward the tentative postulate that the anatomical substrate which underlies conscious processes and serves as a medium for representation of meaning is an omniconnected structure—that is, one in which all individual parts are anatomically capable of influencing all other parts. In many ways this idea is not really a *testable* consequence of the arguments considered. The omniconnection principle itself is inaccessible to direct experimental approaches, since it is much easier technically to study the units (neurones) of which the brain is composed than the relationships between the units, and the omniconnection principle is essentially a statement about these relationships. The omniconnection principle should rather be regarded as offering an alternative view of presently available data on neuronal pathways in the cerebral hemisphere, which is useful in so far as it gives an increased appreciation of the manner by which the brain can function in an integrated fashion to produce behaviour in association with the various processes of consciousness.

In Section 2.2 it was postulated that the concepts of consciousness, meaning, and memory for knowledge are closely linked. Likewise in Section 2.3 it was suggested that consciousness, purpose, and memory for the effect of actions were similarly closely related. Therefore, definition of the biological basis of any of these will have implications for that of others in these two triads. Hence the aim of the present chapter is to show the usefulness of the omniconnection principle in giving an account of the biological basis of learning and memory in sensory and motor systems. It is thereby hoped to extend the present theoretical considerations to the point where they suggest feasible new avenues of experimental investigation.

Right at the outset it is necessary to draw attention to a crucial distinction, which underlies the whole of what follows, between two types of learning process. This is the distinction between *cognitive learning*—that is *learning of information derived directly or indirectly from sensory systems alone*—and *operant learning* (or instrumental learning), in which *new motor responses are acquired as well as the concomitant linking of such responses to associated sensory cues*.* Even though there are a great many similarities between these

* The term 'operant' is sometimes used to identify simple lever-pressing responses, as distinct from larger scale responses involving walking, running or jumping. This distinction is recognized

two types of learning (Hilgard and Marquis 1964), the differences in the necessary logical processes are fundamental in nature. Similarly, although in the present account the omniconnection principle is important in elucidating a possible biological basis of both types of learning, nevertheless, the actual mode of operation to be suggested is radically different for cognitive as compared with operant learning. This situation is made more complex because experimental attempts to observe learning processes usually involve an operant response regardless of whether the learning is primarily cognitive or primarily operant. Moreover, as will become evident later, the twin processes involved in cognitive and operant learning can interact in several important ways, and presumably in the intact animal they seldom operate separately from one another.

In what follows the processes of cognitive and operant learning will be regarded as *associative functions* in which links are established between representations of occurrences which themselves are linked in some way. Since cognitive learning is logically simpler, it will be dealt with before operant learning. For both types of learning the discussion will commence by considering, at a rather abstract level, what logical processes must occur for memories to be acquired. Subsequently these logical processes will be translated into biological terms. In this discussion, a widely-held viewpoint is adopted—that the biological modifications on which learning depends are modifications of the security of synaptic transmission. This premise immediately implies that a substantial proportion of synapses in the brain exist as anatomical entities, while being functionally relatively ineffective. This is a difficult supposition to prove, especially in a neural structure as complex as the cerebral neocortex, or the corpus striatum. However, Mark (1974) has presented evidence in favour of the existence of 'silent' synapses in the peripheral nervous system and Wall (1977) has performed experiments showing their possible existence in the spinal cord.

Once the premise of modifiable synapses is granted, the omniconnection principle shows its importance again because it allows one to explain some of the characteristics of learning processes at the whole brain level (i.e. psychological functions) from the postulated properties of individual neurones and their synapses. Consequently the crucial premises on which this chapter is built are statements of the rules governing synaptic modification during cognitive and operant learning. These statements are selected in order to

---

(See Chapter 7), but the word 'operant' is used in this book to identify voluntary responses, modifiable during learning, as distinct from unmodifiable 'reflex' responses. The term 'cognitive' used in relation to 'learning' commonly signifies the acquisition of some internal trace which does not lead to an immediate behavioural response, but the possession of which can lead to modification of subsequent behaviour. In the present work the term 'cognitive learning' has these implications, but also signifies 'learning occurring within the grasp of consciousness, leading therefore to acquisition of knowledge by that consciousness'. Other varieties of learning (e.g. conditioning of reflexes) are also 'derived from sensory systems alone', but are not the principal phenomena for which I use this label.

explain the logical processes in the two types of associative learning. However, they should not be regarded as the only possible rules of synaptic modification which could explain the processes: they are to be thought of as examples of the way a neural network might operate, rather than as *the* definitive mode of operation. For instance, Mark (1974) lays more emphasis on processes of synaptic suppression than on synaptic strengthening, such as proposed by Hebb. However, bearing in mind that forgetting can occur, as well as learning, it is in any case likely that both processes must eventually be involved in a more complete model of the mechanisms of memory.

The ideas about learning on which this chapter is built are in many ways rather traditional, ignoring work which has emphasized that much learning behaviour is not easily described in terms of associational linking of information. Piaget in his studies of human psychological development repeatedly condemns naïve associationism (see Piaget and Inhelder 1969). Much learning in human beings approximates more to a form of 'modelling' rather than associational linking. The reason for using association as a descriptor of learning behaviour is that, at the most fundamental level, it is not difficult to see a parallel between association as a psychological function and the convergence of signals upon neural elements in a nerve network as a biological function, whereas direct biological parallels of modelling and other high-order psychological schemata are not so easily found. In a brain containing many thousands of millions of neurones it would not be surprising if large-scale properties emerged which were quite unforeseeable from the associative properties of the neural elements as such. With the possibility of a very large number of associational links occurring simultaneously it is not surprising that overall functioning during learning might seem more akin to modelling than to simple classical or instrumental conditioning. A convenient analogy of the process of emergence of these more complex functions is found in the 'pointilliste' style of painting, in which paint is applied as a large number of small points of colour, but can nevertheless represent a fluid and continuous whole. It should also be mentioned here that the derivation of complex emergent properties from simpler basic elements is largely the same problem as the derivation of stable adult patterns of behaviour from paradigms of learning applying throughout development. This chapter is concerned almost entirely with the paradigms of learning—that is with the mode of acquisition, rather than with the integrated whole that is eventually acquired. What is constructed may be incomprehensibly subtle and complex, but this does not mean that the process of construction is also incomprehensible.

In Chapter 7 some suggestions are made about how a few of these more complex properties might emerge. However, this is merely scratching the surface of an enormous problem in explaining the vast variety of learned behaviour in an adult human. Certainly in the case of Piagetian developmental patterns it is only in the very earliest stages of human development that associational mechanisms seem directly applicable. For instance, Piaget does mention examples of infants at age six to eight months who learn of the concept of causality by phenomenological association alone, without understanding the necessity for contact between the interacting elements (Piaget and Inhelder 1969, p. 18). All later stages are described in a quite different language, however—that of a high-order emergent property.

4.2. Acquisition of cognitive memory

4.2.1. THEORETICAL PRINCIPLES

It has been suggested that the process of acquiring cognitive memory is closely linked to the detection of meaning (Section 2.2). 'Meaning' in its simplest form is the clustering of statistically significant associations in space and time. The basic logic of cognitive learning could thus be stated somewhat as follows. *If two or more items of the sensory input display a close juxtaposition in space or time which is repeated sufficiently often to indicate statistically significant linkage in this input, then associative mechanisms in the brain will link together the cerebral representations of the different sensory items, in much the same way (logically) as the environmental stimuli which evoke them are linked. On subsequent exposure to the same cluster of associated inputs, it will no longer be necessary to evaluate the items individually: the cluster can be recognized as a whole.* The basic form of the association registered in this type of learning can be summed up in the word *contiguity*.

Associations based on contiguity may be positive or negative in sign, according to whether the correlations between contiguous portions of sensory input are positive or negative. For instance, a certain group of positively associated items of sensory input may be needed to recognize a Merino sheep; but when this animal is compared with another variety of sheep—say a Jacob sheep—then although most of the associations will also be present in the new variety, a proportion of them (e.g. the shape of the horns) will be negatively associated with the cluster of associations defining the Merino sheep. Moreover, in many situations involving learning on the basis of contiguity, confusion would result unless there were a mechanism of enhancing the contrast between a group of positively-associated items, and the non-associated background (for example when learning to recognize an unfamiliar species of bird, partly camouflaged against its background).

If associations based on contiguity are to be represented in connectionist terms within the brain, the overall operation of the process in which cognitive memory traces are laid down must depend on strengthening those relationships between neurones which define significant associations of sensory input and the clusters of such associations which represent meaning. In addition, since meaning is built up of negative, as well as positive associations, it is likely that processes also exist to strengthen inhibitory relationships between incompatible meanings of sensory input. In other words, a *feedback* process must operate in which some mechanism exists to detect meaningful patterns, which then directs a strengthening influence towards those *excitatory* links of the input pathways which contribute to the expression of that pattern in terms of neuronal activity. This strengthening mechanism will also be directed to those *inhibitory* links in the input pathways which contribute to the expression of incompatible patterns. Such a feedback loop may be put in diagrammatic form as in Fig. 1.

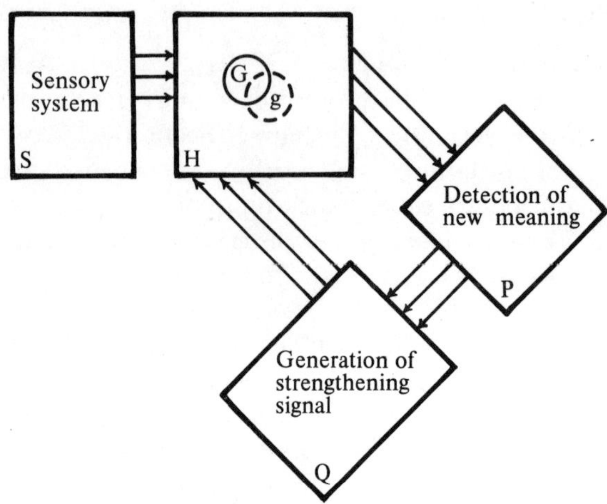

FIG. 1. The block diagram illustrates the following principle: if learning processes are particularly concerned with acquiring a representation of new meaning, there must be a method of detecting new meaning, and of subsequently feeding back a strengthening signal on to the representation of that meaning.

The sensory system (S) provides an input of information to the structure labelled H, in which the omniconnection principle applies, and in which meanings of the sensory input can therefore be represented. In addition, two further functional units are included: one (P) is concerned with detection of the fact that significant new associations of activity occur within H, and the other (Q) is concerned with generation of appropriate strengthening signals directed back towards H. Perceptual psychologists, such as Broadbent (1958), have proposed a model in which a 'filter' is placed at an early stage in the formation of memory, which separates the new meanings contained within sensory input from the familiar meanings. The box P in Fig. 1 is thus one interpretation of this filter. However, as explained in Sections 2.2 and 2.4 'significance' and 'novelty' are concepts applicable on both small and large scale. Here we are dealing with low-level functions. Higher-level assessment of novelty and significance is given more detailed attention in Chapter 7.

The mode of operation could be illustrated by considering two Gestalts—G representing a Merino sheep and g representing a Jacob sheep. The first time that either of these Gestalts was transmitted by S, and represented in H, then P and Q would operate so that the internal excitatory connections *within* G or g would be strengthened, thus imprinting the fact that the cluster of complex associations required to define either of these Gestalts was statistically significant. With further presentation of G and g, the structures P and Q would operate to strengthen inhibitory connections *between* G and g, thus encoding the incompatibilities between these two Gestalts.

In such a model an important constraint derived from the previous chapter, must apply: detection of *new* meaning, in P, requires an anatomical structure of the same omniconnected form as does the representation of familiar meaning, since meanings are by their very nature complex structures. Moreover, if the strengthening signal, generated in Q, is to pick out exactly the right synaptic connections within H when any particular meaning is to be imprinted as memory, then Q also must be a large and complex omniconnected structure, capable of mapping a vast variety of complex Gestalts. At this point the key question can be asked: 'Do the boxes H, P, and Q correspond to physically separate gross structures within the forebrain, or are they solely functionally or logically separate while being merged together within one large structure?' To put the question another way, should one consider H, P, and Q as separate nuclear masses, or are they physiological processes repeated a multitude of times at a much smaller level—say at the neuronal and synaptic level? The former of these alternatives would imply that memory involved a form of reverberating circuit, not so much as a store of information, as has been proposed by some authors, but as part of the mechanism for registering information in the store.

The weakness in the idea of reverberating feedback loops between large nuclear masses is as follows. Consider a neurone, which has, say 50 synaptic terminations in H. Only a small proportion of these, say five, will contribute to the specification of a particular Gestalt in H. The strengthening mechanism, Q, must therefore have under direct point to point control these five specific synapses, so that they may be strengthened independently of any other synapses. Of course, all other synapses which take part in specification of other Gestalts must be under similar control. There is thus a requirement for a phenomenally intricate and specific array of connections between Q and H, which *must be hard-wired*, that is independent of modifications during learning. Any advocate of such a hypothesis has therefore, above all else, to explain the developmental mechanisms by which such an array of connections can arise. This is a problem at least as intangible as that which it is attempting to solve. If, on the other hand, physiological feedback processes, operating throughout one large structure at the neuronal and synaptic level can be suggested, which do not demand anything more than some kind of random neural network, they would be the basis of a much simpler hypothesis. Occam's razor must be used to choose it, rather than the more complex former hypothesis.

4.2.2. SYNAPTIC PLASTICITY AND COGNITIVE LEARNING

4.2.2(a). Plasticity postulates for cognitive learning. In order to explain the associative functions involved in cognitive learning it is proposed that a formally similar relationship exists at the *microscopic* level between the neurone and the various synaptic inputs which converge upon it, as exists at the psychological level between the various components of information which define cognitive learning. Moreover, to explain the capacity in mammalian learning for recognition of differences as well as similarities, and to explain the clear cut distinction which can be established between a sensory gestalt and its background *it is necessary to postulate that inhibitory as well as excitatory synapses are modifiable*, both then being involved in forming cognitive representations of external objects. The basic postulates concern plastic changes in synaptic security. For excitatory synapses one might postulate that *if the impulse frequency in a neurone is temporarily elevated above a 'neutral' level of activity, then this neurone will exert a local influence on all of its own excitatory synapses which are contiguously active, and will tend to enhance the efficacy above a 'baseline' level of efficacy*. With regard to inhibitory synapses a converse relationship may be supposed to hold. *If the impulse frequency in a neurone temporarily falls below a 'neutral' frequency range, then the neurone will exert a local influence on all of its own inhibitory synapses which are contiguously active, and will tend to enhance their efficacy above a 'baseline' level*. These rules of operation may be supposed to influence particularly those synapses with such low security that their contribution to the change in activity was negligible. At any single neurone, those synaptic inputs which tend to fire synchronously will tend to be strengthened. Consequently, in future, a significant change in neuronal activity can be achieved in the neurone with a smaller degree of synaptic activation in the group of synapses, or a smaller number out of the group being active. The more often a synapse is active during the period of changed activity in the post-synaptic neurone, or the greater the change in the neurone's activity, the greater effect it will have in increasing synaptic security.

Such postulates are not original, of course. Hebb proposed a mechanism which, in overall operational terms was virtually identical to that just suggested, including the necessity for increasing the security of contacts whose security was so low that they contributed little to neuronal activity during the learning situation:

> In the intact nervous system an axon that passes close to the dendrites or body of a second cell would be capable of *helping* to fire it when the second cell is exposed to other stimulation at the same point. . . . When the coincidence does occur and the active fibre which is merely close to the soma of another cell adds a local excitation in it, I assume that the joint action tends to produce a thickening of the fibre—forming a synaptic knob—or adds to a thickening already present' (Hebb 1949).

It should be noted here that both plasticity postulates (and also Hebb's formulation) are statements of overall operational characteristics, rather than of the actual mechanism underlying such operation. Hebb formulated his ideas in terms of growth of synapses, but the same logic would apply to physiological changes occurring at synapses without apparent anatomical change. In the present book we focus on learning as a conscious process, and this is so rapid that the physiological model is thought more appropriate than that involving structural change. Possible details of such a mechanism are briefly considered in Section 5.2.

4.2.2(b). Cognitive meaning at the neuronal level. In a random neural network in which all neurones are in potential relationship with all others, neural activity cannot be confined to any small portion of the network, but will spread its influence throughout the network. Provided some form of activity is maintained in the network, all neurones will carry a continual stream of impulses. The frequency of this stream of impulses in any neurone will fluctuate depending on the statistics of coincidence of excitatory and inhibitory influences at any moment, but there will inevitably be limits to the likely frequency, beyond which high frequency bursts or periods of depressed frequency become extremely improbable. However, when a sensory input impinges on such a network, the neurones involved need not be bound by such statistical constraints. Admittedly many of the neurones in the network may receive negligible excitation or inhibition as a result of sensory input, but others may undergo a change of frequency which, in intensity or duration, greatly exceeds those occurrences which are likely to happen in the undisturbed network. The precise distribution of neurones undergoing such a change will depend on the spatial and temporal parameters of the stimulus, and on the indefinable intricacies of the web of connections along which the sensory stimulus spreads its influence. There will undoubtedly be a continuous gradation between cells whose firing does not depart from the range of frequencies expected as a result of endogenous activity of the network, through various intermediate stages, to the smaller number of neurones in which highly significant changes occur. If a continuous barrage of varied sensory input impinges on the network, many of the departures from expected frequency will be defined not so much by the isolated components of the input, but by the possibility of convergence of influences upon neurones from separate but simultaneous portions of the input. *In such a network, the single action potential conveys no meaning. Only when the frequency of the impulse stream deviates outside the expected range for a period long enough to give it statistical significance is it likely that a meaningful signal is being dealt with by a neurone.* Thus, in order to interpret the succession of action potentials and intervening intervals in a single neurone, it is unnecessary to invoke the idea of a complex and sophisticated temporal code (Hydén 1959; John 1967). In any case the quantal nature of transmitter release would introduce statistical variations into the precise timing of successive impulses, and would thus limit the scope of a temporal code to fairly simple forms.

Such a conclusion from theory is well in accord with the behaviour of central neurones in practice. Most of them, indeed, show a continuing discharge which can be described in the statistical terms applied to random processes. Whenever significant correlations are observed between neuronal discharge and sensory or motor function, the signal consists of relatively prolonged changes in frequency, superimposed on a background level of neuronal 'noise' (Burns 1968). It should be pointed out here that the suggestion which was considered earlier, that 'units of information' are handled by single neurones, is consistent with the idea that 'units of information' are represented physiologically by all or nothing action potentials. However, the view advocated here, that information is handled within an omni-connected holographic structure, necessarily implies that meaningful information is represented physiologically by *graded* changes of impulse frequency, in a stream of impulses to be described stochastically. Furthermore, if a meaningful signal at the neuronal level requires a somewhat extended change of impulse frequency, it follows that conscious appreciation, at the subjective level, of even the simplest and most transitory element of meaning must occur on a time scale considerably longer than the millisecond of the single action potential.

The relevance of this for the plasticity mechanism is as follows: *if the plasticity mechanism is to detect a meaningful signal and use it to strengthen associated synaptic contacts, the trigger to this process at the neuronal level must be a relatively prolonged alteration of impulse frequency, rather than a single action potential.* In searching for the physicochemical basis of synaptic plasticity therefore, processes which are triggered by subthreshold synaptic events or single action potentials, can be disregarded, since neither of these is meaningful at the neuronal level. (However, this does not mean that the plasticity mechanism, once triggered, cannot influence synapses which operating alone would have subthreshold effects.) Further, in the operation of the proposed mechanism there must be a clear distinction between changes in frequency likely to be encountered in the undisturbed network, and those which represent meaning and can thus trigger the plasticity mechanism. If this distinction breaks down, appreciation of meaning at the psychological level will be disturbed.

If the single action potential were to be the carrier of meaning, then a stream of impulses would contain no signal which could be used to strengthen inhibitory connections, since the single action potential signifies excitation of a neurone, but cannot signify inhibition. *If, on the other hand, as proposed here, temporary changes in impulse frequency carry meaning, it would be possible to use a significant drop in frequency, or a total silence, to trigger a mechanism for strengthening inhibitory synapses, since activation of the latter would correlate with a fall in frequency, or a silence.* Thus plastic changes in excitatory and inhibitory synapses are envisaged as being triggered by two independent but parallel mechanisms operating within the neurone, relying respectively on significant increases or falls of impulse frequency in the post-synaptic neurone as the adequate stimulus. Any hypothesis dealing with the precise subcellular mechanism for plastic changes in synapses must make suggestions applicable to each type of synapse. In summary, although the

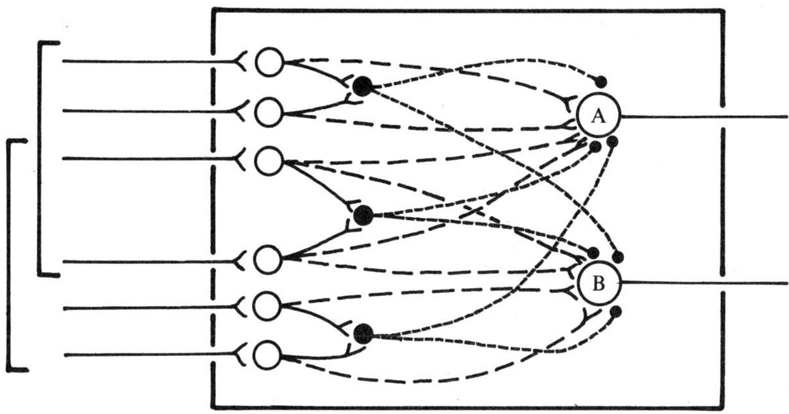

FIG. 2. In this and all subsequent figures, the symbols used have the following significance. *Circles* and *lines* represent interconnections. They may be imagined either as neuronal and axonal elements, respectively, or as more abstract significations of linkages within and between informational representations. *Complete lines* represent connections with secure, unmodifiable synapses. *Broken lines* represent connections which exist in structural terms, but do not exist physiologically until the plasticity mechanism has made their synaptic terminations functionally secure (i.e. they are *modifiable connections*). ——⟨ and ——● represent excitatory and inhibitory unmodifiable connections respectively. — — —⟨ and - - - -● represent excitatory and inhibitory modifiable connections respectively. *Within the square (or rectangular) box, the omniconnection principle may be applied: connections between any circle ('neurone') and any other may be assumed to exist.* In Figs. 2–13 however, only the connections relevant to that figure are depicted. *Input* to square box (or rectangle) is on the left; *output* on the right. For further symbols see Fig. 3 (p. 73), Fig. 5 (p. 79), and Fig. 6 (p. 82).

Fig. 2 represents the sort of network in which similarities and differences can simultaneously be represented. Inhibitory influences are distributed more widely than excitatory ones. If a sensory stimulus activates the upper four inputs, neurone A will be activated by four excitatory synapses and by two inhibitory ones; neurone B will be activated by two excitatory synapses and two inhibitory ones. Given appropriate transfer functions at the various synapses, the plasticity mechanisms discussed in Section 4.2.2(a) would ensure strengthening of the converging group of excitatory synapses upon A, and the converging group of inhibitory synapses upon B. This would allow neurone A to encode the associations contained within the stimulus grouping (upper four inputs), while neurone B would encode the contrasting background to this grouping. With a slightly different stimulus grouping (lower four inputs) neurone B would also be included in the group of neurones in which excitatory convergence exceeded inhibitory convergence.

stream of action potentials in a neurone seems like a binary code of all or nothing signals, its significance for memory and synaptic plasticity is that of a more complex code, where graded frequency changes in either direction can signal associations of opposite sign.

At this point one may ask how impulse frequency in a cortical neurone may temporarily be induced to fall below the 'neutral' frequency. Two mechanisms are envisaged. Firstly, in the case of major sensory systems, particularly those involved in analysis of spatial or quasi-spatial parameters, it is common to find that hard-wired connections in the first- and second-order sensory nuclei produce surround inhibition, or contrast enhancement. Thus, if any region of skin, retina, or cochlea is excited by a stimulus, the neurones in these nuclei directly representing the centre of the stimulus, will be excited, while those representing closely adjacent regions of the sensory surface will decrease their activity (Whitfield 1967; Levick 1972; Brown and Gordon 1977). Such decreases can also be expected to be transmitted to some of the cortical neurones in the corresponding sensory system, and can serve as a focus for strengthening inhibitory cortico–cortical connections which are contiguously active. A corollary of this is that, in the adult, thalamo–cortical connections must be secure and unmodifiable and these connections will thus be a major determinant of the maintained level of impulse activity which is typical of cortical neurones.

The above mechanism cannot operate for enhancing the contrast of the more abstract associations which are not closely linked to the structure of space, and consequently where surround inhibition cannot be hard-wired. To permit acquisition of contrast enhancement in these cases it is necessary to suppose that, in the absence of any synaptic strengthening, active cortical neurones distribute a small net inhibitory influence widely upon other neurones in the network. Without such a postulate there could be no inhibitory influence to be enhanced, when learning to recognize the difference between some complex sensory Gestalt and its background. Figure 2 illustrates the way in which the above principles may operate.

4.2.2(c). Macroscopic consequences of the proposed plasticity mechanisms. Aside from the considerations of the previous section the most important implication of the omniconnection principle is, of course, the connectionist one: whenever two (or more) separate portions of information represented within the brain correspond to events or stimuli in the environment which are statistically associated, axonal connections will always exist whereby this association can be represented, and converted into a functional connection —or elementary memory trace. With this point in mind it becomes very simple to explain the learning of sensory Gestalts, or the association of conditioned and unconditioned stimuli found in classical conditioning. The processes involved may be symbolized as in the diagrams below.

In Fig. 3, spatial summation of many weak synaptic inputs converging on

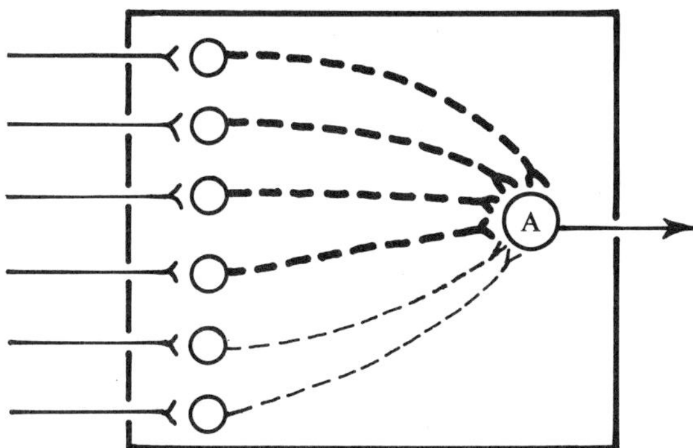

FIG. 3. This represents the learning of a sensory Gestalt, which includes both spatial and temporal information. Thick broken lines = rapidly conducting 'axonal' connections. Thin broken lines = slowly conducting 'axonal' connections. Other symbols as in Fig. 2 (p. 71).

the single neurone A produces a 'meaningful burst' of activity in A, so that the various synapses involved, though singly ineffective at first, become strengthened so that fewer of them will subsequently be required to excite A. In Fig. 4, the statistical association of the conditioning stimulus (CS) and the unconditioned stimulus (UCS) results in activation of synapses b and/or c at a time when neurones B and C are adequately excited by already-secure synapses, and are thus carrying a meaningful signal. Synapses b and c are thus strengthened so that CS by itself will subsequently be able to evoke the response.

It is not intended to work out here all the implications of these postulates in full mathematical detail. However, some further matters of detail do deserve comment.

Firstly, how can the information acquired during cognitive learning represent both the similarities and the differences between two related Gestalts in the flexible way that is implied by animal behaviour? Suppose, for instance, that an animal is trained to perform a response when presented with

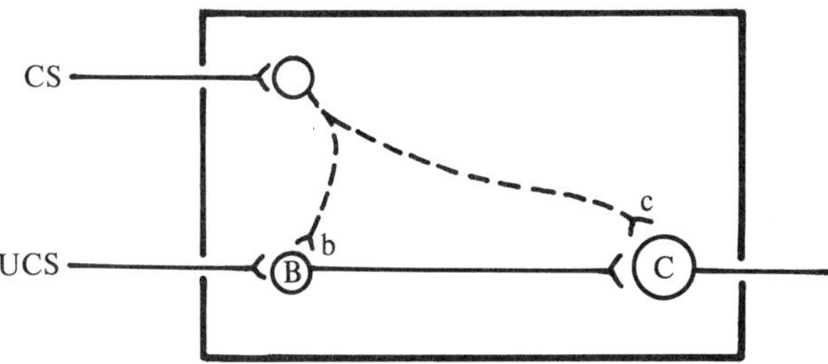

FIG. 4. This represents classical conditioning. UCS = unconditioned stimulus, CS = conditioning stimulus. Symbols as in Fig. 2 (p. 71).

one form of sensory stimulus (say a large triangle) and is then presented with another stimulus which has some features in common with the first (say a small triangle). On some occasions it may be the common properties of the two Gestalts which lead to a response (stimulus generalization) while at other times the distinguishing features of the same Gestalts could determine the response (discrimination). Which of these two occurs is influenced by a number of factors and cannot be easily predicted in absence of empirical testing in an individual behaviour test (Evans 1967; Hilgard and Marquis 1964). The explanation of this is somewhat as follows. For any one neurone there would be a set of sensory circumstances in which excitatory convergence during learning exceeded inhibitory convergence sufficiently to trigger strengthening of excitatory synapses; another set of circumstances is possible in which the reverse happened and inhibitory synapses were strengthened; there might also be a 'neutral' set of circumstances in which neither change occurred. For any one Gestalt, the quantitative specification of these circumstances for different neurones in the network would vary, since the balance of excitatory and inhibitory connectivity might be expected to display considerable random variation between neurones. Thus some neurones would be part of the 'excitatory centre' representing the Gestalt, others would become part of the 'inhibitory surround' representing the contrasting background, whilst a third group of neurones would not be involved either way. For two related Gestalts which were partly similar and partly different, there would be some neurones which were in the excitatory centre of both Gestalts, some in the inhibitory surround of both Gestalts, and others which were in the inhibitory surround of one, and the excitatory centre of the other. Thus different populations of neurones would encode the common properties and the distinguishing features. Figure 2 attempts to illustrate this. The two 'output' neurones receive, by chance, convergences of excitatory and inhibitory connections which are partly the same, partly different. Operation of the plasticity postulates could lead to their encoding similar but somewhat discrepant Gestalts (e.g. a Jacob sheep versus a Merino sheep). In this scheme it should be noticed that, with random connectivity, the many neurones involved in representing any Gestalt would be spatially distributed, so that a memory trace would not be highly localized in the network.

The *second* topic links together three apparently unrelated properties of the proposed network: its information capacity when acting as a memory store, its stability, and the degree to which external objects or events are unambiguously represented within it. It has been argued by Brindley (1969) that the information capacity of a neural network is excessively small if each neurone can encode only one set of associations, whereas if the synapse is the fundamental unit of memory coding, more realistic estimates of information capacity are obtained, since the numbers of synapses per unit volume of cerebral tissue are greater than the numbers of neurones by several orders. In line with Brindley's concept, it is envisaged for the present model that any 'unitary associative operation' in a neurone involves a very small proportion of the synapses in the neurone, so that each neurone can be involved in a variety of 'unitary associative operations'. Consequently, when the network has been in operation for some time, any one neurone can be part of the excitatory centres representing some Gestalts and part of the inhibitory surrounds of others. Thus, there need be no tendency for an unstable positive feedback process to strengthen all the excitatory synapses on a particular neurone, though under pathological circumstances such a process might occur.

The multiple role of each neurone in the network is further linked to the question raised in the previous chapter (p. 47) about whether multisynaptic links within an omniconnected network are valid as independent connections. The fact is that interlinkages between many (probably most) pairs of neurones within neocortex or striatum are not direct, but involve one or more intermediate neurones. Since divergence and convergence is possible at each of these intermediate steps, the specification of information in associative learning in terms of connections is not without ambiguity. Signals arriving at the end of (say) a disynaptic chain could have originated in a range of other neurones besides that from which they actually did originate. If it is assumed that the overall spatio–temporal pattern of activity in the network is broadly similar on two occasions it is likely that a particular stimulus object will activate the same subsidiary network within the total network, because incidental activity at these intermediary links will be the same. However, in a situation where a familiar object has to be recognized in a novel setting, this assumption is unlikely to be fulfilled, and the potential ambiguity of associational representation will be exposed. The vulnerability of a network, such as described here, to changes in context will be mentioned again in Chapter 7, and some suggestions will be made as to how the mammalian forebrain has developed additional functions which may overcome the weakness.

The *third* large scale consequence of the proposed mechanism of cognitive learning concerns not so much the enormous capacity of the memory store, but the limited capacity of the mechanism of information processing during actual learning. As mentioned in the previous section, any one neurone might contribute to the mapping of several independent patterns of associative linkages. Hence if a large number of sensory stimuli are presented to an animal simultaneously, it may happen that convergence at the neuronal level occurs between the representations of independent stimuli, and this may trigger the plasticity mechanism. In this case, the information that is encoded is a confused representation of the stimuli, since on later occasions when the stimuli occur in other combinations, the same convergence is unlikely to occur, and so the stimuli will not be recognized. If, however, the separate stimuli occur singly, the internal relationships defining each of them can readily be encoded; and if later the stimuli occur in combination, discrimination learning, employing inhibitory synapses, can then take place to ensure that their representations are kept separate. In this case the representation is not confused. Thus, during the actual learning process it is easy to overload the mechanism envisaged here. During learning, there is a limited capacity for processing information which does not apply to the routine handling of familiar information. It is interesting to relate this conclusion to the basic plan for cognitive learning shown in Fig. 1. The 'black box' P, for detection of new meaning, corresponds to the set of synapses which, though not yet present as secure functional connections, can become secure as a result of convergent activation of post-synaptic neurones. It has been pointed out (p. 66) that P corresponds to the 'filter' on sensory input suggested by perceptual psychologists such as Broadbent (1958). One of the most important features of such hypothetical 'filters' is their limited capacity. The present model of cognitive learning gives an explanation of this limited capacity.

The final aspect of cognitive learning to be briefly introduced in this section is the *control* of the learning mechanism. In Sections 2.4 and 2.6 it was suggested that capacity for cognitive learning could be adjusted to serve the overall needs of the animal, either to meet the varying demands put on the learning mechanism in strange, as opposed to familiar environments, or because of internal factors leading to fluctuation in level of consciousness during various phases of sleep and wakefulness. How could such control be executed? The account of cognitive learning given here depends on strengthening of selected synapses, and so large populations of synapses which are susceptible to modification are presumed to possess the same machinery (biochemical or otherwise) by which the modification can be accomplished. The most economical way of controlling such a system would therefore be by way of some diffuse influence, rather than by way of a colossal number of 'presynaptic' contacts (which would be more appropriate if it was required to control individual synapses rather than a vast population of them). Such a diffuse influence could be exerted either by way of a diffusely acting chemical transmitter substance, or by way of diffusely acting electrical fields. In the rest of this book, however, only diffuse chemical influences will be considered, since there is far more experimental evidence on this, and therefore more scope for realistic discussion (see Chapters 5 and 6).

4.3. Acquisition of operant memory

4.3.1. THEORETICAL PRINCIPLES

In cognitive learning all that is required is to encode the fact that two sensory Gestalts are significantly associated spatially and/or temporally. Any response which is associated with these Gestalts remains the same before and after learning, though the sensory stimulus which triggers it may be transferred from one Gestalt to the other. However, in operant learning a *new* motor response may be produced. Alternatively even if the motor response is not new, it will appear in totally new relationship to sensory input, rather than merely by transference from one stimulus to another which is statistically associated with the former. In either case a new relationship between sensory and motor information needs to be established, *which is contingent on the effects of the motor response*. The nature of the associative links mediating operant conditioning is thus rather different from, and more complex than those mediating classical conditioning or sensory learning. The basic logic of operant learning could be stated somewhat as follows. *Suppose an animal is faced with environmental circumstances which provide a total sensory input $S+$. If a random fragment of behaviour M exerts an influence on the environment such that $S+$ changes to $S-$, then that fragment of behaviour will become associated with the change $S+ \rightarrow S-$. This change may be motivationally favourable or unfavourable for the animal. If it is favourable, subsequent presentation of $S+$, by virtue of the association formed, will call forth M, and its consequence $S-$. If it is unfavourable, subsequent presentation of $S+$ will suppress M. In either case the response (or its inhibition) will no longer be a random consequence of $S+$, but a causally-determined one.* This form of association can best be summed up by the single word *effect* since associations which are formed depend on the effect of a response.

It will be noticed that in the initial stages of operant learning the new motor response cannot be defined wholly by the pre-existing stimuli from the environment, since it is the modification of these stimuli by the motor act which determines which responses will be learned. No form of causal reasoning can explain the emergence of a fully formed motor act, perfectly matched to a novel sensory input the first time that input is presented, though confusing teleological arguments often appear to provide such an explanation. To explain how operant behaviour originates *de novo* within the animal, as its own creation, *it is necessary to postulate some form of random behavioural activity*. Associative links can then be formed between fragments of this random behaviour and the changes of sensory input consequent on the portion of behaviour. Each time this fragment of behaviour appears in the same sensory context, it must be assumed that it is subject to some random variation of detail, so that by a process of successive approximation the change of sensory input becomes linked with a motor pattern more and more precisely related to the production of that change.

It may be objected that operant responses are too well matched to motivational requirements for them to rely on a random process. However, it should be pointed out that the actual performance of a fully-fledged behavioural sequence is much easier to study than the process of acquiring such a sequence. It is in acquisition rather than in performance that random factors are involved, and during this time the animal's response is not well matched, and may be little different from random exploration. Thus, the high degree of order and specificity seen in the properties which emerge in adult behaviour are deceptive, and do not imply a high degree of order in all the stages of acquisition.

In the earlier years of this century there was a heated debate about whether the associative operations by which learning processes occur are best to be described as stimulus–stimulus association, or associations between a response and a stimulus. The basic logic of cognitive learning is clearly of the former type, that of operant learning (see above) of the latter type. This debate is not now so hotly argued, though it has never been unambiguously resolved. It is closely related to the issue mentioned in Section 2.4 about whether or not a motive is always necessary in learning, since, if all learning proceeds by association of responses with motivationally significant changes of stimulus, then all learning must be related to one or other motive. There has clearly been no need so far in this chapter to regard either of these dichotomies as strict alternatives: both types of association are regarded as occurring in mammalian learning, and it is in working out their interrelationships in the next chapter that a tentative resolution of the debate will be suggested.

Portions of operant behaviour may be welded into much larger behavioural programmes, which subserve some particular motive or goal. Operant conditioning is studied experimentally by putting an animal in circumstances where one or other type of goal-fulfilment is required. Thus animals may be required to fashion a motor act which will avoid a painful stimulus (active avoidance), or to suppress actions which result in a painful stimulus (passive avoidance), or they may be motivated by hunger or thirst (appetitive behaviour). In what follows the basic logic of operant learning suggested above is to be applied, initially at least, regardless of the goals to which the operant task is directed. Thus, an external signal such as pain is regarded as in many ways logically equivalent to an internally originating motivational stimulus such as hunger or thirst. This assumption, made for the sake of simplicity here, will require qualification later on (Section 5.4), because different types of operant learning are not logically identical. For example, pain as a motivational stimulus is often immediate in onset and termination, whereas hunger and thirst develop more slowly and are not dissipated by any single, rapid operant response. Phenomena such as acquired taste aversion (Revusky and Garcia 1970), in which the aversive stimulus is delivered some hours after the eating response which is to be suppressed, also suggest that subdivision within the class of operant learned responses is necessary on logical grounds, and may reflect a parallel subdivision of biological mechanisms.

4.3.2. SYNAPTIC PLASTICITY AND OPERANT LEARNING

4.3.2(a). The plasticity postulates for operant learning. In discussing cognitive learning it was pointed out that in an omniconnected holographic structure a continuous stream of random neural activity would be generated.

In operant learning, such random activity could have the important function of generating the random behavioural activity referred to above. The motor portions of the brain less central than the region where operant learning processes occur, may synthesize certain components of meaning from this random activity, so that coherent motor movements occur, although they do not form part of a coherent purposive behaviour pattern. With such a premise as a basis, there are nevertheless insoluble problems in explaining operant learning by means of the same plasticity postulates suggested for cognitive learning.

The difficulty can be illustrated with a typical example of operant learning —passive avoidance conditioning. In this the experimental animal is placed on a raised platform above the cage floor and is required to learn not to step down on to the cage floor, in order to avoid a painful electric shock. This can be presented diagrammatically as in Fig. 5.

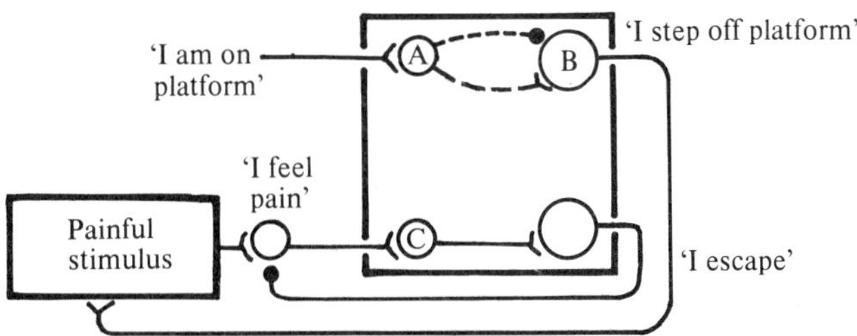

FIG. 5. This diagram illustrates the logical processes that must occur in passive avoidance conditioning. Statements in quotation marks identify the meanings represented when the corresponding unit (neurone or group of neurones) fires a burst of activity. Symbols as in Fig. 2 (p. 71). As a mechanism, this diagram is incomplete because the relationship of unit C to the linkages from A to B is not specified (but see Fig. 6).

'Neurone A' is part of the network of connections which fires as part of the representation of the sensory Gestalt 'I am on the platform'. 'Neurone B' similarly is part of the representation of the motor Gestalt 'I step off the platform'. Initially there will be no definite functional relationship between firing of neurone A and that of neurone B: if neurone B produces a burst of impulses at the same time as unit A is firing a burst, the former is randomly generated rather than causally related to A. (Hence the lines connecting A and B are drawn as broken lines.) Following firing of B, a painful stimulus would be generated at unit C. It is required that, contingent upon the firing of unit C, the *inhibitory* connections from A to B are strengthened until they are fully functional. If, on the other hand, unit A represented a painful stimulus, and unit B indicated a response which avoided this stimulus (i.e. the active avoidance paradigm) then firing of B, and the associated relief of the painful stimulus would be required to strengthen *excitatory* connections from A to B.

The difficulties of explaining such a mode of operation by the plasticity postulate discussed earlier are as follows. (i) The excitation of neurone C occurs *after* the firing of B; hence, if the plasticity mechanism depends on *contiguity* (i.e. *simultaneous* activation of the pre- and post-synaptic elements), it cannot be used to strengthen synapses which are active before the firing of C (i.e. those from A to B). This is referred to as the problem of retroflex action by learning theorists (Hilgard and Marquis 1964). (ii) In operant learning the precise response to be learned (promotion or suppression of a spontaneous act) depends on the effect of the act. It is necessary, therefore, that neurones such as C can give rise to influences strengthening *either* excitatory *or* inhibitory synapses, according to circumstances. For this, further major assumptions are necessary. (iii) Excitation of neurone C must be *potentially* capable of influencing any of a vast multitude of synapses representing sensory–motor relationships, yet paradoxically in any *one* example of operant learning it must be highly specific with regard to the synapses it strengthens.

The first of these problems could be solved if some representation of the initial sensory–motor relationship outlasted the actual performance of a motor act, until such a time that associations could be formed with representations of the subsequent sensory changes. The second of these problems requires the existence of a sensory analyser, to assess the motivational significance of an act, and that this analyser controls two classes of neurones such as C, of opposite significance, one to strengthen excitatory, the other inhibitory synapses. The third of these difficulties remains a paradox. As mentioned in Section 4.2.1 a macroscopic feedback could not *specify* the synapses to be modified, unless quite implausible assumptions are made about the complexity of the connections of the synaptic strengthening system.

In the case of cognitive learning, the twin problems of *specifying* and *strengthening* synapses were solved simultaneously by postulating a mechanism operating solely at the microscopic level, dependent on *contiguous* activation of pre- and post-synaptic elements to trigger a change in synaptic security. In the case of operant learning, such a scheme cannot adequately explain the strengthening of the appropriate synapses, since this must depend on the *effect* of a response, and so must involve a signal fed back at the macroscopic level, and yet a signal fed back at the macroscopic level is also, by itself, inadequate because it cannot specify the synapses to which the strengthening influence should be directed. If, however, the functions of specification and strengthening were physiologically separate (contrasting therefore with the proposed mechanism for cognitive learning), the one occurring at the microscopic level, the other at the macroscopic level, a synaptic basis for operant learning can be suggested which makes use of both types of feedback simultaneously.

Suppose that neurones such as C were capable of spreading their influences widely to all synapses within the structure where operant learning takes place, thereby providing the strengthening signal which is capable of increasing the security of certain synapses; and that they are of two types, those which could strengthen excitatory synaptic connections and those which could strengthen inhibitory ones. Suppose also that the plastic changes involved in strengthening a synapse depended on the following two concomitant relationships. (i) In Fig. 5 it is envisaged that in a particular sensory situation neurone B, by chance, fires a 'meaningful burst' of activity, which is then translated into motor acts, which then change the situation. It must be supposed that the meaningful burst has an influence, *at the neuronal level*, on all of its own synapses which are active at the time, whether excitatory or inhibitory, thereby making a preliminary selection of the synapses to be strengthened, though not yet actually strengthening them. (ii) The strengthening signal from neurones such as C makes the final selection between inhibitory and excitatory synapses, and accomplishes the definitive change in the appropriate synapses. Hence, a synapse, which by mechanism (i) has been 'made ready' for the increase in security, can achieve the actual state of a functionally secure synapse by mechanism (ii). In such a system one could consider that the signal fed back from the active neurone B, at the *microscopic* level would specify all synapses to be strengthened, plus an equal number of irrelevant synapses of the opposite sign, and would render them *susceptible* to plastic change; and the signal fed back from neurones such as C, at the *macroscopic* level would perform the final selection and would initiate the *actual* process of strengthening the relevant synapses. The latter process can now be labelled *reinforcement*, a word which will be used here only when there is a *macroscopic* influence, involving behaviour itself. The opposing influences upon synapses during operant learning may thus be labelled 'positive and negative reinforcements'. (The less specific word *strengthening* is used for the *microscopic* feedback processes, occurring independently in a great multitude of neurones and their synapses during learning.)

It should be noted that these postulates are not the only ones that could explain operant-type learning. With certain other modifications it would be equally plausible for the two reinforcement systems to act the other way round with respect to inhibitory and excitatory synapses. For the sake of simplicity the merits of the various alternatives will not be discussed (but see p. 97 for further comments on this matter). Some aspects of the hypothetical scheme outlined above have also been put forward by Crow (1968). Diagrammatically this scheme can be represented as in Fig. 6.

In this figure, diffusely branching connections are used to symbolize the widespread influence of the two reinforcement systems. However, in the theory put forward there is no need for these influences to rely at all on specific synaptic connections. The two reinforcement signals play a role in specification of the *sign* of synapses to be strengthened, but apart from this the detailed specification of exactly which synapses should be made secure is accomplished by other means. The most efficient way in which selective strengthening of synapses of one or other sign could be achieved is by means of neurotransmitter substances, which after release from nerve endings, spread their influence well beyond the immediate locality from which they were released, so as to influence a great many adjacent synapses. Such a mode of transmitter action is, of course, diametrically opposed to that which must operate in all the major motor and sensory pathways, and which is essential for the 'omniconnection' concept discussed in the previous chapter. In these systems, information would become 'blurred' if transmitters were allowed to spread their influence beyond the immediate confines of the

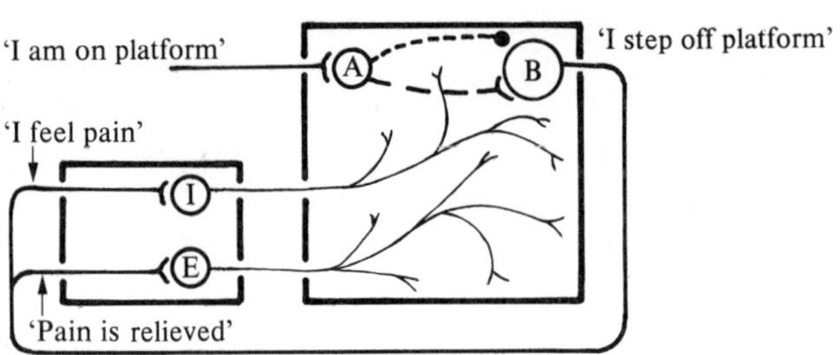

FIG. 6. Diagram of a possible mechanism for learning an operant (avoidance) response (completing the scheme begun in Fig. 5). The units E and I spread diffuse influences (depicted as *branching connections*) within the omniconnected structure (large square box). Unit E strengthens excitatory connections (positive reinforcement system) and unit I strengthens inhibitory connections (negative reinforcement system). The small box in which E and I are located operates as a sensory analyser, assessing the motivational significance of portions of behaviour. Other symbols as in Fig. 2 (p. 71).

synapses from which they were released. The reinforcement signals, in contrast, are in some ways like hormones, the major difference being that true hormones will be capable of influencing any region supplied by the blood stream, whereas the reinforcement signals will be strictly limited to the general region of distribution of the relevant nerve tracts, though within such a region they will be diffusely distributed. Thus, just as in cognitive learning, diffuse influences, as well as point-like synaptic influences have a part to play, and in the case of operant learning this part is a most essential feature of the model proposed. Evidence for the existence of such diffusely acting neurotransmitters will be presented in the next chapter.

A further component introduced into Fig. 6 also requires comment, namely the 'sensory analyser unit' placed between the sensory periphery and the reinforcement units. This is concerned with recognition of the motivational significance (positive or negative) of a particular operant response. In its simplest form this consists of an arrangement of 'hard-wired' (i.e. unmodifiable) connections by which particular features are detected and conveyed to one of the two reinforcement systems. These connections thus correspond to the genetically determined motivational systems necessary for self-preservation or self-expression in an organism, and their pattern of wiring may be likened to that supposed to apply to 'hard-wired' reflex connections. It would be too simplistic to think that this is the only machinery involved in detecting motivational significance. Thus, in order to trigger the reinforcement mechanism it may be necessary for an animal to learn to recognize some new and complex sensory pattern, rather than a basic stimulus such as pain, which presumably requires no learning. Such learning could, however, take place using the principle of contiguity alone, just as in classical conditioning: the complex stimulus would become associated with pain and with its behavioural antecedants, provided it was significantly correlated with a painful stimulus.

It should be noted that, just as the plasticity postulate put forward in Section 4.2.2(a) is an accurate translation of the logic of classical conditioning and sensory learning to the unitary level, so the scheme just proposed is also an accurate translation of the logic of operant learning to the microscopic level. However the latter cannot operate totally within the brain because it inevitably requires a causal link in the environment before appropriate synapses can be strengthened. This inevitably leads to increased complexity of organization of brain structures involved.

To sum up, cognitive learning requires contiguity of the synaptic inputs to be associated, and the strengthening mechanism is a microscopic feedback localized to each individual neuron concerned. Operant learning, however, requires contiguity of synaptic inputs combined with a macroscopic feedback involving the behaviour of the animal. To describe the latter, the terms *reinforcement* or *law of effect* may fairly be used in the same sense as they are used by learning theorists (Tolman 1932; Hilgard and Marquis 1964).

4.3.2(b). Implications of the plasticity postulates for operant learning. The two types of learning which have been dealt with—one dependent on contiguity alone, the other requiring behavioural feedback in addition—are similar in that they both must operate within the context of an omniconnected structure. However, they are very different at the synaptic level.

If the postulates for operant learning are to operate adequately, many of the further details implied by these postulates will be similar to those described for cognitive learning. Thus, meaning at the neuronal level—the adequate signal to create a 'state of readiness' in converging active synapses—will be a relatively extended rise or fall in impulse frequency. The occurrence of these changes is a likely consequence of varied sensory input upon a complex neural network. Similarly, in such a network it will be likely that any one neurone can participate in registration of a number of independent associations of synapses, both inhibitory and excitatory, representing alternative sensory circumstances in which the same element of motor output is required to be activated or suppressed.

Apart from these similarities, the contrasting features of the schemes for the two types of learning imply some important differences in the macroscopic properties of operant learning processes compared with those in cognitive learning. Amongst these are the phenomena of discrimination and generalization, which are features of operant-type learning as much as of cognitive learning. However, their explanation in operant learning is different from that in cognitive learning, and in some respects more complex, because the model of operant learning allows for separate processes of discrimination and generalization to apply to the behavioural act itself, and to the sensory situation in which it occurs.

In Fig. 7 (illustrating discrimination and generalization of the motor component) the output from the structure concerned with operant learning is represented by three neurones, 'X', 'Y', and 'Z', rather than as one.

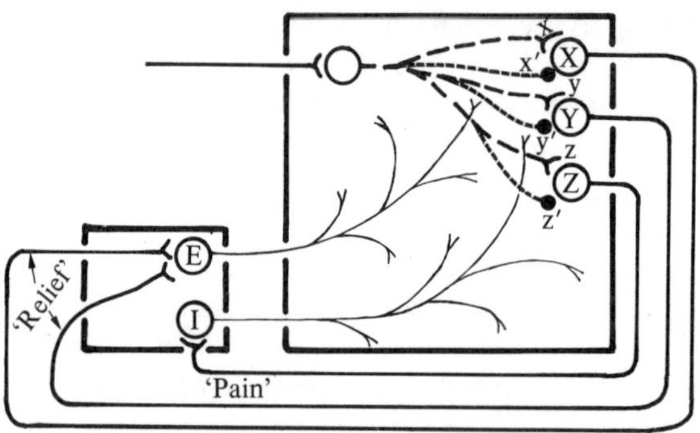

FIG. 7. Diagram to illustrate discrimination learning of the *motor* details of an operant response. It must be imagined that when units X and Y fire, a motivationally favourable motor response occurs, and when unit Z fires, an unfavourable response occurs. Symbols as in Fig. 2 (p. 71) and Fig. 6 (p. 82).

Suppose the consequence of a burst of action potentials in X and Y is a behavioural act which tends to fulfil a certain necessary motive for the animal, but that of activity in Z tends to prevent fulfilment of the goal. If all three neurones fire together, as a result of concomitant afferent activity, it may happen that the consequence of X and Y firing are effectively overridden by that of Z, so that the resultant behaviour is, in total, motivationally neutral. In this case neither of the reinforcement systems will be triggered. On the other hand, if when all three neurones fire, the result is, in total, favourable, the synapses x, y and z, which are excitatory will be strengthened, but not x′, y′, and z′, which are inhibitory. Discrimination between the synapses on X and Y, and those on Z cannot occur until further experience of the situation has been gained, and chance firing of neurone Z has occurred in circumstances where its unfavourable consequences are displayed in isolation.

Discrimination of the sensory context for an operant act depends on a similar process of successive approximation (see Fig. 8). Suppose an output neurone fires on two different occasions, and the pattern of activation of convergent synapses which leads to this firing is slightly different on these two occasions (groups A and B in Fig. 8, representing slight differences in the sensory context in which the act is performed). The motivational significance

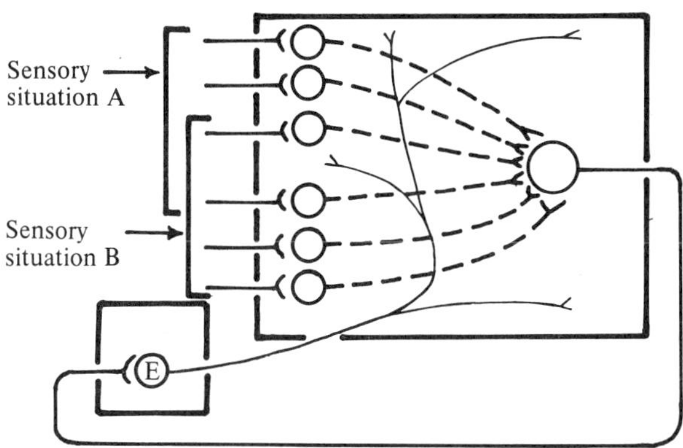

FIG. 8. Diagram to illustrate discrimination learning of the *sensory* details in which an operant response has a favourable outcome. Brackets (A and B) signify sensory situations similar in some respects, but different with regard to the *effect* of a response initiated in each situation. Symbols as in Fig. 2 (p. 71) and Fig. 6 (p. 82).

of the following act may vary according to the differences in context although the act itself is identical on the two occasions. Selection of the most appropriate context in which the act should be performed depends on repeated occurrence of the act in a series of slightly different contexts, so that ultimately the only synapses which are consistently strengthened are precisely those whose activity is associated with a favourable outcome for the act.

In cognitive learning, discrimination and generalization were an immediate consequence of the contiguity mechanisms, which allowed direct coding of the positive and negative correlations in the sensory input. In operant learning, however, although a form of contiguity mechanism is involved in establishing the 'state of readiness' in certain synapses, the final selection is made from a variety of random groupings of active neurones and synapses, by behavioural feedback mechanisms. These may either *tolerate* incidental behavioural components if they are motivationally neutral, *exclude* them, if they are motivationally negative, or *definitively include* them if they are motivationally essential. *Thus, the representation of motor behaviour within this structure will be in a relatively simple form, with none of the reciprocal inhibition, characteristic of motor systems at a lower level*, though undoubtedly the lower levels of the motor systems would use such inhibition to erase some of the incompatibilities generated by the above mechanism.

If this argument is correct, the opposed excitatory and inhibitory synapses within the structure(s) where operant responses are generated must represent directly opposed behavioural tendencies—activity versus quiescence, approach versus withdrawal, advancing a limb versus withdrawal of it. Moreover, if this is so, the population of neurones which forms the immediate output from this structure must represent behaviour essentially by connections all of which have mathematically the same sign—either *all* excitatory or *all* inhibitory. In these parallel output connections, opposing behavioural tendencies would be represented by the contrast between neuronal activity and silence, not by neuronal activity in output fibres of opposite sign. If there were mixtures of excitatory and inhibitory connections at the *terminations* of these output neurones, then the significance of behavioural feedback on to the modifiable synapses upon these neurones would be ambiguous, and operant learning could not occur.

This matter will be discussed further in Chapter 5. For the time being it is sufficient to point out a curious implication of the above statements. In animal and human behaviour it is often necessary to have alternative opposing strategies of response for apparently identical situations. According to what has been said so far about operant learning, the only way in which an opposing response (e.g. approach rather than avoidance) can be encoded is by first suppressing the representation of the first, and then relearning the new task. This is a lengthy procedure, and does not accord with the facts of mammalian behaviour: mammalian species exposed to alternate opposing reinforcement paradigms progressively learn both of the contrasting responses together (Sutherland and Mackintosh 1971, p. 318). This paradox clearly cannot be resolved within the bounds of the present model of operant learning. However, when operant learning and cognitive learning are considered in mutual relation (Section 5.3) it finds a consistent and realistic explanation.

When one considers acquisition of the more skilled, highly co-ordinated motor responses it again becomes apparent that operant learning on the basis of the effect of a response is by no means the only learning process involved in motor mechanisms. The greater the degree of skill required the more unlikely it is that the mechanism of trial and error combined with reinforcement of favourable portions of behaviour could accomplish the necessary task. Certainly, in many instances of animals learning skilled movements (e.g. a horse learning to clear a hurdle), the learning process does not simply depend on the rewards and punishments consequent on success or failure in performing the task as a whole. In such instances it seems that a good deal of cerebral information processing must be involved to register the interrelationship amongst such variables as velocity, acceleration, force, and momentum. These relationships can then be gradually generalized from an easy example of a particular task (e.g. clearing a low hurdle) to more difficult examples (a high hurdle). Thus, an animal faced with a somewhat novel task, which is more demanding than it has hitherto attempted can to some extent calculate—that is predict—the most appropriate sequence of muscle contractions needed to fulfil the motor objective. At this point reference should be made to an interesting paper by Pellionisz and Llinás (1979) on the subject of cerebellar function, in which a theory is put forward about how such predictions might be accomplished. Clearly, in explaining acquisition of skilled co-ordinated movements, there is a large gap between the basic logical properties of operant learning and the most complex emergent properties displayed by the several motor areas in the brain, acting in concert. The role of trial and error learning associated with positive and negative reinforcement may thus be confined to the global aspects of purposive behaviour, rather than all the details of its execution (i.e. strategy rather than tactics).

In a variety of biological problems, ranging from organic evolution to immunology, there has been a debate about whether *instruction* or *selection* is involved in specifying the necessary patterns of information. Edelman (1978) has provided an interesting comparison of selectionist theories in evolution, immunology, and higher brain function. The hypotheses outlined in the present chapter, for operant and cognitive learning, are, in one sense, both selectionist theories, since information is imprinted by selection from a finite (albeit very large) number of connections. In a different sense, however, cognitive learning is instructional, since the environment instructs the brain which connections to strengthen; in this sense operant learning is selectional since the brain generates a random variety of motor responses and then selects those which are motivationally advantageous. Even under the most favourable circumstances, operant learning, like organic evolution, has an element of chance in it, which makes it a rather lengthy process compared with cognitive learning. Much repetition of a response may be necessary before it is gradually approximated to the response which most accurately fulfils the motivational requirements of the situation the animal is in. It is difficult to envisage any other model for operant learning unless one attributes processes of symbolic deductive logic to subhuman animals.

4.4. Temporal aspects of learning

In Section 2.5 mention was made of certain temporal features of learning, as described at the behavioural or psychological level. In Chapter 3 consideration was also given to the anatomical substrate which can allow representation of at least some of the temporal information which is capable of being learnt. In the present section these two threads will be drawn together, to give an explanation of temporal features of learning in biological terms.

The crucial postulate for this section is that put forward in Section 3.2.4: for cortico–cortical, commissural and cortico–striate axonal connections, the omniconnection principle applies to the temporal dimension, at least for intervals of 250 ms or less (in humans). In other words, the individual axonal links within and between the cortices and striata of the two hemispheres may be expected to impose a wide range of conduction delays between synaptically linked neuronal cell bodies, some of these delays being only a few milliseconds duration, with others of various longer durations, up to about 250 ms in the human hemisphere.

Given such a premise, the encoding of temporal information during cognitive and operant learning is easily explained. In Fig. 3, two of the converging connections are drawn as fine lines, to represent slowly-conducting connections which impose (say) a 250 ms delay on their signals. If it is envisaged that a Gestalt is to be represented which consist of one part occurring 250 ms earlier than the other parts, then the plasticity mechanism, triggered from neurone A and employing the connections described, could operate to encode the whole of such a Gestalt. A similar mechanism is at least theoretically possible for operant learning, in cases where the motor response which most accurately fulfils a certain goal involves temporal patterning of the components of the response. In Fig. 9 it is imagined that three output neurones (representing components of a response) each have anatomical inputs from a single source imposing 10, 50, and 200 ms delays on the signal from that source. Firing of the three neurones simultaneously (i.e. without sequencing) might fulfil the necessary goal on a sufficient number of occasions that synaptic connections are to some degree strengthened. Suppose, however, that the most effective fulfilment of the goal requires temporal relationships of the components to be specified—say that component C should fire 200 ms before A and 50 ms before B. In this case after

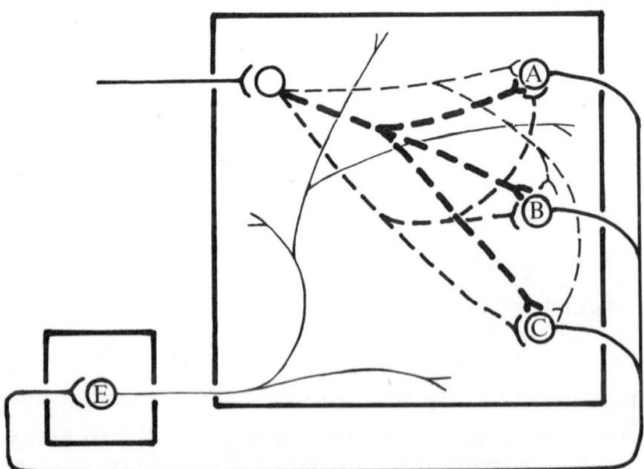

FIG. 9. Diagram to illustrate possibilities for acquiring temporal patterns of operant behaviour. Three output neurones are each influenced from the sensory input, by three connections each having different characteristic latencies. ▬ ▬ ▬ = 10 ms latency. - - - = 50 ms latency. - - - = 200 ms latency. Reinforcement must be imagined to strengthen the combinations of connections required for the most favourable sequence of activation of the three output neurones. Symbols as in Figs. 2 (p. 71) and 6 (p. 82).

some practice, with trial and error, the synapses which were most consistently and powerfully strengthened would be the 10 ms input to neurone C, the 50 ms input to neurone B, and the 200 ms input to neurone A. To what extent this mechanism actually is employed in operant learning is debatable, since as already mentioned many other mechanisms contribute to the learning of co-ordinated movements. It is, however, a potential attribute of the model proposed.

We have already seen several examples of how macroscopic properties of a neural network capable of learning can be derived from consideration of connectivity and plasticity in the network. Introduction of temporal aspects of connectivity into the discussion prompts a similar attempt to explain some of the temporal attributes of learning on the macroscopic scale. As mentioned in Section 2.5 the basic interval over which momentary subjective impressions are integrated (the psychological moment) has been variously estimated to be between 50 and 250 ms (usual value about 100 ms). This accords quite well with the hypothesis just put forward. If the hypothesis is valid, its implication would be that subjective awareness of 'the present' was a wave of integration travelling through time, itself approximately 250 ms in duration. This wave would correspond to the potential for immediate association of events, and its width would be determined by the proportion of very slowly conducting intracerebral axonal connections. Blumenthal (1977) calls this process 'rapid attentional integration'.

Perception of time passing is not universally regarded as a 'travelling wave'. Some writers (see Harter 1967) have proposed that it is a pulsatile awareness, with periods of less efficient information processing between each pulse. A recent biological interpretation of the latter type of theory is given by Edelman (1978) in which emphasis is placed on 'phased re-entry' of output signals back into the structure from which they emanated. Edelman is influenced by evidence of inherent rhythmic activity in some regions of the brain, particularly the thalamus (see Andersen and Andersson 1968), and so he has in mind particularly the reciprocal thalamo–cortical/cortico–thalamic connections as a basis for re-entry. In comment it must be admitted that thalamic rhythms are an important aspect of forebrain function, which may well have an important role in registration of temporal patterns. However, the widely divergent experimental estimates of the integration interval (0·05–0·25 s) provided by different methods of estimation (Blumenthal 1977) seem more easily compatible with the idea of temporal integration as dependent upon distributed axonal conduction times, rather than on a pulsatile and fairly regular thalamo–cortical rhythm.

In Section 2.5 mention was also made of pre-attentive 'buffer delays'—variously estimated at from 0·5–1 s (usual value 0·7 s). Considerable information could be stored for this length of time, but in an evanescent fashion, either to be dealt with by the rapid attentional integration mechanism discussed above (and so to reach consciousness) or to disappear without subsequently affecting consciousness or memory. 'Buffer delays' can also be given a counterpart in the scheme proposed here for temporal aspects of learning. During the long span of life during which an animal can progressively learn more information it may be imagined that representations of information become progressively more and more remote (logically) from the sensory input. Thus, the first associations to be learnt will involve modification of synapses in the cortex only one or a few junctions removed from the primary areas. Later in the adult life of the animal these synapses, now quite secure, form a preliminary network for conducting signals into the logically deeper portions of the brain where active modification of synapses is occurring, mediating the current learning activity. The 50–250 ms interval by which rapid attentional integrations are described corresponds only to the single synaptic linkages involved in current learning. However, it may be expected that rather longer delays may sometimes intervene between the time a sensory signal first impinges on the animal and the latest time when it can register on consciousness. These larger intervals are the conduction time through the logically more superficial parts of the cortical network, until the signals reach the frontier of the securely defined connections where they can trigger new learning. Such longer intervals preceding conscious integration correspond well with the role of buffer delays in Blumenthal's (1977) description.

It is interesting here to refer also to the work of Libet, who has studied the temporal aspects of conscious appreciation of sensation elicited by electrical stimulation of exposed sensory cortex in human beings at operation. Libet (1973) determined a strength–duration curve for conscious detection of the stimulus-elicited sensation. The least intense stimuli which were capable of producing a sensation required a duration of at least 0·7 s. For more intense stimuli a shorter duration stimulus was required, and the threshold intensity rose sharply for durations shorter than 0·1 s. These results can be interpreted as follows. Maximum sensitivity to the cortical stimulus requires maximum convergence. This requires conduction through several synapses, and consequently requires a stimulus sufficiently extended in time that the multisynaptic signals can converge with the directly conducted ones. With more intense stimuli less convergence is required, and this can then rely mainly on monosynaptic connections, which require a shorter integration interval typical of the 'rapid attentional integrations' of Blumenthal.

The third of the temporal features of learning mentioned in Section 2.5 was 'short-term memory', a post-attentive storage of information. If similar impressions are repeated within the span of short-term memory (5–20 s) the likelihood that the impressions will register in long-term memory as well as on momentary consciousness is increased. Otherwise the impression of the moment will be lost from consciousness with no long-term influence. Short-term memory probably has a rather different explanation from that proposed for rapid attentional integrations, and buffer delays. In the account of learning given in Sections 4.2 and 4.3 the actual strengthening of synapses depended on *repeated* occurrence of the situation tending towards their strengthening. In intervals between such repetitions the influence upon synapses may be expected to decay, so that only if the situation recurs before complete decay is there any progressive and cumulative strengthening. Short-term memory would therefore correspond to some biochemical time constant of modifiable synapses, such that cumulative (or multiplicative) biochemical modifications occur only if the strengthening circumstance is repeated prior to the disappearance of the biochemical changes of such a previous circumstance. It would not be unreasonable, therefore, to seek biochemical effects associated with learning situations which have a time constant comparable with that of short-term memory. However, the phrase 'short-term memory' has been used to describe a variety of experimental results, where decay processes take a variety of times. It is possible that any one example of a short-term memory phenomenon is a composite function of a variety of biological processes, only one of which is the decay of some biochemical activation of a synapse.

5. Cognitive and operant learning in real brain structures

5.1. The relative roles of neocortex and basal ganglia

5.1.1. INTRODUCTION

IN the case of cognitive learning it was proposed (Section 4.2.2) that *either* a temporary rise in impulse frequency will strengthen excitatory synapses, *or* a temporary fall in impulse frequency will strengthen inhibitory ones. In the case of operant learning, it was proposed (Section 4.3.2) that a temporary change in frequency (*both* a rise *and* a fall) will influence both excitatory and inhibitory synapses to put them in a 'state of readiness'. The macroscopic feedback mechanism will then determine whether the excitatory or the inhibitory synapses in this state are to be converted into functionally secure connections. It is impossible for both the types of physiological mechanism to occur at the same synapses and in the same neurones. If it is assumed that both of the two types of associative operation are found in mammalian brain mechanisms, and that the structural basis for either of these operations is a random neural network, *it must be concluded that the two processes occur within different networks, i.e. different gross structures within the brain*. This immediately inspires an attempt to identify the hypothetical networks for cognitive and operant learning with real structures in the mammalian brain.

An important postulate for the present account of learning is that the *cerebral neocortex as a whole is concerned with cognitive learning, involving the contiguity principle alone, whilst the basal ganglia, especially the caudate–putamen are one of the major centres concerned with operant learning*, and the generation of the spontaneous rudiments of neural activity which are finally expressed as behaviour. This statement should not be taken to imply that these regions are the only ones in which the two modes of learning can occur. The ability to learn in some sense may be a much more widely distributed property of nervous tissue (see Oakley 1979*a*). However, these two regions are taken to be the most highly evolved structures mediating the two types of learning. It should be mentioned that the suggestion that the cortex is the site of contiguity-based associations has been made before by Pavlov (1927). His suggestion related specifically to the associations by means of which conditioned reflexes are established. It now seems likely that the cerebral neocortex is not essential for conditioning of reflexes, particularly if the demands on sensory discrimination are not great (Gastaut 1958; Ross and Russell 1967). The present suggestion applies principally to contiguity-based associations which are readily available to consciousness, as in conscious recognition of complex spatial and temporal patterns.

5.1.2. THE ROLE OF THE NEOCORTEX

Consider firstly the neocortex. This contains all the primary receiving areas for sensory information, and it also contains a number of partially independent areas of association cortex to which the former send major inputs. The areas of association cortex, are usually assumed (e.g. Creutzfeldt 1978) to deal with higher level convergences of information originating in the primary sensory areas. The existence of these regions of partial functional segregation within the overall organization of the neocortex is entirely consistent with the idea that a major neocortical function is the detection of contiguity within its afferent activity: different aspects of sensory contiguity need not be intermingled in a totally uniform cortical network, but can be partially segregated in specialized regions, which are quantitatively, if not qualitatively, different in their potentiality. To be more specific, it seems likely that the different regions of neocortex, while having the same general function of encoding contiguities, can operate on different classes of contiguities, in so far as their input connections may be to varying degrees segregated. The existence of an important motor area within the neocortex of mammals deserves special comment since a cortex principally concerned with storing associations amongst sensory stimuli has no obvious need of a motor region integrated with it in the same structure: a motor region would be expected to be more closely involved in operant functions rather than cognitive ones. However, the function of the motor cortex, to be suggested shortly, is not the *acquisition* of operant responses, but rather the *storage* of the information so acquired, and this will be seen to depend solely on contiguity, as in other neocortical functions. The motor cortex is thus one example of a number of cortical regions where signals enter the cortex after a considerable amount of prior information processing. Although these signals are not sensory ones, their contiguity with other signals held within the cortex can still be registered.

A variety of physiological experiments have been carried out, over several decades, which demonstrate the modifiability of cortical functions following repeatedly applied contiguous stimuli. The older parts of this literature were reviewed by John (1967). In recent years, a number of workers (e.g. Woody and Black-Cleworth 1973; Baranyi and Fehér 1978) have described increases in excitatory synaptic efficacy in cortical neurones, produced by repeated activation of groups of synapses. These effects are not simply a function of use of synapses, since they may influence synapses other than those where activation is greatest (hetero-synaptic facilitation). Moreover, in one instance (Baranyi and Fehér 1978) repeated pairing of activity in pre- and post-synaptic elements produced the most effective facilitation. These investigations seem to be clear examples of the principle of contiguity, operating at the neuronal level, upon excitatory synapses. It is interesting to note here that experimental demonstrations of the role of the cortex in encoding contiguities in the sensory input include examples in which temporal patterns of stimulation are encoded as temporal patterns of electrical activity (Morrell and Jasper 1956; Yoshii and Hockaday 1958) as would be predicted from arguments advanced in earlier chapters.

The postulate made in Section 4.2.2 for modification of inhibitory synapses in cognitive learning has less direct experimental support. However, in experiments on slabs of isolated cortex Bliss, Burns, and Uttley (1968) produced evidence which is compatible with this postulate. They investigated 'conductivity' for input pathways to single neurones in the cortex and found, on repeated stimulation of an input, that conductivity changes correlated with frequency changes in the input. Some of these correlations were positive (implying perhaps enhancement of the efficacy of excitatory synapses converging on the neurone). The majority, however, were negative correlations, implying perhaps the enhancement of efficacy of converging synapses from inhibitory interneurones linked to the input pathway. The preponderance of negative effects in an experiment of this sort could be taken as an indication that the representation of an inhibitory surround for a newly encoded Gestalt involves *in toto* a more pervasive and widespread influence than the representation of the sharply focussed contrasting excitatory centre. This finding is thus compatible with the suggestion made in Section 4.2.2(c), that active cortical neurones have a net inhibitory effect that is distributed within the surrounding cortical network.

In other recent experiments of a somewhat different nature, changes have been demonstrated in the response properties of single cortical neurones after imposition of abnormalities in sensory input. The earlier of these experiments (Hirsch and Spinelli 1970; Blakemore and Mitchell 1973) involved grossly abnormal sensory environments, but in one of the most recent examples (Spinelli and Jensen 1979) the sensory environment was relatively normal, and the changes in response properties of the neurones studied were those needed to encode contiguous features of the imposed sensory input. It should be admitted that these examples of plasticity were observed in immature animals, before the onset of a 'critical period', and they probably depend at least to some extent on anatomical plasticity, rather than modification of synaptic efficacy without apparent anatomical change (Innocenti and Frost 1979). However, in so far as they are elicited merely by modifications of sensory input, or occur regardless of the effect of any operant response which is performed, they should be included in the definition of cognitive learning used here.

5.1.3. THE ROLE OF THE STRIATUM

The proposed role for the striatum in operant learning is also consistent with a good deal of macroscopic physiological evidence. (i) Much experimental and clinical data suggests the close involvement of this structure in the initiation of voluntary (i.e. operant) behaviour (Poirier *et al.* 1975). (ii) As predicted of a structure in which operant motor programmes are 'discovered', the striatum is one of the sites in the forebrain which controls spontaneous locomotor activity (Jung and Hassler 1960; Laverty 1974). (This region has even been called the *nodus cursorius*.) (iii) The conclusion derived in an earlier section, that the structure in which operant learning occurs should represent opposing behavioural tendencies in a relatively simple form, without reciprocal inhibitory connections, seems to hold true for the striatum. A number of experimental modifications of the striatum (particularly pharmacological modifications) have simple clear-cut influences on locomotor activity or related behaviour (Jung and Hassler 1960; Laursen 1963; Ungerstedt 1971*b*; Laverty 1974; Schallert, Whishaw, Ramirez, and Teitelbaum 1978) and this is in strong contrast with the mechanism of the more peripheral parts of the motor system. (iv) It was deduced (p. 86) that for the network concerned with operant learning the immediate output neurones should be of mathematically uniform sign. Electrophysiological evidence generally confirms this inference: the pathway from putamen to globus pallidus appears to be overwhelmingly inhibitory in sign (Malliani and Purpura 1967; Yoshida, Rabin, and Anderson 1972; Levine, Hull, and Buchwald 1974). Subsidiary excitatory components of pallidal responses to striatal stimulation (which have been described) may have other explanations than direct striato–pallidal connections – such as branching axons from other regions, supplying both striatum and pallidum. An alternative route from striatum to thalamus – i.e. via the substantia nigra – also appears to have an initial link which is uniformly inhibitory in sign (Yoshida and Precht 1971). (v) In contrast to the theory put forward for cognitive learning, the model outlined for operant learning demands a very thorough and intimate convergence upon output neurones. It leaves little room for areas of partial functional independence as found in the neocortex. In view of this, the identification of the striatum as the site where operant programmes are discovered receives some support from a consideration of the functional and anatomic organization of the striatum. As mentioned in Section 3.2.3 there is considerable overlap of striatal regions receiving inputs from quite separate cortical regions (Kemp and Powell 1970; Blake, Zarzecki, and Somjen 1976) and no precise topographical sensory or motor map has been found in the striatum by physiological means (Jung and Hassler 1960). It is perhaps not surprising that a three-dimensional structure such as the striatum should undertake the function of operant learning, rather than a structure such as the cortex which is in origin a laminated superficial layer: for topological reasons the type of convergence required can be achieved more easily in the former type of structure.

Apart from such circumstantial evidence, it has been possible to provide further evidence, some of it more direct, in favour of the role of the striatum in reinforced behaviour, using electrophysiological methods (i.e. stimulation and/or recording) in a number of ways to probe the striatum and associated circuitry. The most thoroughly investigated phenomenon revealed by such methods is the intracranial self-stimulation phenomenon first described by Olds and Milner (1954) in which an animal with stimulating electrodes implanted in appropriate parts of its brain, will repeatedly perform operant responses in order to deliver stimuli through these electrodes. This phenomenon clearly has a close logical relationship to operant learning processes. Its discovery by Olds and Milner was a direct development from the debates about learning theory which flourished in the earlier years of this century, and so it is not surprising that it is also directly predictable from the theory of operant learning elaborated here. Thus, if an animal, by its operant responses can directly control the positive reinforcement system, without the prior discriminative action of the hypothetical sensory analyser of the motivational significance of behaviour, then behaviour which leads to activation of this reinforcement system will be reinforced indiscriminately, regardless of its usual motivational significance (see Deutsch 1963).

A variety of electrode placements in the brain will support intracranial self-stimulation, including sites in the brain stem, the diencephalon, the basal ganglia, and the cerebral cortex. It is now clear that this phenomenon is not a unitary one, but involves a number of related behaviours, and a number of fibre systems (Gallistel 1973; Rolls 1975; Olds 1977). The striatum is not in fact the most obvious of the sites from which self-stimulation can be elicited: this is the medial forebrain bundle, a region containing a great many fibre pathways, both ascending and descending. However, a number of reports make it clear that the striatum will also act as a self-stimulation site (Brady and Conrad 1960; Olds and Olds 1963; Justesen, Sharp, and Porter 1963). In addition the septal nuclei and nucleus accumbens septi (i.e. the limbic striatum) are commonly found to be self-stimulation sites (Olds 1958; Routtenberg and Huang 1968). The latter structures are in many ways related to the neostriatum, and recent analyses of connections of the limbic striatum also suggest that they may not be very sharply distinguishable from the neighbouring neostriatum (Nauta, Smith, Faull, and Domesick 1978). The identity of the postulated positive reinforcement system will be discussed in more detail in the next section. For the time being it should be pointed out that the various sites mentioned correspond to the course and regions of termination of the ascending pathway of dopaminergic axons from substantia nigra to striatum. Cortical sites which support self-stimulation also appear to correspond mainly with regions possessing dopaminergic innervation (Collier, Kurtzman, and Routtenberg 1977; Phillips, Mora, and Rolls 1979), though whether this innervation arises as branches from axons innervating the striatum or from independent neurones is not clear. The region where these fibres are most densely crowded—the medial forebrain bundle—is the most clear-cut self-stimulation site.

Just as positive feedback occurs when an animal can directly control the positive reinforcement pathways in its brain, so it could be predicted that self-limiting negative feedback would occur, if the stimulating electrodes were placed in the course of the negative reinforcement pathways. This converse phenomenon has certainly been observed: animals, with stimulating electrodes in certain areas of the brain, systematically avoid actions which would lead to activation of the electrodes (Olds and Olds 1963). The evidence that the latter phenomenon is a function of the striatum is not particularly striking, but it should be born in mind that the avoidance phenomenon may be hard to demonstrate satisfactorily in a region where both positive and negative reinforcement systems are intermingled, and where the distribution of the negative reinforcement fibres, near their terminations, is not dense. The real justification for mentioning both these phenomena at this point is that their existence is predicted by the hypothesis. In the real brain interpretation of the available evidence is not simple, partly for reasons just mentioned, partly because other fibre systems almost certainly contribute to these phenomena. Some of these other fibre systems will be briefly mentioned later (p. 118 and p. 140).

A second line of electrophysiological investigation of mechanisms of operant learning has been undertaken by Keene (1975, 1978). From the postulates put forward in Section 4.3.2 it would be predicted that activation of one or other of the reinforcement systems by electrical stimulation in an acute animal preparation should strengthen a proportion of the synapses in the striatum, if their neurones are currently in a state of elevated or lowered activity. Consequently it would be expected that neurones should change their firing rate following activation of the reinforcement systems. More specifically, the plasticity postulates, as stated, imply that activation of the positive reinforcement pathway should increase the firing frequency of neurones it directly influences, and activation of the negative reinforcement pathway should lower the firing frequency of neurones it directly influences. However, these predictions may not apply in quite such a simple sense, for two reasons. Firstly, in a network of excitatory and inhibitory connections, observed changes in firing frequency may be indirect effects, with sign reversed because of the intervention of an inhibitory link in bringing about the change. Secondly, it should be noted that the postulated influences of positive and negative reinforcement systems upon excitatory and inhibitory striatal synapses could be interchanged without seriously weakening the hypothesis. (The only associated change that would be necessary would be reversal of the sign of one of the synaptic links in the sequence by which striatal output finally is expressed as behaviour.) Indeed, the reversed relationship could well be the true one: bilateral striatal lesions lead to hyperactivity rather than inactivity (Laursen 1963) so it is likely that the effect of impulse activity levels in striatal output neurones is the suppression of behavioural activity, rather than its initiation. If such were the case it would be necessary for the positive reinforcement system to strengthen inhibitory effects on the output neurones, in order to selectively initiate behavioural items. It seems premature to debate these more detailed matters of striatal function, until firmly established electrophysiological and neurochemical data permit a more complete formulation of striatal synaptic mechanisms. The postulates of Section 4.3.2 will therefore suffice here, since they allow somewhat simpler arguments than their alternatives.

In spite of these uncertainties it may reasonably be predicted, from the general form of the plasticity postulates put forward for operant learning, that the activity levels of individual neurones, in the structure concerned, should be influenced in antagonistic ways when the positive and negative reinforcement systems are activated. With the evidence of self-stimulation and avoidance phenomena in mind, Keene (1975, 1978) has investigated the electrophysiological basis of reinforcement in this way, and has thus provided further direct evidence of the participation of the striatum in generating reinforced behaviour. Following stimulation of brainstem sites from which self-stimulation and avoidance could be elicited, prolonged changes in firing frequency were observed in neurones in various forebrain loci. In many regions there was rarely any obvious antagonism between the effects of stimulation of the hypothetical positive and negative reinforcement sites. However, in the striatum, and in the loci in its efferent pathway (globus pallidus, nuclei ventralis anterior and ventralis lateralis of the thalamus) such antagonism was commonly observed (in up to 50 per cent of neurones). This is a further indication that the motor consequences of electrical activity in these structures represents motivational consequences of behaviour in a fairly direct fashion, as required in the present theory. Potentially this antagonism could be displayed in both a positive sense (i.e. positive reinforcement leading to increases in frequency in a neurone, and negative reinforcement leading to falls in frequency) and in a negative sense (where the opposite effects would be observed). Keene (1978) mentions that the 'positive antagonistic' effects were commonest in the medial pallidal units. Unfortunately the proportions of 'positive' and 'negative' antagonisms in striatal units are not given in this paper. This would be of particular relevance to the present theory not only with respect to concepts of reinforcement and synaptic plasticity but also with regard to the uncertainties mentioned in the previous paragraph. Such additional information would give more precise insights into the patterns of relationship of excitatory and inhibitory mechanisms which develop in the mature striatum and could lead to a more precise model than that put forward here. It could also help to resolve a paradoxical aspect of the theory of operant learning: the striatum, by virtue of its own random impulse activity is supposed to generate behavioural activity, yet the striatum actually has very low levels of spontaneous activity compared with many forebrain regions. (Compare Hyvärinen (1966) with Hull, Levine, Buchwald, Heller, and Browning (1974); Schultz and Ungerstedt (1978); Garcia-Rill, Hull, Levine, and Buchwald (1978).) Even as it stands, however, Keene's evidence strongly supports the idea that the striatum and associated circuitry are closely involved in generation of motor signals related to motivationally significant portions of behaviour.

A third strategy of electrophysiological investigation of operant learning is to arrange that firing of a single neurone in a forebrain locus is equivalent to the operant response itself in that reward (or punishment) is directly contingent upon electrical activity in the neurone (or upon some derivative of this activity). A number of experiments have shown that the pattern of firing of single neurones is capable of modification under these circumstances. One of the first to show such effects was J. Olds (1963, 1965) who reported that it was 'far easier . . . to use reinforcement to create a change in the spontaneous discharge rates of units recorded from paleocortical and caudate placements, than to cause similar changes in spontaneous rates of neocortical units'. More recent investigations of this phenomenon (Fetz 1969; Shinkman, Bruce, and Pfingst 1974; Schmidt, Bak, McIntosh, and Thomas 1977; Wyler and Burchiel 1978) have not followed up this particular comment, but have concentrated upon operant control of neocortical neurone discharge. That this should also be observable is not inconsistent with the present theory: any region which is under the influence of the striatal output, even if indirectly, should potentially be modifiable, as a result of synaptic modifications occurring in the striatum. It might be expected that the time course of modification, as the rewarding stimulus is repeatedly presented, might be shorter for striatal units, than for those less directly involved. However, in the absence of detailed comparisons of operant conditioning in striatal and neocortical units this type of study furnishes no further decisive evidence of the primacy of the striatum in correlating motor signals with their motivational significance.

5.2. Reinforcement systems, and other diffuse influences on learning mechanisms

In the last fifteen years a great deal of experimental work has been devoted to defining pathways in the brain containing as neurotransmitters the various monoamines, viz. dopamine, noradrenaline and serotonin (5-hydroxytryptamine, 5HT) (Hillarp, Fuxe, and Dahlström 1966; Ungerstedt 1971*a*; Hökfelt, Ljungdahl, Fuxe, and Johansson 1974; Fuxe and Jonsson 1974). Of the various structures involved in the circuitry of the striatum, there are good reasons for identifying monoamine containing axonal pathways with the reinforcement systems. Specifically, it is suggested that the *substantia nigra, which provides the striatum with dopaminergic innervation, is the positive reinforcement system, and that the midbrain raphe nuclei, particularly the dorsal raphe nucleus, which provides the striatum with serotonergic innervation* (Fuxe and Jonsson 1974), *is the negative reinforcement system*. The present section is mainly concerned with summarizing some of the evidence for these statements.

In the model put forward for operant learning, the two antagonistic reinforcement systems were required to *act diffusely* upon the structures they innervate. Attention will therefore be focussed on evidence suggesting that monoamine neurotransmitters act diffusely. It will be remembered, however, that diffuse influences have a role to play in control of cognitive learning (p. 76) as well as in operant learning. On grounds of economy and simplicity it is attractive to suggest that monoamines in the neocortex have a facilitating effect upon synaptic change in that structure, somewhat similar to that of the striatal amines. (It should be noted here, however, that the major catecholamine present in the neocortex is not dopamine, but noradrenaline (Hillarp *et al.* 1966; Ungerstedt 1971*a*).)

An important part of the evidence indicating the involvement of striatal and cortical amines in synaptic plasticity, learning, and memory, is behavioural in nature. Since the behavioural pharmacology of monoamines is such a complex field, discussion of this evidence is left until Chapter 6. Here we shall concentrate on simpler aspects of the evidence. At the end of this section some suggestions are made about how monoamine neurotransmitters might interact with other biochemical events in synapses to bring about changes in synaptic efficacy. These suggestions are meant to apply as much to plasticity of cortical synapses as to that of striatal ones.

The diffuseness or otherwise of the action of monoamine neurotransmitters is a topic of considerable theoretical importance and currently a matter for vigorous debate. The most striking evidence to suggest that monoamines act diffusely, rather than by way of precise points of synaptic connection is ultrastructural: axons and varicosities labelled in various ways for monoamine neurotransmitters, in several brain regions, display remarkably few regions of synaptic specialization, compared with the majority of other axonal profiles in the neuropil (Descarries, Watkins, and Lapierre 1977; Dismukes 1977). Evidence of this kind has also been obtained for striatal aminergic axons, both dopaminergic (Tennyson, Heikkila, Mytelineou, Côté, and Cohen 1974; Pickel, Joh, and Reis 1976) and serotonergic (Calas, Besson, Gaughy, Alonso, Glowinski, and Chéramy 1976), though other experimenters advocate the presence of conventional synapses for dopaminergic striatal axons (Hattori, Fibiger, McGeer, and Maler 1973; Arluison, Agid, and Javoy 1978). Experiments of this type are beset with considerable technical problems, and it is possible that transmitter release sites for striatal amines are not of a single homogeneous type. It is to be hoped that, in the future, histochemical studies of distribution of monoaminergic receptor sites may help to clarify the evidence derived from electron microscopy.

Besides the ultrastructural evidence, however, a good deal of circumstantial evidence indicates diffuseness of action of amines in the striatum and elsewhere.

(i) Monoaminergic pathways in the forebrain are distributed in a much more diffuse fashion than are most of the forebrain pathways which have been demonstrated neuroanatomically. There is evidence that a small cell group such as the locus coeruleus can supply noradrenergic axons to neocortex, hippocampus and cerebellum, and indeed single noradrenergic neurones may possess all these projections (Hillarp *et al.* 1966; Ungerstedt 1971*a*; Olson and Fuxe 1971; Nakamura and Iwama 1975). It is unlikely that such profusely branching fibre systems originating from relatively small nuclei could have sufficient afferent synaptic contacts to preserve intact any intricate pattern of sensory or motor information. Probably, therefore, they have a more diffuse function.

(ii) There is much evidence that monoamines in the forebrain are subject to negative feedback control mechanisms, operating partly through neuronal feedback loops, and resulting in control of the levels of pharmacologically active amines within forebrain structures (Nybäck 1972; Costa and Meek 1974). Such negative feedback controls would be most inappropriate in a system where carriage of information was dependent on a large number of discrete connections, but would be highly relevant for a system which modifies and controls the chemical environment of a region of brain tissue, in a diffuse and holistic sense. It should be noted here that if monoaminergic systems act as behavioural reinforcers, they must operate in a unified manner, rather than as a set of independent components, since reinforcement is under the control of items of behaviour taken as a whole. Likewise, any controlling influence exerted upon cognitive learning is likely to be a unified switch-like response, rather than a multiplicity of independent controls, since such an influence would be needed to serve a requirement of the whole animal (e.g. the control of sleep and wakefulness or control of 'arousal' in the face of a novel environment). Some of the neurochemical evidence referred to above strongly points to such a unified mode of action. In particular, partial destruction of the dopaminergic component of the substantia nigra is followed by biochemical hyperactivity of the remaining neurones (Agid, Javoy, and Glowinski 1973). This unification of function applies not only within a single substantia nigra, but between the substantiae nigrae on opposite sides, since unilateral modification of nigral function results in compensatory changes in the contralateral nucleus (Leviel, Chéramy, and Glowinski 1979). Evidence of the same nature has apparently not been sought for the serotonergic systems originating in the midbrain raphe nuclei, but corresponding findings are predicted. Exactly how the unification of function in the monoaminergic nuclei might be achieved is uncertain. However, there has been much discussion of the role of dendrites in the substantia nigra, since the discovery that in this region and elsewhere dendrites are capable of transmitter release (Björklund and Lindvall 1975; Geffen, Jessel, Cuello, and Iversen 1976; Sloper and Powell 1978; Leviel *et al.* 1979). A dendritic mechanism of unification is also suggested by the findings of Cummings and Felten (1979) that neurones in the brainstem raphe nuclei possess bundles of dendrites running together in close alignment.

(iii) Behavioural evidence also suggests that the physiological role of one monoamine (dopamine) does not depend greatly on the specification of axon terminals from which it is released. Thus, therapy for Parkinson's disease with L-DOPA can be effective even when degeneration of the nigro–striatal tract has reached such an extent that only 10 per cent of normal levels of the dopamine synthesizing enzymes can be measured *post mortem* (Lloyd, Davison, and Hornykiewicz 1975).

A further prediction which should be true if the striatal dopaminergic and serotonergic innervations are in fact the two reinforcement systems, is that the input to the above two neuronal groups should carry motivationally significant signals. Evidence on this is scant. It has, however, been observed that the midbrain raphe nuclei receive thermal inputs (Jahns 1976), and that neurones in the substantia nigra are influenced by noxious stimuli (Barasi 1979). Both of these may be examples of motivationally significant signals. Whether dopaminergic neurones are specifically activated by motivationally favourable *changes* in input (or serotonergic neurones by motivationally unfavourable ones) remains to be determined.

In most electrophysiological studies of monoamine neurotransmitters the role envisaged for the amine—that is, excitation or inhibition at a synapse—is rather different from that proposed here. In much of this work, where iontophoresis of the amine is the principal technique employed, it is difficult to be certain where the site of action of the drug is in relation to the electrode tip, and it is therefore impossible to know the effective concentration of the drug at that site, and whether it is a physiological or a pharmacological action (Szabadi and Bradshaw 1974; Maillis 1974; Kelly 1975). In other examples, the action of an amine is investigated by stimulation of aminergic cell groups and recording excitations and inhibitions (Sasa and Takaori 1973; Nakai and Takaori 1974; Zarzecki, Blake, and Somjen 1977; Richardson, Miller, and McLennan 1977; Olpe and Koella 1978). How such actions are related to those postulated here is uncertain. Monoamine neurotransmitters are known to act by way of more than one pharmacological receptor type for each amine, in any particular region of brain tissue, so it is possible that direct excitations and inhibitions are physiological functions independent of the proposed roles of monoamines in facilitating synaptic strengthening. On the other hand, some of the electrophysiological effects of monoamines which have been described are rather unusual, if regarded simply as excitation or inhibition. For instance, in the cerebellum, noradrenaline has the effect of suppressing most of the spontaneous impulse activity in Purkinje cells, while leaving intact the bursts of activity due to climbing fibre discharge. The biophysical effects of catecholamines here are also rather unusual in that membrane potential changes may be accompanied by increase rather than decrease of resistance (Hoffer, Siggins, Oliver, and Bloom 1971). These unusual features may be indications of the function of monoamines in governing synaptic plasticity. Outside the central nervous system (i.e. in a sympathetic ganglion preparation), where more closely controlled experiments are possible, a more striking example of the role of a monoamine (dopamine) in modulating inputs from other synapses has been investigated by Libet, Kobayashi, and Tanaka (1975).

The postulates put forward in Chapter 4 concerning synaptic modification in cognitive and operant learning are statements of *overall operational characteristics* rather than the detailed mechanism for the modifiable junctions. The validity or otherwise of these postulates, therefore, does not depend on what their precise mechanism may be. However, the characteristics proposed for the two types of learning, although different in important ways, have features in parallel which permit some speculation about the detailed mechanism. In operant learning it has been seen that the final strengthening of appropriate synapses can be accomplished by a combination of: (i) the integrated activity in a neurone, resulting from multiple converging excitatory and inhibitory synaptic inputs; and (ii) the concomitant pharmacological activity of monoamine neurotransmitters in the immediate environment of the neurone. In cognitive learning, strengthening of appropriate synapses also depends on integrated impulse activity in a neurone (though the rules supposed to govern this process were different from those governing operant learning). The suggestion has also been made that cortical amines may have a facilitatory effect on this process (though the detailed behavioural evidence for this has yet to be considered). In both types of learning it is likely, therefore, that a similar convergence of influences brings about synaptic strengthening.

One possible locus at which these two influences could converge is at the level of phosphoproteins in the synaptic membrane. Some biochemical evidence suggests that these compounds may be influenced both by pharmacologically active amines in the extraneuronal environment, and by the impulse activity of a neurone. Thus, it is known that catecholamines can influence phosphorylation of synaptic proteins (see Nathanson 1977), via an intermediate step involving activation of adenyl cyclase. There is also evidence that depolarizing stimuli of various types can also influence phosphorylation of these proteins (Reddington, Rodnight, and Williams 1973; Williams and Rodnight 1976). In addition it has been observed that some of the synaptic phosphoproteins alter their degree of phosphorylation during learning situations (Ehrlich, Rabjohns, and Routtenberg 1977) and during situations in which modifications of synaptic security are detectable (Browning, Dunwiddie, Bennett, Gispen, and Lynch 1979). Finally, it has recently been observed that pharmacological receptors for the widely occurring transmitter candidate—glutamate—are regulated by cation concentrations

(Baudry and Lynch 1979). It is possible, therefore, that both in the neocortex and the striatum the mechanism of synaptic strengthening involves prior phosphorylation of synaptic proteins, leading to changes in the pharmacological receptors for non-monoaminergic transmitters. These processes in turn are under the dual control of monoamine neurotransmitters, and intraneuronal concentration of common ions (which are themselves influenced by excitation and inhibition in the neurone).

5.3. The combined operation of neocortex and basal ganglia

If the roles suggested above (Section 5.1) for the neocortex and basal ganglia in cognitive and operant learning respectively are accepted, an important relationship between the two structures can be clearly envisaged. This depends on the axonal pathways linking the two structures. The major input to the caudate–putamen is from widespread areas of neocortex (Kemp and Powell 1970; Poirier *et al.* 1975). The major output from caudate–putamen is, by various routes, to the thalamus, and hence to the neocortex, particularly the motor cortex and regions in front of it (Poirier *et al.* 1975; Faull and Mehler 1978). Within the cortex it is assumed that the contiguity principle applies, without additional involvement of reinforcement related to the effect of a response. Assuming that motivationally useful operant responses are by some means (see Chapter 4) acquired in the striatum, then subsequently, when a particular operant response is performed (depending on crucial functional connections within the caudate–putamen), numerous internal excitatory and inhibitory connections would be established in the neocortex between different contiguous fragments of the motor representation. Furthermore, both the input to the striatum and the output from it will pass through the neocortex. However within the neocortex, the relationship between sensory input and motor output will be purely one of contiguity, and will not involve the effect of the response. Hence the neocortex can treat its input from the striatum as any other sensory input, and connections can be formed between it and other sensory inputs on the basis of this contiguity. Thus, effective cortical connections will be formed which have the same functional significance as the initial striatal connections. *Thus, the neocortex can function as the final store of information, whether it was initially acquired by contiguity learning, or by operation of the law of effect within the striatum.* It should be noted here that the role envisaged for the motor cortex implies no sharp functional segregation of it from neighbouring cortical regions. This is compatible with the known sensory functions of the 'motor' area (Lemon and Porter 1976) and with other evidence that, in several ways, it merges gradually into the main somatic sensory cortex (Heath 1978).

Figure 10 gives a more detailed illustration of how the above process could operate with respect to avoidance learning (see legend) by making use of the models of cortical and striatal function suggested in Chapter 4. The essential point is that, once particular synapses in the striatum have been strengthened by the reinforcement mechanism, this will inevitably give rise to new combinations of contiguously activated neurones in regions of sensory and motor cortex. For instance, if a newly strengthened inhibitory connection in the striatum is activated by an impulse, it will inevitably induce a fall in impulse frequency in a population of cerebral cortical neurones. This fall will be concomitant (i.e. contiguous) with the activation of inhibitory cortico–cortical connections of the neurones which also accompanied the activation of the striatal connection, and this contiguity can then lead to strengthening of these inhibitory cortical synapses.

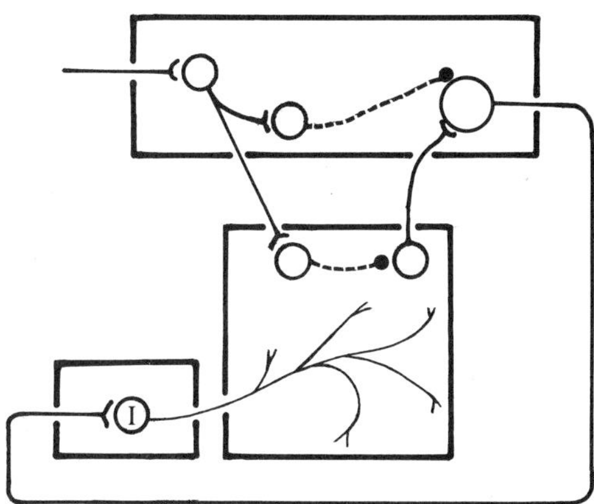

FIG. 10. Diagram to illustrate the relative roles of caudate–putamen and neocortex in formation of a permanent record of an operant response. In the large square box (representing caudate–putamen) strengthening of synapses depends both on contiguity and the effect of a response (see p. 81). In the upper rectangle (representing the neocortex) strengthening of synapses depends on contiguity alone (see p. 68). Although the neocortex has no means of acquiring a purposeful operant response, it can encode a permanent version of responses discovered in the caudate–putamen. Symbols as in Figs. 2 (p. 71) and 6 (p. 82).

In this scheme of learning an interesting parallel is apparent. Just as the sensory information entering an organism from the environment is, at the sensory periphery, represented in a simple form without surround inhibition to sharpen contrasts, so at the site of genesis of operant behaviour the representation is also simple, without the reciprocal inhibition and other interconnections present elsewhere in motor systems. It is only when the two types of information have been channelled upwards towards the cortex via the thalamus that these additional features are incorporated.

The proposed relationship of neocortex to neostriatum is again consistent with important features of the macroscopic physiological organization of these two structures, as well as with their manner of interconnection. If the cortex were concerned with cognitive learning in isolation, it could never become linked to output pathways mediating behaviour, and a motor cortex would be redundant. Moreover, an argument of an evolutionary nature also favours the above interpretation of the relative role of basal ganglia and neocortex. The caudate–putamen does not expand in the course of phylogeny to the same extent as does the neocortex. The large relative size of the neocortex (particularly in higher primates) is consistent with its being the final store of information, whatever the means of actually acquiring that information.

It should be pointed out that the transference of the representation of an operant programme, although most easily visualized as occurring after successive repetitions of the response, might not be absolutely dependent on such repetition: provided the appropriate synapses in the striatum have been made secure, then spontaneous activity in appropriate neurones of sensory cortex might still evoke contiguous activity in the motor cortex, although the total pattern of this spontaneous activity in the motor cortex has not the completeness, or coherence, to represent any actual behavioural programme.

In the basic model for operant learning (Chapter 4) the apparent assumption so far has been that once certain synapses are strengthened, during the acquisition of a particular task, they would remain strengthened, and thus form the permanent representation of the task. With the interrelation between operant and cognitive learning just proposed, we can now dispense with this assumption and increase the flexibility of the learning mechanism. Synaptic strengthening in the striatum could be merely a temporary phenomenon. With such an additional feature, the basal ganglia would function *only* during acquisition of a response, and the permanent record would be stored in consolidated form within the neocortex, leaving the basal ganglia unencumbered by stores of operant information, and ready to fashion further new motor programmes. This division of function is also suggested by evidence, to be considered in Chapter 6, on the role of different monoamine transmitters in learning.

As explained on p. 75 the neural network for cognitive learning can simultaneously represent a large variety of sensory situations, because each neurone can be the site of a number of different convergences, each to be used in a different context of overall neural activity. This concept can now be applied to sensorimotor representations as well as to strictly sensory ones. In the mature adult, the neocortex will contain representations of very many previously learned motor programmes, and if the animal's experience has been varied, these will include more than one strategy of response for any particular sensory circumstance. In such an animal, one may therefore envisage that the functions of the striatum include not only the detection of correlations between a response and its effect, and the process of transferring a representation of this correlation to the neocortex, but also a third function: the short-term selection of cortical programmes, so that a particular programme which is already laid down, may be used when relatively transient patterns of reinforcement, appropriate only to the temporary circumstances, require it to be used. What is more, it is at least potentially possible for cortical programmes to override striatal ones, so that behaviour is not rigidly tied to immediate goal-fulfilment. Thus we find that the striatum and cortex in combination have, as a property which develops in the adult, the ability to take a multitude of rapid decisions. These decisions may seem to be based on 'foreknowledge' of the consequences of action, but in reality are derived from long experience of situations which in one way or another have similar features.

The relation between neocortex and striatum outlined in the last few pages is the central theoretical statement in this monograph. Many of the postulates put forward in the earlier or later parts of the book may be incomplete, or replaceable by alternative postulates serving the same theoretical purpose. Some of them may simply be wrong. However, the model of forebrain function put forward here must stand or fall by this crucial scheme of cortico–striatal interdependence. To close this section a few more instances will be given of the explanatory power of the theory. Others will be mentioned in later sections. Others yet may remain to be discovered. In any event this scheme is testable.

One such instance is the phenomenon of latent learning. This was first described by Blodgett (1929) and has since been widely investigated (Tolman and Honzik 1930; Thistlethwaite 1951). In latent learning an animal is exposed to the test situation to be used in an operant conditioning experiment, but initially the reinforcement is omitted. Subsequently, when the reinforcement is introduced, the animal learns the task faster than control animals not given prior exposure to the test situation. This phenomenon, which is (*prima facie* at least) inexplicable in terms of reinforcement theory, is frequently regarded as a crucial test of the rival versions of learning theory—those dependent upon the law of effect (S–R associations), and those dependent upon contiguity (S–S associations) (Seward 1947; Thistlethwaite 1951). The present theory provides an easy explanation of latent learning, and simultaneously provides a rational reconciliation of the opposing schools of learning theorists. In ordinary operant learning tests it may be expected that animals require a number of preliminary trials to familiarize themselves with the experimental situation, that is to encode the various features present, a proportion of which are later to be singled out as aspects of the desired response, or as a source of reinforcement. The association of response with reinforcement is a secondary process dependent to some extent on this prior assimilation of the test environment. Thus in many, perhaps most, operant learning situations, there may be a prior phase of learning involving contiguity rather than reinforcement. This is in fact depicted in Fig. 10, by the fact (consistent with neuroanatomy) that the main pathway by which information can reach the striatum is via the overlying cortical mantle. This component of cortical learning would involve neurones widely spread within the cortex, including some with direct connections to the motor outflow areas of cortex. In principle, this phase of learning can occur without reinforcement itself being applied, as in the latent learning situation. When reinforcement is introduced, after such prior cognitive learning, faster-than-normal learning can occur, because contiguity between signals from the direct intracortical connections to the motor cortex, and those which are recurrent from the striatum can be established more readily than in the naïve animal. Interestingly, a theoretical formulation of latent learning rather similar to that outlined above was made by Seward (1947) who wrote: 'Response to stimulation is held to involve an intervening variable, the surrogate response, conceived as a central mechanism capable of being conditioned on the afferent side to concurrent stimuli, and on the efferent side to concurrent responses'. The present formulation arose more from knowledge of neuroanatomical relations between cortex and striatum, than from knowledge of latent learning, and so expresses Seward's concept in clearly biological terms.

A second instance of the value of this theory concerns various facts obtained by temporary disablement of brain regions by application of potassium chloride to cause 'spreading depression' (Bureš and Burešova 1960*a*). Using this method it has been possible to show that the memory trace for operant responses is represented cortically (Bureš and Burešova 1963; Travis and Sparks 1963; Pearlman 1966), and it has also been possible to localize the memory trace to a single cortex by training animals under conditions of unilateral depression (Bureš and Burešova 1960*b*; Russell and Ochs 1963; Ross and Russell 1964). These results were obtained using a variety of operant tasks—active avoidance, passive avoidance, reversal of a left–right discrimination, and appetitive lever-pressing.

This method has also been used to investigate interhemispheric transfer of memories. For this, unilateral cortical depression is induced and the animal trained to a criterion level, and then, after recovery of the depressed cortex the opposite cortex is disabled and the animal is retrained. Typically, if the animal is given no trials with reinforcement in the intervening period when both hemispheres are functioning, there is no indication that prior learning has occurred: the animal has to learn again from scratch during the retraining session. There is thus no evidence of interhemispheric transfer. However Bureš and Burešova (1960*b*) found that substantial saving could occur in the retraining situation if a small number (ten) of reinforced trials occurred while both hemispheres were normal. Subsequently Russell and Ochs (1963) and Ross and Russell (1964) showed that savings could occur if there was only a single reinforced trial with both hemispheres functioning, but to demonstrate this the depression of the contralateral hemisphere had to be delayed for an hour or more, whereas in the experiments of Bureš and Burešova, contralateral depression was induced within 30 minutes.

The experimental situation is represented in Fig. 11 which depicts a bilateral version of Fig. 10, complete with commissural connections between the two cortices. If cortex B is depressed during an operant learning situation, acquisition of the required task will depend on the gradual strengthening of striatal connection x, followed by the strengthening of parallel cortical connections a and b, to form the permanent memory of the required task in cortex A. If, subsequently, cortex A is depressed and cortex B is normal, retraining will involve an identical series of events, involving striatal connection y, and cortical connections c and d. Retraining will take just as long as the initial training. If however a few intervening reinforced trials are allowed with both hemispheres intact, retraining can occur in a different way which does not depend critically on the gradual prior strengthening of the contra-

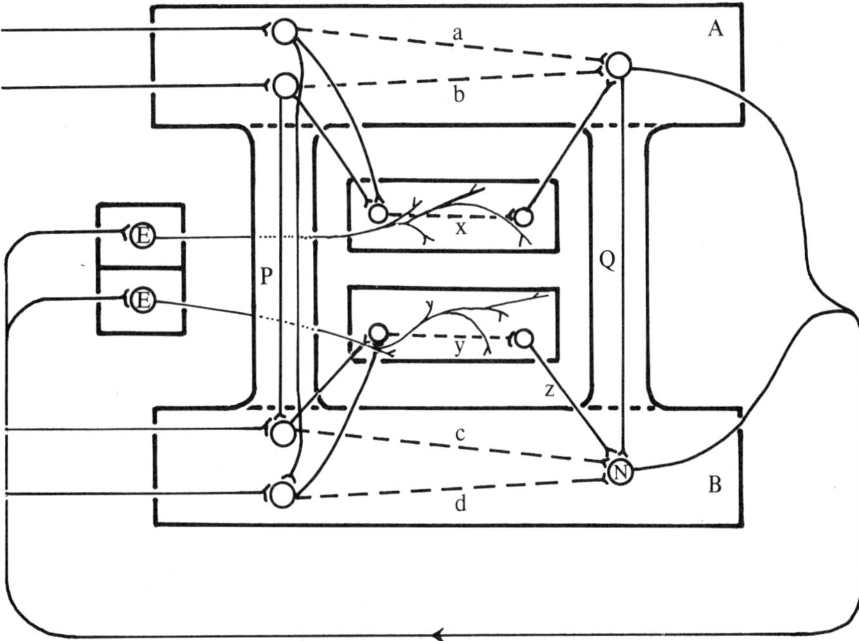

FIG. 11. Diagram to illustrate interhemispheric transfer of the memory of an operant task (e.g. an active avoidance response). The diagram is a bilateral version of Fig. 10, in which the two striata are placed centrally, enclosed by the two cortices A and B and their callosal connections. The two positive reinforcement systems (labelled E) are to the left of the diagram. Normal operant learning depends on the initial strengthening of striatal connections (x and y). In the interhemispheric transfer situation this is impossible on the untrained (depressed) side, but the pre-established callosal connections (P and Q) can nevertheless facilitate operant learning when this hemisphere is normal. Note that callosal connections are drawn passing only from hemisphere A to hemisphere B, because these are the relevant ones in the asymmetrical transfer situation. Symbols as in Figs. 2 (p. 71) and 6 (p. 82). The dashed lines separating the cortices from their callosal connections indicate that cortical spreading depression is confined to one hemisphere in the circumstances of this experiment.

lateral striatal connection y. Under normal circumstances when any motor act is performed, it may be expected that both hemispheres participate, and a large number of contiguities are encoded between neuronal activities in opposite hemispheres which contribute to similar motor functions. In Fig. 11 therefore one may postulate the existence of a connection Q, which links neurones in the trained motor cortical region with ones in the untrained cortex which initiate similar motor acts. All that is then required in training the untrained hemisphere to use this motor act towards the particular requisite goal, is the establishment of further contiguities with the sensory input, via links such as c and d (Fig. 11). Subsequent successful performance of the response may lead to strengthening of striatal connection y, but this is not the decisive factor in training the untrained hemisphere. Essentially what is happening here is that the connection x, established in the trained striatum, and its corresponding cortical links, are used to 'read' equivalent connections into the untrained cortex. Connection Q (which is already functionally established) replaces the hard-wired striato–thalamo–cortical link z.

According to the above argument, one might also suppose the existence of functionally effective commissural connections between contiguous aspects of sensory representation (depicted as P is Fig. 11). In theory these would allow the contiguity between sensory and motor signals (c and d, and Q) to be encoded in neurone N without *any* 'transfer' trials with both hemispheres functioning. This would be an elementary example of the modelling functions considered in Section 7.2.4—the ability to predict the course of an action prior to actual performance, in this case prior to performance mediated by the untrained hemisphere. Amongst the various phenomena described using cortical spreading depression a somewhat similar transfer effect has actually been described by Schneider and Ebbesen (1967): a single reinforced trial *after* depressing the trained hemisphere served to increase subsequent levels of performance during extinction. The circumstances in which such a result is obtained are difficult to define precisely, and Schneider (1973) suggests that it may depend on the precise variety of operant task involved.

An interesting counterpart to this older literature has recently been given by Prado-Alcalá and Cobos-Zapiáin (1979) providing direct evidence that memory for an operant act is located initially in the striatum, but comes to have another location after further training. Performance of a newly-acquired task, but not of an overtrained task, could be disrupted by injections of potassium chloride into the caudate nucleus. It may be suggested that the main locus to which the memory trace is transferred, as a result of over-training, is the neocortex.

Some of the evidence obtained using cortical spreading depression suggests that operant learning can occur without the involvement of the neocortex. Rats can acquire active avoidance responses during bilateral cortical depression, though more slowly than normally (Thompson 1964). They can also show retention of a passive avoidance response if they are tested with the trained hemisphere disabled, and this occurs even if the corpus callosum is severed (Bureš, Burešova, and Fifkova 1964). This evidence is compatible with more recent results indicating that operant learning is possible in decorticate animals (Oakley 1979*a*, *b*; Oakley and Russell 1979; Oakley 1980). According to these experimenters not all varieties of operant learning can occur in decorticate animals (food reinforced behaviour being less vulnerable than avoidance behaviour), and special training methods may need to be employed. Moreover, decorticate animals, though sometimes demonstrating very vigorous operant responses, appear in some respects to be less versatile than normal animals. For instance they tend to confuse the lever in an operant test with the food tray which is the source of reward (Oakley 1980) and they do not learn to respond correctly in a 'GO–NOGO' test, which demands more discrimination on the sensory side than simple lever pressing. These two examples may be indications of deficits in cognitive learning associated with the operant response, rather than of operant learning itself. What the neural substrate of subcortical operant learning is, is uncertain. It is possible however that initial acquisition of the operant task is still a striatal phenomenon, and that alternative input and/or output pathways to the striatum are employed in either relaying or storing the patterns of behaviour thus acquired. Such a suggestion would be consistent with recent anatomical findings of descending pathways from the striatum to the tectum and pontomesencephalic tegmentum via the substantia nigra (*pars reticulata*) (Faull and Mehler 1978; Beckstead, Domesick, and Nauta 1979). It is also consistent with findings (Crossman, Sambrook, Gergies, and Slater 1977) that other behavioural phenomena usually regarded as striatal functions, can also be performed after bilateral removal of sensorimotor cortex. In view of the fact that much simpler animals, without well-developed cortices, are capable of operant learning it is hardly surprising that there are subcortical links with the striatum capable of performing somewhat similar functions to those through the neocortex. Schneider (1967) has in fact produced some evidence that subcortical learning is less important if the neocortex is normal during training, than if it is depressed by potassium chloride application. The fact that learning can occur under abnormal circumstances in pathways other than those emphasized here does not affect the proposed role of cortex and striatum in the intact brain.

A further instance of the use of this theory for cortico–striatal interrelationship concerns some physiological aspects of 'voluntary action'. The term voluntary was used in Section 2.3 in close linkage with the conscious processes of operant learning and goal fulfilment. The present section has given rise to a rather wider concept of voluntary action and volition, which may be more autonomous than previously suggested, and only indirectly related to reinforcement. With this wider concept of volition, it is possible to link together the psychological idea of volition with physiological data about voluntary action. A voluntary act in this experimental situation may be thought of as one performed in response to a stimulus, which has previously been paired with a reward provided the animal performs the response; and physiological recordings may then be made in the period before and after the stimulus is delivered. The usually accepted criterion for distinguishing a 'voluntary' response from a reflex one is that it should have a minimum latency of about 100 ms following the stimulus in man, or a little less in higher primates other than man. However, Evarts (1973) has established that for motor tasks involving a triggering stimulus to muscle receptors, a highly trained response involves a component whose electromyographic latency is 35–40 ms (in monkeys)—too long for spinal reflex action, yet much shorter than a conventionally defined voluntary response. There is some circumstantial evidence for a similar component in man (Marsden, Merton, Morton, and Adam 1977). This component develops gradually with training, and can be modified by prior 'instructions' about the nature of the response to be expected of the animal. The electromyographic response is preceded by activation of neurones in the motor cortex and so it seems likely that it is of cortical origin. One may thus hazard the guess that the 80–100 ms latency response utilizes the pathway established during initial learning, via cortex, striatum, thalamus, and motor cortex, to the corticospinal tract; and that the shorter latency component of the well-learned response utilizes a short-circuit pathway involving merely the adjacent regions of sensory and motor cortex, without involvement of the basal ganglia. 'Cortical-loops' for an operant behaviour (such as suggested by Phillips 1973) may thus represent 'automatized' versions of an oft-repeated voluntary act.

The experiments of Mountcastle *et al.* (1975) also provide some glimpses of the proposed role of the neocortex in storing information about operant behaviour: a proportion of the neurones in parietal association cortex appear to respond consistently during the performance of goal-directed exploratory movements, as might be expected of a region of association cortex integrating purely sensory information with representations of operant behaviour.

It has already been mentioned that the transference of an operant programme from striatum to cortex might be possible even without rehearsal of the task itself. In this context it is relevant to mention again a body of evidence (reviewed by Dru and Walker 1976) which indicates that memory traces represented in the cortex may also have a fluid and fluctuating location. Thus memories which are abolished by single-stage ablation of a region of neocortex, are less severly disrupted by *sequential* ablations limited to the same area of cortex. The preservation of function in the serially-lesioned animals is improved by non-specific enrichment of the sensory environment in the inter-operative period. (An analogous example of flexibility of representation—observed in the brain during development, rather than in the adult brain—has been provided by Spinelli and Jensen (1979): in kittens in which one limb was repeatedly subjected to noxious stimuli, the region of somatosensory cortex representing that limb became enlarged compared with the normal side.) It thus appears likely that cortically encoded memories, just as much as striatally encoded ones, are not static, but may be subject to a certain amount of continuing reorganization. This dynamic state might be predicted from the present theory: any cognitive memory trace would result in contiguous firing of some neurones in the cortex, which could lead to recruitment of yet other neurones into the memory trace, which received convergent inputs from the former. This might be particularly likely to happen at a time when other cognitive learning is occurring, for instance during a period of sensory enrichment.

The process of 'consolidation' of a memory, at least in mammalian species, may thus be a rather complex process, involving transferences from one structure to another, transference within a single structure, as well as any consolidative process occurring at the level of synaptic biochemistry. It would therefore be unlikely that neat correlations could be established between the time-course of consolidation and the time-course of synaptic changes underlying acquisition and permanent recording of a memory.

In Chapter 4 separate theoretical accounts were given of cognitive and operant learning. The picture we have now constructed, however, is one in which these two modes of learning operate together in such close harmony that it is very difficult to separate the two. This accords well with ideas of central nervous function derived from a variety of standpoints. Thus, students of learning in animals usually have to make their observation upon operant behaviour, regardless of whether the actual learning process is operant in nature or cognitive (as in latent learning) (see Hilgard and Marquis 1964). Piaget and his school, in studying the psychology of human development, repeatedly emphasize that learning is not a passive acquisition of information (equivalent to pure cognitive learning) but is an active assimilation, in which action and learning are interdependent (see Piaget and Inhelder 1969). Likewise, at a physiological level neither sensory nor motor function can be properly understood, except in relation to the other. For instance, Brown and Gordon (1977) discuss the function of neurones in primary sensory nuclei which are both rapidly adapting and have inhibitory surrounds to their receptive fields. In such neurones, the inhibitory surround could act to enhance contrast only if the receptive surface is continually moving with respect to the field of environmental stimuli, such as when an animal engages in tactile exploration. Here, then, is another example of the interplay between voluntary motor activity and sensory processing.

5.4. 'Drives', and the acquisition of sequences of operant behaviour

In Section 4.3.2 it was suggested that for operant learning to be accomplished, it was necessary that synapses (of either sign) which are active when a neurone by chance carries a burst of activity, will be put in a 'state of readiness', or susceptibility, and they can then become fully functional synapses, dependent on the subsequent effects of behaviour. How long will the 'state of readiness' last, during which it can successfully interact with the reinforcement signal generated by behaviour?

To accord with the rest of the theory presented here, it should decay rather rapidly. Otherwise, a number of quite different 'states of readiness' would come to co-exist in the striatum, and it would be impossible for the reinforcement systems to act selectively upon the neural trace of a single favourable (or unfavourable) portion of behaviour. For similar reasons one would also expect the reinforcing influence to endure for a relatively brief period after activation of the reinforcement systems. Short duration of the 'state of readiness' and the reinforcement influence present no problems when one is dealing with the reinforcements involved in avoidance learning (the usual example of operant learning considered so far). In these, there is usually a close temporal proximity between the action of an animal and the subsequent reinforcement of the action. However, if one considers appetitive behaviour, there may be a long sequence of actions required to fulfil a certain goal, and therefore considerable temporal delay between the first act in a sequence and the goal fulfilment which is supposed to reinforce this act. What is more, there is evidence that when animals are learning such a complex sequence of behaviour they record not only a representation of the behaviour, but also its association with the particular motive which it is intended to fulfil. Thus, when an animal is trained while simultaneously hungry and thirsty, in a T-maze with food in one arm and water in the other, the animal will, on subsequent testing when motivated by only one of these two, go immediately to the arm appropriate to its need at the moment (Kendler 1946). If operant actions are controlled solely by the twin reinforcement signals, which could merely assign positive or negative motivational significance to neural representations, without specifying which particular biological motive they are related to, this observation cannot be explained.

In order to explain these features of appetitive learning we require all previous premises—omniconnected networks, and neural models of cognitive and operant learning, interrelated to one another—and we require a further concept, that of a 'drive' (see Morgan (1979) and Deutsch (1979) for conflicting views about this concept). Gallistel (1973) writes that whereas '*reward* usually refers to the effects of *goal attainment* on the direction and avidity of behaviour . . . *drive* usually refers to the effects of *internal conditions*, such as tissue needs and hormone levels on the direction and avidity of behaviour.' That drives are in fact important in determining direction and avidity of behaviour is clear from simple observations: a rat will not learn to work for a food reward unless he is hungry—a word referring to an internal state. In purely logical terms one might regard changes in internal states as capable of exerting a similar effect on the reinforcement systems as does the attainment of some external goal. However, another difficulty arises here.

Attainment of an external goal is detected by sensory systems and encoded as impulses in patterns of connections within the nervous system. On the other hand, it is far from obvious how internal conditions, such as tissue needs and hormone levels, can be encoded in connectionist terms within the nervous system, yet the process of *association*, which according to the evidence cited in the previous paragraph, applies as much to motivational states as to sensory representations, has, throughout Chapters 4 and 5, been explained in terms of modification of connections in a richly interconnected network.

Have we therefore reached the limits of the connectionist assumption? Possibly not. There is evidence for the existence of receptors placed within the central nervous system, which can monitor at least some central states, such as blood glucose levels, temperature or osmotic pressure, for instance (Hayward 1977). It is entirely plausible that these internal sense organs could deliver an output to the rest of the brain in terms of impulses in axonal connections. In what follows 'drives' or 'motivational states' could be viewed in such connectionist terms. Using this assumption a scheme is presented whereby extended sequences of goal-directed behaviour can be built up, and in which motivational coding of a sequence of behaviour is also achieved. However it is recognized that the argument is now taking us close to the limits of what connectionism can explain and an alternative biological interpretation of the concept of drive will also be considered.

In Fig. 12 it is required to explain how an animal can learn, when hungry, to explore for food, to approach food when it sees it, and then to ingest it when it has smelt it. It must be assumed initially that ingestion of food when it is actually in the mouth is a hard-wired reflex, part of an inbuilt negative feedback system which tends to remove the state of hunger (depicted in Fig. 12 as the solid connecting line in the right-hand square box). It must also be assumed that this reflex triggers the positive reinforcement signal, and in Fig. 12 this is depicted as occurring partly indirectly by inhibiting messages signifying hunger and partly directly (and therefore more or less immediately). (In Section 6.2.4(a) justification will be given for the assumption that some fragments of behaviour can activate reinforcement mechanisms directly, without actual behavioural feedback.) Any motor response which occurs, with regular association, preceding the 'food in mouth' circumstance, and the linked eating response will thus become associated with eating, by operation of the reinforcement principle. Any sensory occurrence, such as the smell of food, which happens, with regular occurrence, before and during the 'food in mouth' circumstance will also become associated with 'food in mouth' by operation of the contiguity principle. Hence, the smell of food will also come to trigger the positive reinforcement signal, and will reinforce any motor response which leads up to 'the smell of food' — such as approaching a food object which is already visible. (In the latter example of association, the signal indicating that the animal is actually hungry — H — is also included

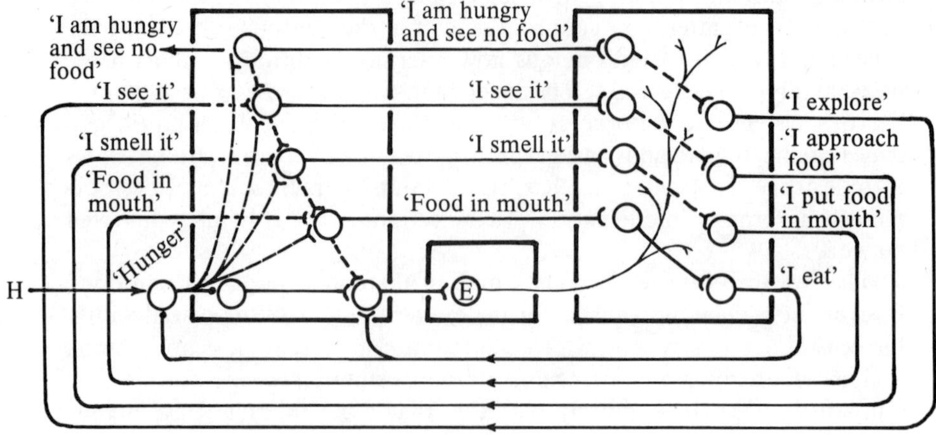

FIG. 12. Diagram to illustrate the sequential learning of behaviour leading to satisfaction of the hunger motive. In the left-hand rectangle (hypothetically the neocortex), the plasticity postulates for cognitive learning (p. 68) apply. In the right-hand rectangle (hypothetically the striatum), the plasticity postulate for operant learning (p. 81) apply. It is assumed that eating, when food is already in the mouth, is a hard-wired reflex, which also activates the positive reinforcement mechanism, partly directly, and partly indirectly (though with larger time delays) through reduction of the hunger signal (H). The hunger signal is depicted as if it is relayed by a branching set of modifiable connections (left-hand rectangle). However, as discussed in the text, this signal need not be of a connectionist nature at all. Motor acts which precede 'food in mouth' are encouraged by means of reinforcement signals. Also each sensory situation which is regularly associated with eating, or with reduction of hunger, will become sequentially linked to the positive reinforcement mechanism, and will thus reinforce the motor act which preceded this situation. Symbols as in Figs. 2 (p. 71) and 6 (p. 82).

in the convergence of inputs upon the neurones, some of whose synapses are to be strengthened.) By exactly similar reasoning one can explain how, when food, for the first time, becomes visible, this will reinforce the behaviour which led to this happening, namely, exploratory behaviour, when the animal is hungry and can see no food. Thus, the sensory pattern which is most remotely related to the final goal fulfilment ('I am hungry and see no food'), could become linked to the positive reinforcement system, and could come to trigger the least specific behavioural response—exploration*—a response which is scarcely different from the random activity which is the substrate of all operant behaviour. In summary, sequential association of various sensory correlates of a long sequence of behaviour, and consequent reinforcement,

* Exploration is of course not simply an increase in random locomotor activity: it involves the deliberate focussing upon certain items—especially the novel or the incongruous. These features, which are dealt with in Section 7.2, will modify locomotor activity under most normal circumstances. As far as the above argument is concerned hunger would become associated simply with an increase in locomotor activity. Realistically, however, in the intact animal this would show itself as an increase in exploratory rather than random activity.

can lead to the behavioural sequence becoming laid down in the memory, although the beginning of the sequence precedes the final goal fulfilment by a very long interval. In this process the response which is least directly related to goal fulfilment is the last to be learned, since its learning depends on all the succeeding learned responses. That sequences of behaviour are in fact learned in this way has been known for many years since Hull (1932) developed the concept of a 'goal gradient factor': in maze learning, the errors at choice points nearest the goal are eliminated at an earlier stage in learning than those at the start (see Hilgard and Marquis 1964).

One way of describing the processes illustrated in Fig. 12 is as the accumulation of secondary reinforcing stimuli, on the basis of their association with a primary reinforcer, and for such an interpretation the 'internal state' or 'drive' (i.e. hunger) is equivalent to any other stimulus. However, certain distinguishing features, to be considered now, make it likely that drives have a biological basis of a different type from other stimuli. The signal indicating hunger can associate with a great many other signals by converging on a multitude of neurones in both the major structures in Fig. 12 (hypothetically the neocortex and striatum). However, this signal is itself surprisingly simple compared with the sensory signals provided by most *external* sense organs. Just as with the reinforcement systems, there is no need here to postulate connections with every neurone in these structures: a diffuse chemical influence delivered from a widespread axonal network might suffice. The chief difference between this chemical influence and the reinforcement signals would be that the latter should be capable of signifying rapid temporal changes, so that the immediate effect of a response can trigger reinforcement of that response, whereas the 'drive' signal would probably be a more prolonged one, incapable of conveying rapid phasic changes in an internal state. Thus, learning of sequences of behaviour related to a single goal involves both rapidly decaying processes ('state of readiness', and reinforcement signal) combined with tonic drive signals which are likely to build up and decay rather more slowly.

How can one obtain evidence about these temporal gradients associated with learning? In theory the rapid decay process associated with reinforcement should be discernible in experiments where the interval between response and reinforcement is the independent variable and some measure of learning is the dependent variable. Two particular experimental situations lend themselves to this approach: (i) in standard operant conditioning tests; and (ii) in the intracranial self-stimulation situation. In neither of these cases is the experiment quite as simple as might be imagined, and in fact the factors which complicate the issue (particularly with regard to self-stimulation) themselves give indications of the slower type of decay process—that relating to drive.

In operant learning, experiments carried out by a variety of workers give divergent estimates of the temporal gradients associated with reinforcement

(Hilgard and Marquis 1964). Such inconsistency is, however, probably largely due to secondary cues associated with the behavioural choice an animal makes, which effectively reduce the relevant time interval during which the state of readiness must last, and therefore make it appear as if the gradient is much slower than it actually is. When precautions are taken to reduce these secondary reinforcing stimuli to the minimum, the delay of reinforcement gradient seems to be rather short, with a 'half-time' of 2–3 seconds in rats (Hilgard and Marquis 1964).

The intracranial self-stimulation phenomenon in its simplest form should avoid the effect of secondary reinforcers because, in theory at any rate, the reinforcement system is activated directly. The actual evidence points to a more complex situation, however: different processes with different temporal gradients are mingled together in a way which varies from animal to animal and from one experimental situation to another. In some experiments the rate of extinction when stimuli are discontinued seems to follow a remarkably similar time course to that observed in conventional operant learning situations (Howarth and Deutsch 1962). Therefore, for inter-trial intervals much longer than 5 seconds, an animal needs 'priming' (i.e. actually to be placed on the goal lever by the experimenter) before it will recommence self-stimulation (Gallistel 1973). These rapid decay effects are not found by all experimenters and in all animals, however: with longer trains of brain stimulation reward, animals have been observed to continue responding with inter-reward intervals of 15 mins or more (see Gallistel 1973). There is indication that these slowly decaying internal states are generated by stimulation of more medial sites in the medial forebrain bundle than the rapidly decaying rewarding effects (Kent and Grossman 1969).

Gallistel (1973) has reviewed evidence which indicates that there may be a drive component associated with the rewarding effects of brain stimulation. In particular he makes a detailed comparison of the parameters of electrical stimulation required to 'prime' a rat for self-stimulation (the 'drive' component), and to support the self-stimulation itself (the 'reward' component). For both these components it was possible to detect a 'refractory period' whose duration was typical of that of axonal refractory periods. However, the refractory periods of the two components were significantly different. In addition, whereas the reward component integrated electrical activation over quite short periods of time (around 1 s), the drive component integrated activity over periods of 10 s or more, and required much more intense activation to reach its maximum effectiveness in 'priming' situations. The interaction of rewarding effects of brain stimulation and natural drives is indicated by the fact that many stimulation sites not only support self-stimulation, but also elicit stimulus-bound eating or drinking (Margules and Olds 1962; Hoebel and Teitelbaum 1962; Mogenson and Stevenson 1966). It has also been shown that in rats deprived of food the decay of brain stimulation reward is slower than in control rats (Deutsch and Di Cara 1967).

However, as Gallistel (1973) points out, the precise relationship of the drive component of self-stimulation and individual natural drives is still far from clear.

It should be added here that there is good evidence for an entirely different temporal gradient for reinforced behaviour—in which reinforcement is effective even when applied a long time after the performance of the behaviour to be reinforced. The best known example of this is acquired taste preference, in which aversion to the taste of a food can be acquired if the taste is associated with an aversive stimulus of 'sickness-producing' nature (such as Lithium salt injection, or X-radiation), applied several hours after the food was ingested (Revusky and Garcia 1970). No doubt learning of this sort is very valuable to an animal in natural conditions, not only so that it can avoid noxious foodstuffs, but also so that it can learn to regulate food and water intake to fit its needs, even when satiation by these factors is not an immediate consequence of ingestion. The mechanism of such long-delayed reinforcers is not discussed further here.

At this point brief and tentative consideration will be given to the actual pathways and transmitters which might mediate the various drive signals. In the last few years much information has been accumulating about neuropeptides, and their behavioural effects, and there are hints that they may be involved in signalling drives within the brain. To establish such an identity for any or all of the various neuropeptides which have been discovered, the following criteria would seem to be appropriate. (i) The neuropeptide under consideration should act diffusely rather than by way of points of synaptic contact. (ii) It should have a relatively long duration of biological action, compared for instance with monoamine neurotransmitters. (iii) Its behavioural effects either on 'innate' habits or on learning should be particularly focussed with respect to a single aspect of motivation. (iv) In so far as it reinforces a particular behavioural tendency, it should do so not in the immediate manner of the direct positive and negative reinforcement systems, but in a more prolonged fashion, so that a habit which is encouraged by the action of a neuropeptide is not dissipated until many seconds (or even minutes) after withdrawal of the neuropeptide influence.

It would be quite inappropriate to try to review data here concerning these points. Only a few indications will be given of the evidence which might become available. A variety of neuropeptides have been shown to have powerful effects on motivated behaviour (Maddison 1977; de Caro, Massi, and Micossi 1978; Phillips 1978), the best known example being the naturally occurring enkephalin analogues—the opiates. Recent experiments show that opioid peptides have reinforcing properties (after intraventricular injection), formally similar to the self-stimulation phenomenon (Stein and Beluzzi 1979). In such observations, there is obviously the makings of an attractive theory for opiate addiction. It is uncertain from experimental studies how fast this reinforcing tendency decays, but it is clear in comparing opiate addiction with self-stimulation that opiates are reinforcing in a much longer term sense than brain stimulation usually is. It is likely that neuropeptide transmitters are metabolically more 'expensive' to synthesize than the simpler molecules and it has been argued by Barker (1976) that they are in fact the mediators of long-term effects of neural activity. The evidence about refractory periods mentioned above indicates that drive signals are conveyed, at least in part, by electrically excitable components of the brain; in fact, immunohistochemical demonstration of peptide-containing cells in the brain shows that these cells have axonal processes typical of neurones in general. There have been, as yet, very few ultrastructural studies of neuropeptide-containing nerve terminals in the brain, and therefore there is no evidence about the extent to which they might form synaptic contacts. At present, therefore, there is no clear evidence that neuropeptides are diffusely acting, as suggested for the drive signals above.

To conclude this chapter some comments will be offered on the extent to which the connectionist premise, for neural representation of information, applies. In most sense organs, a large number of sensory receptor cells are involved in providing independent inputs to the central nervous system, and in almost all cases the biologically meaningful signals are complex patterns of activation within these many inputs. Representation of such complex patterns is possible only so long as the vast number of individual input channels are distinguishable from one another until the stage at which they interact and are integrated. This is achieved by proliferation of connections. When, however, a 'sense organ' can provide a biologically meaningful signal directly, without prior analysis of patterns, it can dispense with some aspects of this connectionism: a diffusely distributed chemical signal can convey the information, provided that sufficiently specific pharmacological receptors are available. The limit on the latter type of information representation is the number of independent pharmacological receptor types which might be present on any neurone. In the case of visual or somatosensory systems, the number of independent sensory cells is so great as to be clearly beyond this limit, so individual connections of each group of sensory cells is required. In simpler systems, including motivational drives, the possible variety of signals is far more limited, so a coding which is basically chemical becomes a practical proposition. Basically, therefore there are two ways in which information may be coded in the brain. One is a code in terms of patterns of synapses, specificity of represented information being achieved mainly by specificity of connections. The other is a code in terms of diverse quasi-humoral chemical signals, and specificity is achieved by specificity of pharmacological receptor types.

6. Monoamines in the basal ganglia and neocortex, and their relation to behaviour

6.1. Introduction

In the previous chapter, diffusely acting transmitter substances (monoamines, possibly some of the neuropeptides) were postulated to have important roles in the functions of reinforcement and motivation. If these postulates are valid it would follow that these substances would have most significant influences not only at the biological level, but also on many of the psychological processes under discussion here, and should therefore play a major part in shaping behaviour and the characteristics of conscious processes in general. There is an enormous literature on psychopharmacology, particularly that relating to the monoamines. The present chapter is an attempt to find coherent interpretations of some of the available evidence on the role of these substances.

Ideally, discussion of the significance of diffusely acting transmitter substances should come after all the regions of the central nervous system have been allotted their role in the co-operative functions of the intact brain. This is quite beyond the aim of the present work, although one further structure, the hippocampus, is to be considered in the next chapter. It therefore seems appropriate to deal with the psychopharmacology of monoamines at this point. The role of hippocampal amines in behaviour, though certainly relevant here, cannot usefully be discussed in the present state of knowledge. It is not yet possible to formulate any coherent synaptic model of hippocampal function. Moreover, there has been scarcely any work in which hippocampal amines have been selectively depleted.

The discussion deals entirely with the three monoamine transmitters—dopamine, noradrenaline and 5-hydroxytryptamine (5HT, serotonin). Though neuropeptide transmitters have been given a tentative theoretical role (see Chapter 5), there is as yet inadequate evidence to warrant any detailed assessment of their role in behaviour. However, a very large number of behavioural phenomena, related to monoamines, have been reported. At first sight many of them seem to be no more than interesting empirical observations, but with the help of the preceding theoretical constructs it is hoped to place much of this evidence into a broader interpretative scheme. Where existing evidence is inadequate, it is possible to make some predictions (of varying precision).

The literature on the behavioural pharmacology of the monoamines is not only voluminous but is also exceedingly complex. There are several reasons for this complexity. It is now well known from the histochemical studies of Hillarp *et al.* (1966), Ungerstedt (1971*a*) and many others that monoamine-containing pathways are widely distributed throughout much of the brain. Attempts to investigate the role of monoamines in behaviour are thus made very difficult because any drug which mimics or antagonizes the actions of monoamines may be acting in any of a variety of brain sites. An alternative approach to administration of drugs is to destroy monoamine-containing neurones or pathways, either by electrolytic lesions, or with specific neuro-toxic substances—but again, it is not always possible to be anatomically as specific as might be wished. A number of intriguing phenomena have been discovered by combining the anatomical lesion technique with the administration of drugs which alter monoamine activity. Here, however, the interpretation depends critically on the detailed mode of action of the particular drugs used (e.g. whether it acts directly on 'post-synaptic' receptor sites or indirectly on 'pre-synaptic' release mechanisms). Interpretation also depends on precisely which transmitters a drug affects, since many drugs act on more than one of the monoamine transmitters. Furthermore, there is evidence that the various neuronal systems utilizing monoamines as transmitters project upon one another and are capable of influencing one another's function (Pujol, Keane, McRae, and Lewis 1978; Sakai, Touret, Salvert, and Jouvet 1978; Simon, Le Moal, Stinus, and Calas 1979; Stern, Johnson, Bronzino, and Morgane 1979; Phillipson 1979). In addition to all this, accounts of experiments in behavioural pharmacology often read as catalogues of apparently unrelated findings, because, although accurate and detailed description of behavioural phenomena is presented, the wider significance of the particular portion of behaviour to the overall patterns and strategies of an animal's behaviour is usually ignored.

One way of presenting ideas about the behavioural pharmacology of monoamines would be to give an interpretative review. However, there are still so many inconsistencies in the literature that, in order to achieve some sort of coherence, it would be necessary to make excessive use of *ad hoc* arguments. The alternative, adopted here for the sake of brevity, is to give emphasis to predictions derived from the previous sections rather than attempt an exhaustive review of presently available experimental results. These predictions will deal with the role of a particular transmitter *for behaviour originating in a particular brain structure*—and in fact the most precise predictions will concern striatal amines only, since predictions of the role of monoamines in cortical function is much more difficult. Even in the case of the striatum, there may be discrepancies between predictions and observed facts, because brain structures other than the striatum contribute to the total behavioural pattern. The predictions start with the most clear cut case—the acquisition of operant tasks themselves. In addition to this, however, there are a number of behavioural phenomena which are more or less directly related to operant processes. Tentative interpretations of these behavioural patterns will be suggested which allow further predictions about the influence of monoamines upon them. Finally, the role of monoamines in neocortical functions will be discussed, though, as will be seen, the theory put forward here is inadequate to make very precise predictions. The subject matter of this chapter has many implications for human illnesses as well as for animal experiments. A number of these implications will be briefly touched upon.

6.2. Striatal monoamines in operant and quasi-operant behaviour

6.2.1. OPERANT LEARNING AND STRIATAL AMINES

If the striatal dopaminergic innervation mediates positive reinforcement in operant learning, by strengthening excitatory synapses, the following prediction can be made: destruction of this dopaminergic innervation would lead to inability to acquire an active operant behaviour, such as an appetitive task, or active avoidance task. Likewise, if striatal 5HT mediates negative reinforcement, by action on inhibitory synapses, it would be predicted that destruction of the serotonergic striatal innervation would lead to deficits in acquisition of a passive avoidance reaction. Conversely, one would predict that in dopamine-depleted animals, the negative reinforcement system would be acting without its normal opposition, so acquisition of passive behaviour would be enhanced. Likewise in 5HT-depleted animals the positive reinforcement system would be acting without the normal opposition, so acquisition of active behaviour would be enhanced. The latter two predictions should not, of course, be thought of as an improvement in learning ability, since they are a reflection of reduced flexibility of the learning mechanism.

The first of these predictions is confirmed by two recent publications (Zis, Fibiger, and Phillips 1974; Ranje and Ungerstedt 1977). In the first of these two it was also shown that the acquisition deficit produced by destruction of dopamine neurones in substantia nigra could be reversed by systemic administration of the metabolic precursor of dopamine, L-DOPA. Moreover, the active operant responses acquired in such animals during L-DOPA substitution, was retained after the effects of the drug had worn off—so the deficit was clearly restricted to acquisition, rather than some sensory or motor deficit involved in performance of the response. The above two papers are also supported by the experiments of Mason and Iversen (1974, 1977). Depletion of both dopamine and noradrenaline disrupted acquisition of an active operant task, but depletion of noradrenaline alone did not have this effect. Since the major part of forebrain dopamine is in the striatum, and that of forebrain noradrenaline is in cortical structures, it is unlikely that dopamine and noradrenaline have complex direct interactions. Hence, by elimination it seems that dopamine is necessary for acquisition. Recent evidence also supports the converse prediction about dopamine depleted animals. Oei and Ng (1978) depleted catecholamines by intracisternal injection of 6-hydroxydopamine and demonstrated a subsequent enhancement of passive avoidance learning, in a multiple-trial learning task. Similar behavioural observations have been made in animals depleted specifically of forebrain dopamine (Miller and Laverty, unpublished results).

Evidence of this nature has developed from a large amount of pharmacological work, which, though anatomically less precise, shows the importance of dopamine in acquisition of operant tasks. Curiously, much of this evidence indicates that dopamine is necessary for performance of an active operant task, as well as its initial acquisition (Seiden and Peterson 1968; Ahlenius and Engel 1971). This might indicate that dopamine had an additional role in *maintaining* excitatory synapses in a functionally secure state as well as in triggering the initial change to this state. On theoretical grounds this would probably be necessary, if the suggestion made in Section 5.3, that synaptic changes in the striatum are relatively temporary, is true.

The predictions concerning striatal 5HT depletion are supported by rather more fragmentary evidence. In many experiments in which attempts have been made to destroy striatal 5HT innervation (Srebro and Lorens 1975; Hole, Fuxe, and Jonsson 1976; Lorens, Guldberg, Hole, Köhler, and Srebro 1976), the behavioural tests performed have not included passive avoidance learning. However, Tye, Everitt, and Iversen (1977) depleted forebrain 5HT with the selective neurotoxin 5,7-dihydroxytryptamine and showed that subsequent acquisition of behavioural suppression was retarded. Other experimenters have reduced forebrain 5HT by pharmacological means rather than by lesions. Stevens and Fechter (1969) showed that administration of *p*-chlorophenylalanine (which depletes brain 5HT) retarded passive avoidance learning. Recent experiments on mouse-killing by rats provide further confirmation of the prediction. Most rats do not naturally kill mice, but depletion of cerebral 5HT (e.g. with *p*-chlorophenylalanine) will precipitate mouse-killing (Di Chiara, Camba, and Spano 1971). Marks, O'Brien, and Paxinos (1977) induced mouse-killing in rats by a stereotaxic injection of 5,7-dihydroxytryptamine to deplete forebrain 5HT. If, however, the rats were exposed to mice pre-operatively the subsequent appearance of mouse-killing behaviour was prevented. Clearly the suppression of mouse-killing could be acquired, by familiarization with the mice, prior to 5HT depletion, but not after it.

The converse prediction also has some experimental support. Steranka and Barrett (1974) found that 5HT depletion caused an increased rate of acquisition of an active avoidance task. Consistent with the prediction put forward here, they attributed this to a decrease of the behavioural suppression occurring when an animal is given a shock, rather than an increase of the positive reinforcement associated with a successful avoidance response.

A few experiments give hints of the special role of *striatal* 5HT in acquired suppression of operant tasks. These experiments depend on selective destruction of the different serotonergic nuclei supplying the forebrain, the dorsal raphe nucleus, and the median raphe nucleus, the former of which appears to be the principal supplier of serotonergic fibres to the striatum (Fuxe and Jonsson 1974; Lorens and Guldberg 1974; Miller, Richardson, Fibiger, and McLennan 1975). Jacobs and Cohen (1976), using electrolytic lesions, compared the effects of median raphe lesions with those of dorsal raphe lesions, with respect to two forms of behaviour: locomotor activity, and the tendency of rats to become aggressive when exposed to unavoidable painful footshocks (shock-induced aggression). Of these two behavioural measures, only shock-induced aggression is a response acquired as a result of motivationally significant stimuli, and thus it bears a closer resemblance to the operant learning paradigm than does locomotor activity. Rats with median raphe lesions showed a long-lasting increase in locomotor activity, whereas dorsal raphe lesions caused a long-lasting increase in tendency towards shock-induced aggression. Similar experiments have been carried out by Waldbillig (1979) using radiofrequency lesions of the different raphe nuclei.

Graeff (1974) and Schoenfield (1976) found that after pharmacological procedures which decrease 5HT activity there is an increased rate of responding with behaviours previously suppressed by punishment. This is not exactly the effect predicted (i.e. inability to *acquire* a behavioural suppression response), but if 5HT had the role of *maintaining* inhibitory synapses in a secure state—comparable to that already suggested for dopamine with respect to excitatory synapses—it could constitute circumstantial evidence in favour of the prediction. Additional evidence for an antagonism between 5HT and dopamine in operant behaviour is the finding of Green and Harvey (1974) that lesions of ascending 5HT pathways will enhance the effect of indirect dopamine agonists (such as amphetamine) on a variable-interval schedule of positive reinforcement.

Classically (see Hilgard and Marquis 1964), operant learning is seen as the interaction of a spontaneously emitted behavioural item and a reinforcement influence, the rate of learning depending on both the frequency of spontaneous occurrence of the item and the intensity of the reinforcement. In most of the experiments quoted above, disruption of cerebral aminergic mechanisms influences general locomotor activity levels in parallel with the changes in acquisition or performance of operant tasks. In some work on active and passive operant learning, these activity levels are regarded as an important incidental variable for which controls need to be provided if 'learning' is to be studied in isolation. However, the scheme of operant learning put forward here suggests that random activity and operant learning are in many situations so closely linked as to be inseparable. Although a particular level of activity does not guarantee that learning will occur, nevertheless learning an operant task cannot occur *without* an appropriate level of activity. An active animal (e.g. one under the influence of a stimulant) would be expected to learn an active task more easily, and a relatively passive animal would be expected to learn a passive task more easily, simply because spontaneous activity (or passivity) is the non-committed substrate from which purposeful behaviour is moulded. Thus, suppression of a specific item of active behaviour, when it is punished, might be explained by the triggering of a negative reinforcement system, specifically linked to a noxious stimulus. However if this explanation is true, then it is equally likely that suppression of motor activity in general can be induced by any level of maintained impulse activity in this system, even when not specifically linked to individual unfavourable items of behaviour. Thus, frequency of spontaneous occurrence of some form of behaviour (e.g. spontaneous crossing between cages) and reinforcement may be mutually interdependent variables. The fact that alterations of striatal monoamines influence motor activity as well as learning does not, therefore, weaken the evidence linking monoamines with operant learning. However, as will be mentioned later, amines in other forebrain regions than the striatum have a significant additional influence on levels of motor activity.

6.2.2. INTRACRANIAL SELF-STIMULATION AND STRIATAL AMINES

The close relationship of operant learning to the intracranial self-stimulation phenomenon and the converse avoidance phenomenon has already been mentioned. If it is correct to identify the positive reinforcement system with the dopaminergic pathway ascending to the striatum, and the negative reinforcement pathway with the serotonergic pathway ascending to the striatum, then the two amines should be closely involved in these phenomena. Some of the evidence has already been mentioned.

The role of catecholamine pathways in self-stimulation has been reviewed more comprehensively by Crow (1972*a*) and by German and Bowden (1974), the most direct evidence being the correlation of brain sites supporting self-stimulation with the location of dopamine-containing neurones and their ascending axons, and the fact that specific destruction of these pathways with the neurotoxic substance 6-hydroxydopamine will prevent the self-stimulation phenomena occurring from these brain sites. Discrepant data, which indicate that more than one system may be involved in this phenomenon have been emphasized by R. A. Wise (1978). It should be pointed out in this context that there is also evidence relating ascending noradrenergic pathways to self-stimulation which complicates interpretation here. This will be briefly considered in the section on monoamines and cognitive functions.

The converse phenomenon—avoidance of performance of an operant response which causes brain stimulation—has also been observed (Olds 1958) with electrodes in other brain regions. Moreover, another closely related form of avoidance behaviour can occur: if it is arranged that lever pressing by an animal temporarily switches off the intracranial stimulation, electrode placements exist in the brain which will favour such lever pressing (Olds and

Olds 1963). There have been few attempts to define the anatomical pathways involved in such negative reinforcement, and there has been no concerted effort to establish correlations between sites of negative reinforcement and the 5HT pathways ascending to the striatum. Furthermore, evidence has been presented that midbrain regions containing 5HT neurones can support self-stimulation, rather than avoidance (Miliaressis, Bouchard, and Jacobowitz 1975). However, pharmacological evidence in most cases supports the present prediction, that 5HT should have an antagonistic action to dopamine in intracranial self-stimulation behaviour: depletion of forebrain 5HT by use of the drug *p*-chlorophenylalanine (Blum and Geller 1969; Poschel and Ninteman 1971) or the toxin 5,6-dihydroxytryptamine (Poschel, Ninteman, McLean, and Potoczak 1974) will markedly enhance self-stimulation (but see also Gibson, McGeer, and McGeer 1970).

6.2.3. THE CONTRASTING ACTIONS OF DIRECTLY AND INDIRECTLY ACTING DRUGS

The two types of operant function considered so far also lend themselves to further rather precise predictions which particularly concern the contrast between directly and indirectly acting dopamine agonists. For both operant learning and intracranial self-stimulation (or avoidance of the same) *the theory put forward in this book assumes, of necessity, that the twin reinforcement pathways carry temporal sequences of signals related to the temporal sequence of positive or negative reinforcement. A steadily maintained elevation in the level of pharmacologically active monoamine cannot substitute for this temporal pattern*, because it would reinforce all synapses of a particular sign, whether or not they were activated concomitantly with a motivationally significant fragment of behaviour. Hence, it would be predicted that indirectly acting dopamine agonists, such as amphetamine, which potentiate the actions of only that dopamine which is released presynaptically by impulses (von Voigtlander and Moore 1973), would have an enhancing effect on active avoidance learning and intracranial self-stimulation. The same would also be true of the metabolic precursor L-DOPA, provided that its conversion to dopamine, and subsequent release at its sites of pharmacological activity occur in and from dopaminergic terminals. In contrast, directly acting dopamine agonists, such as apomorphine, or dopamine itself, would strengthen the excitatory synapses involved in any portion of behaviour, and would not *selectively* reinforce lever pressing or any other positively rewarding behaviour. Parallel predictions for the hypothetical negative reinforcement pathway, employing 5HT, could also easily be suggested.

The actual experimental verification of all these predictions concerning striatal function is far from easy, because amphetamine would affect cortical noradrenaline as well as striatal dopamine, and any pharmacological agent which affected serotonergic function would influence cortical as well as striatal function. Nevertheless, what evidence is available supports these predictions well, though little is available for negative reinforcement systems, compared with positive ones. Amphetamine improves acquisition of operant tasks (Rensch and Rahmann 1960; Kelemen and Bovet 1961; Banerjee 1971). Amphetamine and cocaine will also enhance intracranial self-stimulation (see evidence summarized by Crow 1972*a*). On the other hand, apomorphine seems to have only a slight effect in improving operant learning (see Davies, Jackson, and Redfern 1974) which is greatly overshadowed by learning *deficits*, when the dose is slightly increased. In any case, slight improvement might be anticipated, not because reinforcement was increased, but because general levels of excitation would be increased by apomorphine (see below), and this would result in a more fertile substrate of random behavioural activity from which responses could be selected during the learning process. The actions of apomorphine on self-stimulation are complex, and in different animals self-stimulation may be either increased or decreased (Wauquier and Niemegeers 1973; St. Laurent, Leclerc, Mitchell, and Miliaressis 1973; Broekkamp and Van Rossum 1974; Mora, Phillips, Koolhaas, and Rolls 1976), but, as predicted, there is no strong and uniform potentiation. Similarly, after self-stimulation has been abolished by intracerebral administration of 6-hydroxydopamine, intraventricular injection of dopamine will not reinstate it (M. E. Olds 1975).

6.2.4. STEREOTYPY, LOCOMOTOR ACTIVITY, AND CIRCLING BEHAVIOUR

In addition to operant learning and intracranial self-stimulation, there are several other types of behaviour in which striatal monoamines are to a greater or lesser extent implicated. These include the stereotyped behaviour patterns observed after administration of amphetamine (Randrup and Munkvad 1967), changes in non-specific locomotor activity, and the circling behaviours produced by administration of dopamine agonists after asymmetrical lesions placed in the substantia nigra or elsewhere. Laverty (1974) has reviewed the role of catecholamines in some of these behaviours. Interpretations of the general psychological significance of such behaviour patterns may be less easy than for those already considered. However, in the case of the stereotyped behaviour it has been suggested (Randrup, Munkvad, Fog, and Ayhan 1975) that these particular behavioural acts (e.g. sniffing, licking, gnawing in rats) in some way 'provide their own reward', and such a relationship was therefore built into the model of acquiring feeding behaviour, illustrated in Fig. 12. From this it would be predicted that procedures which enhance positive reinforcement mechanisms (e.g. administration of amphetamine) would increase this stereotyped behaviour (or reveal it when it was otherwise absent). Such action of amphetamine would, to some extent be dependent on the integrity of the nigro–striatal pathway, since temporal patterning is presumably involved in the reinforcement of stereotyped behaviour. Hence, if the interpretation of Randrup and Munkvad is accepted, it is predicted that directly acting dopamine agonists would have less of a tendency than the indirectly acting ones to produce stereotypy. On the other hand the directly acting drugs, by non-specific reinforcement of excitatory synapses, would be expected to cause a general increase in locomotor activity. A qualification is appropriate here however. If an animal spends a substantial portion of its time performing one of the stereotyped behaviour patterns, such acts are in any case likely to be encouraged by a dopamine agonist, even if it is a directly acting one. The converse predictions, with respect to the negative reinforcement systems and 5HT, are as follows: procedures which decrease striatal 5HT should increase general activity levels, and might under some circumstances reveal stereotyped behaviour patterns hitherto suppressed.

The evidence on the above predictions may be summarized as follows. Both amphetamine (Randrup and Munkvad 1967) and apomorphine (Ernst 1967) can induce stereotyped behaviour. Lesion experiments (Creese and Iversen 1972; Fibiger, Fibiger, and Zis 1973) indicate that neostriatal dopamine is involved in stereotyped behaviour, though there is also evidence that limbic striatal regions also contribute to its appearance (Costall, Naylor, and Neumeyer 1975). It is not clear from the literature whether differences exist between amphetamine and apomorphine induced stereotypy. It might be expected that the latter behaviour would be more continuous, with fewer interruptions (if it occurred at all) compared with the former, though it would require detailed observations to establish this.

An interesting aspect of this stereotyped behaviour is worth mentioning in this context. It has been observed (e.g. Segal 1975) that with repeated daily administration of *d*-amphetamine the stereotypy effect increases progressively in magnitude, a phenomenon which could be termed reverse tolerance. However, this phenomenon is not found when apomorphine is the inducing agent (Flemenbaum 1979) and it thus seems likely that the effect is more complex than simple receptor sensitization. The interpretation which can be offered, based on the present theory, is that amphetamine, because of its indirect mode of action, will potentiate a genuine operant learning component of stereotypy. The stereotyped behaviour will become linked to some aspects of the sensory situation in which it is elicited, and with repetition, this sensorimotor representation will be gradually transferred to the cortex. A gradual increase in the strength of this habit might thus be expected. On the other hand, apomorphine cannot provide a temporal pattern of stimulation contingent on the animal's behaviour and so cannot act as a true reinforcing signal. The learning aspect of stereotypy (including the transference of representation to the cortex) will thus not be shown by this drug.

As predicted, apomorphine injection causes an increase in locomotor activity (a behaviour in which learning is not involved) (Jalfre and Haefely 1971). Amphetamine will also increase locomotor activity, but this effect appears to be mediated largely by amines other than striatal dopamine

(Creese and Iversen 1972; Fibiger, Fibiger, and Zis 1973; Laverty 1974) (see Section 6.3). Exploratory activity in particular appears to be related particularly to noradrenaline (Corrodi, Fuxe, Ljungdahl, and Ögren 1970).

Evidence about the converse predictions (concerning the hypothetical negative reinforcement system) largely supports the theory, with some discrepancies. Experiments in which lesions are placed in midbrain regions rich in 5HT-containing neurones generally demonstrate increased activity, as predicted here (Kostowski, Giacalone, Garattini, and Valzelli 1968; Srebro and Lorens 1975), though this may not be due entirely to decreased forebrain 5HT. Similarly, it has been shown that 5HT agonists, or 5HT uptake inhibitors potentiate the actions of the dopamine antagonist haloperidol in causing catalepsy (Balsara, Jadhav, and Chandorkar 1979). Lucki and Harvey (1979) showed that after midbrain raphe lesions which caused over 90 per cent forebrain 5HT depletion, amphetamines (particularly *d*-amphetamine) have a more potent effect than normally in increasing activity levels and in initiating stereotyped behaviour. Furthermore, Costall, Naylor, Marsden, and Pycock (1976) showed that hyperactivity induced by direct injections of dopamine into nucleus accumbens could be antagonized by simultaneous injections of 5HT.

In contrast to these results Tenen (1967) showed that decrease of 5HT synthesis with *p*-chlorophenylalanine lowers activity levels, though it increases sensitivity to painful stimuli. Hole, Fuxe, and Jonsson (1976) also found decreases in locomotor activity after depletion of forebrain serotonin. Grahame-Smith (1971) has shown that increase in whole brain 5HT (by loading with tryptophan after inhibition of monoamine oxidase) will cause gross hyperactivity. More recently it has been shown that this hyperactivity is dependent upon the integrity of forebrain dopaminergic systems (Green and Grahame-Smith 1974). Such results may thus be a consequence of the interactions which are known to be possible between the various monoamine nuclei in the brainstem (see Phillipson 1979). Evidence on the relation between midbrain raphe lesions and stereotyped behaviour is rather confused. Kostowski *et al.* (1968) reported the appearance of stereotypy while Costall and Naylor (1974*a*) reported a reduction of amphetamine-induced stereotypy after such lesions.

Unilateral lesions of brainstem regions containing monoaminergic neurones produce a variety of examples of asymmetrical motor behaviour, both in posture and during locomotor activity. These may be regarded as special examples of the behaviour discussed above: in so far as the reinforcement of behaviour is asymmetrical, so motor activity will display asymmetries. It is, however, tentatively predicted that differences should exist between the asymmetrical behaviour induced by *directly* and *indirectly* acting dopamine agonists, the former producing only steadily maintained circling behaviour (corresponding to general levels of motor activity, or steadily maintained stereotypy in the intact animal), whereas the latter should promote only certain specific features of asymmetrical behaviour, and would thus not produce a steadily maintained behavioural pattern. Ungerstedt (1971*b*) and others have in fact shown that, after unilateral lesions of the nigro–striatal pathways, amphetamine will cause rotation *towards* the lesioned side, presumably because motor activity originating in the intact striatum is potentiated when presynaptic dopamine release on that side is increased. However, in such lesioned animals, directly acting agonists produce rotation *away from* the lesioned side (Ungerstedt 1971*c*; Corrodi, Fuxe, and Ungerstedt 1971) which was taken to indicate 'post-synaptic' supersensitivity to dopamine agonists on the denervated side. L-DOPA, which can be converted to dopamine extraneuronally (Constantinidis, Bartholini, Tissot, and Pletscher 1968), has a similar effect. In comparison with these results, Andén, Dahlström, Fuxe, and Larsson (1966) showed that in animals with unilateral lesions of the nigro–striatal pathway, both L-DOPA plus a monoamine oxidase inhibitor, and reserpine plus a monoamine oxidase inhibitor would produce turning *towards* the lesion, indicating that each of these drug combinations increase dopamine release from the intact side. They also remark that, in the animals treated with L-DOPA plus monoamine oxidase inhibitors, rotation was not as continuous as in animals treated with reserpine plus monoamine oxidase inhibitors. This could be an indication that the former drug combination permitted impulse associated dopamine release, whereas with the latter combination, transmitter 'spilled over' from the dopamine containing varicosites, regardless of impulses. Recently, the availability of inhibitors of dopamine reuptake has provided the possibility of a further test of the above arguments. These drugs should be regarded as comparable to amphetamine, in that they will potentiate the actions of impulse-associated dopamine release, without exerting any direct action themselves. In fact, as expected, they induce rotation ipsilateral to a one-sided nigral lesion (Duviosin, Heikkila, and Manzine 1978).

In animals with asymmetrical lesions of regions of the midbrain raphe, containing 5HT neurones, systemic administration of either directly or indirectly acting dopamine agonists will initiate turning away from the side of the lesion (Costall and Naylor 1974*a*). In these animals the striatal dopamine on the lesioned side only, will outweigh the 5HT whose actions normally oppose dopamine, and so will produce turning in the direction opposite to that in animals with lesions in substantia nigra. Since no supersensitivity to dopamine can develop in these animals, directly and indirectly acting dopamine agonists will have the same effect. One result which is however difficult to explain, is that of Costall and Naylor (1974*b*) that 5HT injected unilaterally into the striatum had the same effect as a unilateral striatal dopamine injection, i.e. contralateral turning. In the experiments of Jacobs, Simon, Ruimy, and Trulson (1977), unilateral damage to serotonergic fibres in the medial forebrain bundle was produced with 5,7-dihydroxytryptamine. Subsequent administration of *p*-chloroamphetamime (a 5HT uptake inhibitor, analogous therefore to an indirect agonist) induced ipsilateral rotation, while 5-hydroxytryptophan (which could be converted to 5HT in non-serotonergic fibres, and is therefore analogous to a direct agonist) produced a contralateral rotation. These effects are similar to, rather than antagonistic to, the corresponding effects of indirect and direct dopamine agonists, and they are therefore difficult to explain.

6.2.5. PARKINSONISM

In the human condition of Parkinsonism, an important element in the pathology is degeneration of some or all of the ascending pathways supplying the striatum with dopamine (Bernheimer *et al.*, 1973). The discussion in the earlier part of this chapter is therefore relevant to understanding some at least of the phenomena found in this illness. The three cardinal features of this syndrome are tremor, rigidity, and akinesia (or bradykinesia). Of these three the last (inability to initiate voluntary movement in normal fashion) is a directly predictable consequence of the striatal dopamine deficiency: these patients will experience difficulty with any form of active movement, whether it is non-specific spontaneous activity, learning a new activity, or decision-making about which already-learned activity should be initiated in any particular circumstance (see Chapter 5, p. 107).

Therapy of Parkinson's disease commonly makes use of the metabolic precursor of dopamine—L-DOPA—and the major limitation of such therapy is the development of the 'on–off' effect: it becomes impossible to find a dose, which will ameliorate the akinesic symptoms, without causing uncontrollable hyperkinesia (Sweet and McDowall 1974; Sacks 1974). There is much speculation about the cause of this phenomenon. One body of opinion holds that its occurrence is related to the stage in the natural course of the disease, rather than to a trophic effect of prolonged L-DOPA therapy itself (Duvoisin 1974). In line with Duvoisin's viewpoint, the following tentative interpretation is offered, arising from the above discussion about the contrasting properties of directly and indirectly acting dopamine agonists. If the nigro–striatal tract has partially degenerated, akinesic symptoms arise because this pathway cannot effectively transmit to the striatum the normal temporal pattern of signals which reinforces active operant behaviour, by strengthening excitatory synapses. L-DOPA can to some extent restore the effectiveness of the remaining dopamine releasing varicosities, but if nigro–striatal degeneration has progressed beyond a certain degree, most of the dopamine formed within the striatum will not be synthesized within, and released from, nigro–striatal axons, but will be formed elsewhere (e.g. in 5HT-containing axons which also possess the necessary decarboxylating enzyme (Hockman, Lloyd, Farley, and Hornykiewicz 1971)). In this circumstance dopamine cannot be released in the temporal pattern expected of a positive reinforcement signal, but may give rise to a steadily maintained strengthening of all excitatory synapses within the striatum—leading to hyperkinesia. The prediction from this line of argument is clear: the degree of degeneration of the nigro–striatal system, as detected by neurochemical means *post mortem*, should correlate with the occurrence of the 'on–off' effect before death. (It would likewise be expected that in the animal experiments of Zis *et al*. (1974) which have already been mentioned, restoration of learning deficits by administration of L-DOPA should not be possible in animals with *complete* destruction of the striatal dopamine-containing axons.)

In recent years, a number of other agents which influence dopaminergic mechanisms have been given limited trials as therapeutic agents in Parkinsonism. These include: short-acting dopamine agonists (Cotzias, Mena, Papavasiliou, and Mendez 1974); long-lasting dopamine agonists, such as bromocriptine and lergotrile (Shaw, Lees and Stern 1978; Yahr 1978; Klawans, Goetz, Volkman, Nauseida, and Weiner 1978); inhibitors of monoamine oxidase, type B (which metabolizes dopamine) (Yahr 1978; Birkmayer 1978; Rinne, Siirtola, and Sonninen 1978); and inhibitors of dopamine reuptake (Park, Findley, and Teychenne 1977; Bedard, Parkes, and Marsden 1977).

It would be expected that for a drug to be effective, it should potentiate impulse-associated dopaminergic effects. On such theoretical grounds it is difficult to see how directly acting dopamine agonists could be as effective as L-DOPA. On the other hand, the other two groups of drugs might, under certain circumstances, potentiate the temporally patterned dopamine release, and thus contribute to effective therapy, either alone or in combination with L-DOPA, and they might be expected to avoid at least some of the 'on–off' effects of L-DOPA. However, these drugs could also potentially lead to 'flooding' of the striatum with dopamine, so that no appropriate temporal patterning of dopaminergic influence would be received by the striatum, even though the transmitter was released there in a temporal pattern.

None of these new therapies has yet been fully tested. Bromocriptine and similar drugs have been said to be useful in some cases, but possibly for reasons irrelevant to the present argument. Yahr (1978) writes: 'In our experience neither [Piribedil nor Bromocriptine] used alone in full therapeutic dosage has comparable anti-Parkinson effects to that of Levodopa . . . nor do they overcome its limitations'. Initial experience with monoamine oxidase inhibitors (e.g. deprenyl) is, however, more encouraging, and such drugs seem to improve significantly cases of 'on–off' effect.

In concluding this section it is perhaps pertinent to comment that on theoretical grounds there must be limitations to what can be achieved by way of transmitter replacement therapy. Anatomical pathways as well as neurotransmitters are required for proper function to occur. In the case of a diffusely acting transmitter (hypothetically dopamine), axonal pathways are necessary merely to allow temporal patterning of transmitter release, which can presumably be maintained even after fairly severe degeneration of the nigro–striatal pathway. In the case of transmitters acting through specific synaptic junctions, spatial patterning as well as temporal patterning is required, and this is likely to be more severely disrupted by moderate degrees of axonal degeneration in a pathway. In such cases it is unlikely that transmitter replacement can improve the functional deficits a great deal.

6.3. Neocortical monoamines in cognitive and quasi-cognitive functions

6.3.1. NEOCORTICAL AMINES AND LEARNING

The basal ganglia contain dopaminergic and serotonergic innervation which, according to the present hypothesis, have opposing functions as synaptic modulators. In other major structures of the forebrain, notably the neocortex and hippocampus, the monoamine innervation also consists of both a catecholamine (i.e. noradrenaline, or in some regions, noradrenaline in conjunction with dopamine) and 5HT. There is, therefore, a certain attraction in the idea that, in a more general way than hitherto suggested, catecholamines are modulators of excitatory synapses, and 5HT is a modulator of inhibitory ones. The function of such synaptic modulators in neocortex and elsewhere would, of course, relate to other aspects of brain control than the reinforcement of operant behaviour. One of the most obvious functions in which diffusely acting modulators could be involved, is in control of the level of consciousness in the varying conditions of wakefulness and sleep, though they could also play a role in more structured control processes, such as the enhancement of cognitive learning in novel situations. In Chapter 2 it was argued that consciousness and learning were closely related. If general synaptic modulators existed without which any form of change in synaptic security could not occur, then control of the activity of such modulators could control the level of consciousness as such.

If such were in fact the role of neocortical monoamines then, in contrast to striatal monoamines, it need not involve much temporal patterning of the signals in the aminergic pathways, and in fact the transmitters might be released quite steadily during a steadily maintained level of consciousness. Evidence supporting the idea that noradrenaline has an important role in controlling wakefulness, and that 5HT is similarly important in controlling sleep, has been reviewed by Jouvet (1972). Amongst the evidence cited are direct neurochemical data that 5HT turnover is elevated during slow wave sleep, and that procedures which promote abnormal wakefulness increase noradrenaline turnover.

Unfortunately, it is not possible to explore these ideas with any precision within the confines of the present work. Interpretation of the role of monoamines in hippocampal function cannot start until a more complete model of hippocampal function has been suggested than the tentative one advanced in Chapter 7. Moreover, when neocortical function is considered in these definite terms, the limitations of the present theory become obvious. In the scheme of anatomical and physiological relationships suggested for cognitive learning (contrasting with operant learning), synapses of opposite signs (excitatory or inhibitory) do not have an easy and definite antagonistic relationship to cognitive processes 'of opposite sign'. In order to make predictions about the effect of disturbances of monoamines on cognitive functions, the following questions need to be answered. (i) Does the omniconnection principle apply equally to inhibitory and excitatory neurones? It would hardly seem so, since most cortical inhibitory neurones are probably short axon interneurones (Szentágothai 1978*a*). (ii) Does the plasticity postulate for cognitive learning apply equally to synapses upon the excitatory neurones and to those upon inhibitory neurones? Questions such as these demand a more precise model than that put forward here (and probably a mathematical model).

Despite this, certain pieces of experimental work support the idea of a role for cortical monoamines in memory, in a way consistent with the present suggestions about synaptic modulation. A variety of experimental evidence supports the idea of the involvement of cortical noradrenaline in cognitive learning. The postulated role of cortical serotonin is not, as yet, supported by any direct evidence, partly because it is very difficult to separate the effect of striatal and neocortical serotonin. The hypothesized role of serotonin, therefore, stands as a prediction. The behavioural role of neocortical dopamine, in those regions where it is present, has only recently come under scrutiny. Finally, the possible complicating effects of alterations of hippocampal amines when assessing the behavioural role of neocortical amines cannot be known, since it has not yet been possible to deplete neocortical and hippocampal amines selectively. With these limitations to the available data, the postulates made above for the role of neocortical amines are nevertheless of some value in explaining some amine-related behavioural disturbances, particularly where cortex and striatum should be operating together.

The primary prediction from the theory is that neocortical noradrenaline (and also serotonin) should be involved in the formation of a permanent record of an operant task, but not in the initial acquisition phase. Unfortunately, much of the work on learning and cortical noradrenaline (e.g. Anlezark, Crow, and Greenway 1973; Mason and Iversen 1975; Amaral and Foss 1975) has employed behavioural tests where learning is accomplished slowly in a series of daily trials or sessions, and is thus not well suited for distinguishing the acquisition phase from a subsequent phase of consolidation. In such experiments, where rate of learning presumably depends on both components, animals depleted in forebrain noradrenaline have been variously reported to show learning deficits (Anlezark, Crow, and Greenway 1973), or normal learning (Mason and Iversen 1975; Amaral and Foss 1975; Roberts, Price, and Fibiger 1976), while Sessions, Kant, and Koob (1976) observed learning deficits in one test, but not in several others. In other work the influence of noradrenaline upon consolidation (considered as a separate variable from acquisition) has been studied. In the experiments of Randt,

Quartermain, Goldstein, and Anagnoste (1971), in which whole brain noradrenaline was depleted by inhibition of its synthesis, rats acquired a passive avoidance task normally, but deficits of retention of the memory were observable at times ranging from 1 to 24 hours after the initial learning. Fulginiti, Molina, and Orsingher (1976) and Spanis, Haycock, Handwerker, Rose, and McGaugh (1977) have shown that these deficits also apply to retention of active operant tasks. It has also been shown (Stein, Beluzzi, and Wise 1975) that central injections of noradrenaline immediately after learning can abolish such deficits. Crow and Wendlandt (1976) demonstrated that animals depleted in forebrain noradrenaline, as a result of stereotaxic injections of 6-hydroxydopamine into the locus coeruleus, acquired a passive avoidance reaction, but showed deficits of retention three days later. Furthermore, in at least one category of human amnesia–alcoholic Korsakoff syndrome — it has been shown that there is a highly significant lowering of the level of the noradrenaline breakdown product, 3-methoxy, 4-hydroxyphenyl glycol (MHPG) in cerebrospinal fluid, as compared with control groups of psychiatric patients (McEntee and Mair 1978). Interestingly, noradrenaline also appears to be involved in developmental aspects of cortical plasticity: Kasamatsu and Pettigrew (1976) have shown that the normal process of reversal of ocular dominance, which occurs in visual cortical cells of kittens after unilateral eye closure did not occur in animals depleted in cortical noradrenaline, while infusion of this amine could restore the process (Pettigrew and Kasamatsu 1978).

As mentioned above, one of the complicating factors which makes interpretation of the behavioural effects of cortical amines difficult is that in the present theory, cortical synapses of opposite sign (excitatory or inhibitory) do not have a simple antagonistic relationship to cognitive processes of opposite sign (as is postulated for striatal synapses and operant processes). A synapse of one or other sign may contribute to the representation of meaning in a variety of ways, depending on the signs of the succeeding synapses in the network by which it finally expresses itself. However, this observation helps to explain several additional strands in the behavioural evidence. (i) It explains the fact that noradrenaline appears to be involved in retention of both active and passive operant tasks. Presumably 5-HT in the cortex would also have a non-specific involvement in both types of task, which could help explain some of the contradictions in the data presented on the role of 5HT in quasi-operant behaviours. (ii) It also helps to explain the inconsistency of reports about learning deficits following noradrenaline depletion, since a cortex devoid of noradrenaline may still have some capacity for learning, by modulation of inhibitory synapses, in the presence of intact serotonergic innervation. (iii) An extensive series of investigations by Mason and others demonstrates that for many learning tasks, although acquisition and retention are normal after forebrain noradrenaline depletion, nevertheless, the flexibility of the learning mechanisms is reduced: during subsequent extinction trials (i.e. with the reinforcing stimuli removed) the acquired habit persists longer than in normal rats (Mason and Iversen 1975, 1977, 1979; Mason and Fibiger 1978; Mason 1978). It seems that reversal of a sensorimotor linkage by strengthening antagonistic connections occurs more slowly than normal. This would be expected if an influence has been removed which enhanced the strengthening of positive (excitatory) influences, while negative (inhibitory) influences could still be strengthened in a normal manner. The situation is more complex than this, however. If both the opposing stimulus–response sequences have been learned before extinction trials begin, either in a partial reinforcement schedule (Mason and Fibiger 1978) or by previous extinction experience (Mason 1978), or if an operant response has been acquired selectively to only one of two related stimuli (Mason 1978), then the delay of extinction in the noradrenaline-depleted animals does not occur.

It is instructive to consider some of these findings in rather more detail, because the explanation is somewhat different in each case; to this end Fig. 13 is given to aid thought about the problem. In the case of a normal animal, performance of a *continuously reinforced task* presumably depends on the convergent influence of striatal connections and synergistic cortical ones (connections x and y in Fig. 13(a)), acting upon neurones in the motor cortex. On removal of reinforcement, extinction occurs relatively quickly because the striatal component is then absent, and the cortex can readily establish another set of linkages, of opposite sign, to represent the relation between sensory circumstances and the non-performance of the response. In the noradrenaline-depleted animal, however, extinction is delayed because it is difficult to establish a cortical synaptic linkage opposite in sign to that which already exists. (Note that it is *difficult*, but not *impossible*: if only inhibitory synapses remain modifiable, then a sequence of even numbers of modifiable inhibitory synapses–connection z in Fig. 13(a)—would be logically equivalent to a modifiable excitatory synapse, provided all neurones involved could maintain some level of impulse activity from other inputs.) In animals which have had previous extinction experience, or have acquired an operant response selectively to one of two related stimuli there is no need for modulation of further antagonistic synaptic connections in the cortex additional to those established during the learning period: change of the reinforcement contingency merely switches off one already established cortical pathway and switches on another, by alteration of the pattern of striatal inputs to the motor cortex. There would thus be no difference between normal animals and those depleted of cortical noradrenaline. (This would be depicted in Fig. 13(a) by drawing both y and z as unbroken connecting lines.)

In the case of animals trained on a *partial reinforcement schedule* (Fig. 13(b)) the absence of the extinction effect has a rather different explanation. In normal animals, a partially reinforced task has to be executed even in the

(a)

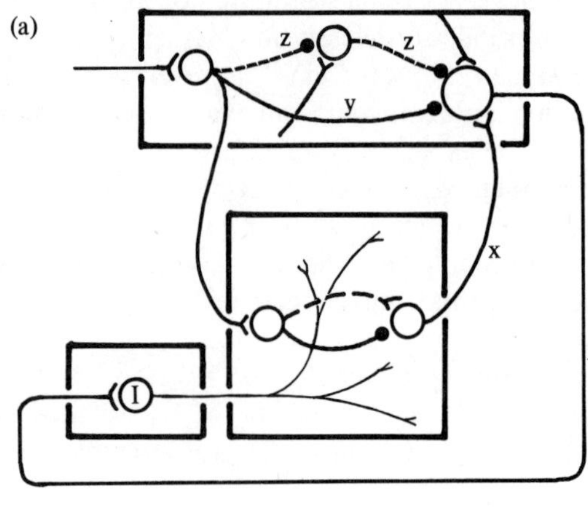

(b)

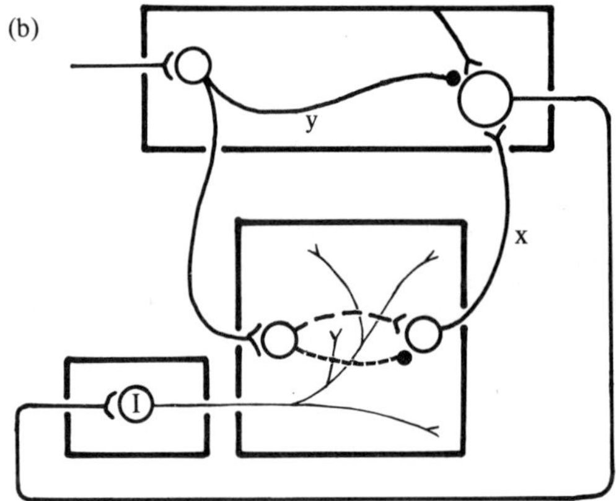

FIG. 13. Diagram to illustrate extinction deficits after cortical noradrenaline depletion. It is assumed that, under these circumstances cortical inhibitory synapses are still modifiable, whereas excitatory ones are not. All cortical learning must therefore be mediated by the former. Secure unmodifiable excitatory connections are assumed to exist, however, maintaining impulse frequencies in cortical neurones high enough for inhibitory influences to be able to have significant effects. These are depicted as unconnected synaptic terminations in the two figures. The diagrams illustrate extinction of a passive avoidance response. Symbols as in Figs. 2 (p. 71) and 6 (p. 82).

FIG. 13(a). *Continuous reinforcement.* The motor program for a passive avoidance response is maintained by secure inhibitory connections in both striatum and neocortex, the former requiring continuous reinforcement to maintain their strengthened form. Change of the reinforcement contingency, so that responses are no longer punished, may lead to extinction, since there is no longer a contiguity between fall in activity in the striatal excitatory input to the motor cortex (link x), and the activation of the inhibitory link (y) through the neocortex. In the normal animal such extinction will involve the strengthening of an alternative direct excitatory link through the cortex, to match the equivalent striatal link. However, in the noradrenaline depleted animal, absence of reinforcement, so when the task is adequately learned it will depend more on a cortical set of linkages than on a striatal one. Therefore, on removing reinforcement, extinction will depend principally on the time-course of decay of strength of cortical synapses. We have already seen that this is probably much more protracted than that of striatal synapses, and we therefore have an explanation of the well known finding that extinction after partial reinforcement is much slower than after continuously reinforced schedules (Hilgard and Marquis 1964). In the noradrenaline depleted animal, trained on a partial reinforcement schedule, the change of striatal input will have little influence on the process of extinction, because the striatal input plays only a minor part in the permanent maintenance of the necessary cortical linkages. (Hence in Fig. 13(b) both striatal connections are drawn as broken lines.) Formation of alternative antagonistic cortical pathways corresponding to alternative striatal pathways which become strengthened, is therefore not a major factor in extinction here. No alternative route through the cortex is therefore drawn in Fig. 13(b).

Mason and Iversen (1979) explain their own findings by postulating a deficit of selective attention. The explanation offered here can also be expressed in terms of the concept of attention, defined as 'the states of an internal control mechanism which determines to what extent learning occurs'. Both hypotheses should predict some deficiencies in actual learning (as well as in extinction) even though it may be far from an absolute deficit, and as mentioned above some of the evidence demonstrates such a deficiency. However, Mason and Iversen (1979) give little emphasis to this aspect of their hypothesis. The theory offered here is itself, however, not completely satisfactory, and it is likely that some of the findings of Mason and co-workers reflect dysfunctions additional to those discussed above, e.g. those resulting from hippocampal noradrenaline depletion.

Some of the behavioural evidence about cerebral noradrenaline points to a role for this amine in retrieval as well as in the phases of memory already considered. Deficits in retention performance have been shown in animals depleted of cerebral noradrenaline (using a dopamine β hydroxylase inhibitor), when this is carried out immediately prior to testing, as well as during the period of gradual acquisition. Such deficits could be reversed by injection of a noradrenaline agonist at this time (Hamburg and Kerr 1976; Botwinick, Quartermain, Freedman, and Hallock 1977). To explain such findings it must be assumed that transference of a memory from striatum to

---

extinction requires simultaneous strengthening of two inhibitory synapses (link z) to override the effect of link y.

FIG. 13(b). *Partial reinforcement.* The motor program is maintained mainly by secure neocortical inhibitory synapses (link y). Changes of reinforcement contingency does not greatly influence the motor cortical output neurones. Extinction depends more on the decay of effectiveness of link y—which will be very slow—than on formation of an alternative, antagonistic, cortical link, as with continuous reinforcement.

neocortex is a gradual process, so that, for an incompletely 'corticalized' memory, the cortical synapses involved are not effective enough to express their information unless noradrenergic activity is present in the cortex at the time of actual performance. It might be expected that longer established or overtrained memories would have no such dependence on noradrenaline for their expression.

6.3.2. NEOCORTICAL AMINES, SELF-STIMULATION AND AVOIDANCE

As mentioned earlier, the self-stimulation phenomenon has also been related to noradrenergic mechanisms (presumably to large extent in the neocortex), as well as to dopaminergic ones. This may seem difficult to place in the present theoretical framework, since operant behaviour is presumed to originate as random neural activity within the striatum. However, an interesting difference has been observed between the acquisition of self-stimulation from noradrenergic and from dopaminergic stimulation sites. In the latter case, self-stimulation is acquired very rapidly, but for noradrenergic pathways self-stimulation is only seen after a period of up to 30 min, in which the animal is 'shaped' or otherwise encouraged to perform the lever-pressing response (Crow, Spear, and Arbuthnot 1972; Ritter and Stein 1973; compare with: Amaral and Routtenberg 1975; Simon, Le Moal, and Cardo 1975). Crow *et al.* write: 'responding (from the locus coeruleus) generally took at least one 30-minute session to establish, and the very rapid acquisition of self-stimulation behaviour which often occurs with the ventral tegmental electrode placements was not seen.' This effect is in fact directly predictable from the present theory, since this prolonged acquisition period would allow transfer of the representation of a response from striatum to cortex, and its encoding in the cortex would then be favoured, since noradrenergic pathways are activated by the response. However, it should be pointed out that Crow *et al.* place their observations in a rather different theoretical framework from that developed here (Crow 1972*b*). Moreover, it should be added that the relationship of noradrenergic pathways to self-stimulation sites has been questioned (see Corbett, Skelton, and Wise 1977; Corbett and Wise 1979).

It is possible that some of the inconsistencies noted earlier (p. 127) in the literature about 5HT in relation to self-stimulation and avoidance behaviours might have an explanation similar to that given in the preceding paragraph. It is predicted that for some serotonergic pathways which support avoidance behaviour, the acquisition of such behaviour would be relatively rapid, because it would involve striatal function and the serotonergic pathways projecting to the striatum. On the other hand, for serotonergic pathways projecting to the cortex, the situation might be more complex. For reasons outlined in the previous paragraphs, cortical 5HT would be involved in maintaining *either* self-stimulation *or* avoidance behaviours, whichever were predominant at a particular time. 5HT and catecholamine fibres are intimately mixed in the medial forebrain bundle (a common site for self-stimulation), and if maintained performance rather than acquisition of self-stimulation were under study, it is likely that cortical 5HT as well as noradrenaline would be involved in maintaining the behaviour. Presently available evidence is not sufficient to disentangle the precise factors involved amongst the various conflicting reports. Moreover, even the above complex arguments are not sufficient to explain the findings of Miliaressis *et al.* (1975) who could initiate and maintain self-stimulation (i.e. positive reinforcement) from stimulation sites in the median raphe nuclei (which supply other forebrain regions than the striatum, including the neocortex).

It is probable that the self-stimulation and avoidance effects which are dependent upon cortical noradrenaline and 5HT do not *require* a temporal patterning of signals in the ascending noradrenaline system (though such a pattern would in fact be present), since cortical functions, by hypothesis, require merely *contiguity* of activation in pre- and post-synaptic elements rather than a temporally patterned reinforcement signal. On this, however, the evidence is currently ambiguous: Wise and Stein (1969) show that after depletion of the forebrain catecholamines with a dopamine β hydroxylase inhibitor, intraventricular noradrenaline can restore self-stimulation (apparently by direct action on the receptor rather than by uptake and release from remaining noradrenergic boutons). M. E. Olds (1975) found that after destroying catecholaminergic pathways with 6-hydroxydopamine, intraventricular noradrenaline (in contrast to dopamine) could restore self-stimulation. On the other hand, Shaw and Rolls (1976) found that directly acting α adrenergic agonists would not reinstate self-stimulation after depletion of forebrain noradrenaline with a dopamine β hydroxylase inhibitor.

6.3.3. CORTICAL DOPAMINE AND BEHAVIOUR; PSYCHOTIC MANIFESTATIONS

Certain regions of the cortex contain dopamine as well as noradrenaline. These include parts of the frontal cortex and the cingulate cortex (Hökfelt *et al.* 1974; Berger, Thierry, Tassin, and Moyne 1976; Lewis, Molliver, Morrison, and Lidov 1979). Sometimes these regions are included with the limbic structures such as the hippocampus, rather than with the neocortex. However, it is readily apparent from consideration of gross structure and histological appearance that they bear closer structural resemblance to the neocortex than the varied entities which make up the limbic system. A recent study (Brozovski, Brown, Rosvold, and Goldman 1979) has investigated the behavioural role of dopamine in the frontal region of the cortex. This region is already known to be involved in behaviours where temporal delays are necessary before a behaviour is carried out (e.g. delayed alternation between two arms of a maze). Specific depletion of dopamine in this region causes deficits in such behaviour almost as profound as those caused by a lesion of the same area. It is impossible to give a clear account of what might be happening here. If behaviours of this sort came under the general heading of 'associations based on contiguity' they must be high-level functions where contiguity is established between extensively processed portions of information. Possibly, in tasks such as this, cortical dopamine is somehow involved in relatively temporary associations of the contiguity type, just as in the neostriatum dopamine is supposed to mediate short-lived associations of the operant type.

The role of dopamine in associative processes based on contiguity is relevant in certain psychiatric disease-states in humans. In major psychotic illness (mania, schizophrenia) one of the more dramatic manifestations is the 'thought disorder', a general loosening of associations which can give rise to delusional systems of thinking. It has been pointed out (Miller 1976) that any mechanism performing operations of associative logic must have built into it a sort of 'set point', to enable a distinction (perhaps rather arbitrary) to be made between those conclusions which should be accepted as valid, and those which are to be rejected as coincidental. This 'set point' is analagous to the probability values by which the significance of a statistical inference may be decided. In psychotic thought disorders one might therefore imagine that this 'set point', or 'critical level of statistical significance' has become altered. Various suggestions could be made concerning the biological counterpart of 'a critical level of significance'. It could depend on the precise parameters of impulse activity needed to trigger synaptic change, or on the profuseness of axonal branching in the relevant regions of the particular individual's brain. A more interesting suggestion, however, is that it depends on the level of pharmacological activity of amines involved in the synaptic changes which are assumed to underlie the processes of associative logic taking place. Much evidence suggests in fact that in acute psychotic illness there is some form of hyperactivity of dopaminergic mechanisms. At present it seems rather more likely that supersensitivity of pharmacological receptors is implicated, rather than a direct overactivity of dopaminergic neurones themselves (Crow 1978; Owen, Cross, Crow, Longden, Poulter, and Riley 1978). Since the main site of dopamine is the striatum, it was previously suggested (Miller 1976) that striatal functions are the principal ones involved in genesis of such acute psychotic symptoms. This would restrict the symptomatology to disturbance of associations based on effect, i.e. operant functions. However, psychotic mental disturbances involve both overtly expressed behaviour, as well as more covert underlying thought disorder. The former seems describable as a deranged operant function and could result from indiscriminate activation of superabundant pharmacological receptors in the striatum. The latter, however, is clearly related to cognitive processes as defined here, relying solely on association of contiguous signals. Hence, to accord with the theory presented in this book it should involve cortical mechanisms. The presence of behaviourally influential dopamine innervation in the cortex thus becomes of great interest.

As pointed out earlier (Miller 1976), one serious paradox about acute psychotic illness is resolved with a hypothesis such as that outlined above, that psychotic thought disorder is a disturbance of a memory acquisition process: antipsychotic drugs apparently owe their therapeutic activity to their dopamine-blocking potency (Crow 1978, 1979) and yet their time-course of action is slower than that of transmitter blockade by many orders of magnitude. If, however, it is assumed that excessive dopaminergic stimulation results in formation of 'erroneous' associative links in the memory which are nevertheless established as if they represented truly contiguous occurrences, then these pathological links will not disappear the moment that neuroleptic therapy is initiated. They will be erased far more slowly than this, if at all.

Finally, it should be mentioned that the disturbances of consciousness occurring after intoxication by hallucinogens may fall within the scope of the present theory. Hallucinogens, such as LSD, are thought to act by inhibition of serotonergic mechanisms in the brain (Haigler and Aghajanian 1976), though it is also known that these drugs can influence receptors other than serotonergic ones (Whitaker and Seeman 1977). The cognitive aspect (as defined here) of hallucinogen intoxication is the dramatic disturbance of perception. Possibly this reflects an imbalance of the mechanisms by which inhibitory surrounds to the representations of sensory data are acquired. It seems likely that a disturbance of memory processes is involved here, for the same reason as in acute psychotic illness: recovery from hallucinogen intoxication may be a protracted affair, with flashbacks to the mental state during intoxication occurring long after the strictly pharmacological effects of the drug have subsided.

7. Higher-order functions of the brain

7.1. Introduction

THE earlier chapters of this book have covered a wide variety of topics related to the interlinked concepts of consciousness, learning, and memory, but only occasionally has the discussion come within reach of what the man in the street would recognize as learning and memory, as processes of which he is consciously aware. The enormous gap between plastic functions at the neuronal and synaptic level, and the functioning of the entire human brain, with perhaps 10^{11} neurones and 10^{14} synapses, seems scarcely bridgeable if only one conceptual language is to be used throughout. Some suggestions have been made concerning the concerted action of large numbers of units in two of the major components of the forebrain, the striatum and the neocortex, but this is far from a complete account of whole brain function, even in animals, let alone in man.

In the present chapter, consideration will be given to some aspects of higher nervous function which extend the concepts developed in earlier chapters, towards the concepts which are appropriate in describing human behaviour. Three main topics will be included.

(i) The functions discussed in Section 2.4 concerning novelty and familiarity of information within its large-scale context, and the related controlling processes which can enhance learning if novel patterns of information are detected, or can promote recall of half-forgotten detail if familiar patterns are detected.

(ii) The process of introspection, as it exists in humans, together with certain related phenomena in the literature about animal experiments (Section 2.7).

(iii) The possible means by which human intelligence, as it is normally understood, can arise from all the features of brain function considered so far.

7.2. Novelty, curiosity, and contexts

7.2.1. RELATIONSHIP OF RELEVANT CONCEPTS

The model of forebrain function constructed so far gives an account of acquisition of memory by postulating a physico–chemical embodiment of the ideas developed by learning theorists. It incorporates both of the principal rivals in learning theory (i.e. associations based on contiguity versus those based on effect) into one model, in which the two are closely integrated in most learning situations. In so doing it presents a model of learning which avoids some of the more obvious pitfalls of either brand of learning theory taken alone; and thus avoids the necessity to adopt extreme positions in order to maintain logical consistency. Nevertheless a variety of evidence can be cited which is not readily accounted for by this model, and demands additional postulates if a more realistic account of consciousness and forebrain function is to be given.

First among these anomalies is the novelty-detection function mentioned in Section 2.4. In that section the discussion was based mainly upon introspective data; but the same function is revealed by many observations upon experimental animals. Observation shows that locomotor activity in mammals is seldom random (as assumed hitherto) but is exploratory in nature, deliberately seeking out aspects of the environment which are in some way novel, incongruous, or complex (Fowler 1965). There thus appears to be an 'exploratory drive' which makes animals in many situations systematically concentrate on aspects of the environment where they have most to learn. It has been questioned whether this really is a drive separate from those such as hunger and thirst, the alternative suggestion being that it may be acquired by prior association with primary rewards such as food. Some evidence exists that this is not the case: in infant monkeys, exposed to solid food for the first time (a situation in which the hypothetical novelty-seeking drive should be in operation as well as the food-seeking drive) investigation of different types of food is correlated not with its attractiveness as a food, but by other of its prominent sensory attributes (Mason and Harlow 1959). As pointed out on p. 28, the inclusion of exploratory behaviour (novelty seeking) amongst the other drives seems valid in so far as it, like other drives, is a focus for goal-directed behaviour, but it is nevertheless unique amongst those drives in that the goal is learning itself. In any case, the mechanisms concerned with this unique drive must be capable of assessing the environment as a whole in order to discover which parts of it contain most unknown elements. The existence of this drive is anomalous, in that it has no counterpart in the model constructed in Chapters 3–6.

The second anomaly is that man and other animals appear to make use of contexts, i.e. superordinate information groupings which help in identification and correlation of other smaller-scale portions of information. The anomaly here relates directly to the omniconnection principle, for it was argued in Chapter 3 that only if this principle applied was it possible to represent all the associations by which the environment could be described. The distinction between a 'context' and a smaller-scale grouping of information ('an item') would then seem to be redundant. Nevertheless, as pointed out on page 27 commonplace experiences of the circumstances favouring correct recall of memories lead one to suspect that contexts are separately dealt with by the brain. Moreover, animal experiments also suggest the need for a concept of this general nature. In a recent monograph, O'Keefe and Nadel (1978) review a large body of behavioural literature which suggests that tasks dependent on contexts may be differentially disrupted compared with those dependent on smaller scale groupings of information. The particular case which these authors advocate is that the primary context which can be represented in the brain (specifically they argue, in the hippocampus) is that of *spatial location* or *place*, and that any other contexts which can be encoded, are done so on the basis of their similarity to spatial contexts. From the point of view of behavioural experiments this has a distinct advantage, because a place is capable of precise definition, whereas the more general notion of a context is much more difficult to demarcate, even though it is necessary on theoretical grounds (see below). The case put forward by O'Keefe and Nadel is a strong one, but in the opinion of this author it is not sufficient to rule out a wider notion of context than that of spatial location (though spatial location is likely to be biologically one of the most significant of contexts, and experimentally the easiest to investigate, especially in territorial animals). Indeed, introspection seems to indicate that contexts other than spatial ones may be powerful aids to memory recall and related behaviour: I walk through a shop doorway, and as I do so an electric bell rings because I have interrupted a light beam directed at a photoelectric cell. I may notice the bell, but it may still be far from obvious to me that the bell rings only when I am in a certain *place*. This is because the usual context in which I can 'locate' the ringing of an electric bell is not a place context, but the motor context of 'pressing a button or switch'. Likewise when I meet an acquaintance whom I cannot instantly name, it is not necessarily *where* I last met him that triggers my memory, but it could be his occupation or a variety of other types of context.

One particular aspect of context representation is the phenomenon of 'selective attention'. That it is possible for a person to direct attention at a particular range of possible stimuli, simultaneously ignoring a wide range of others, is a matter of common experience; and it is well substantiated by experiment that man can establish in his cerebral activity a 'set', or internal state which allows him to perform particular sensory or motor tasks with optimal efficiency, while other tasks could not be performed well under the same circumstances (Sutherland and Mackintosh 1971). Such phenomena have however no clear counterpart in the scheme of Chapters 3–6.

The third anomaly is closely related to the second. In many accounts of learning and memory it is felt useful to regard the processes of 'read-in' (acquisition) and 'read-out' (retrieval) as necessarily separate. This tendency owes something to the fashionable analogies which are drawn between brains and computers, and something to commonplace acts of introspection (see below). The important puzzle about this way of thinking arises from the adoption, throughout Chapters 4, 5, and 6 of the basic premise that information was stored by modification of security of transmission in selected connections, for it would follow from this premise that the process of 'read-in' necessarily implies the process of 'read-out'. According to this premise, when a pattern of information is presented which is similar to that present during an earlier learning experience, then the pattern of connections strengthened during that learning will once more be used. There is no need to postulate different macroscopic functions of acquisition and recall in such a scheme. Nevertheless, such a subdivision of memory functions corresponds well with everyday notions about learning and memory: we are all aware of distinct processes of 'committing to memory', and of 'recalling a memory', and it is a commonplace experience that a particular detail or word may be 'on the tip of one's tongue', suggesting a failure of information processing restricted only to 'read-out' functions. (Such an interpretation need not be incompatible with the usual 'explanation' that is given for this experience, namely that it is a sort of 'physiological aphasia'.) Moreover, descriptions of memory disturbances in man are frequently analysed in terms of selective failure of one or other of these categories (Piercy 1977).

Some of the concepts used above—e.g. 'novelty' and 'context'—are difficult to define precisely in the circumstances of a behavioural experiment. In the paragraphs below it is nevertheless hoped to show that they are theoretically necessary, and might therefore be definable with respect to other aspects of the theory put forward here. Some of the properties ascribed earlier to the cortical network may be thought of as its 'weaknesses'. One is therefore prompted to postulate a further function which is designed to make good the deficit. At the same time the above anomalous features of the functioning of the intact brain become logically related to one another as aspects of this additional function.

Let us recapitulate the model which has been constructed so far. We have a cortex and striatum which can form associations of simultaneous and sequential events, occurring either spontaneously in the environment, or initiated by the organism itself. In other words, a network of functionally effective connections is formed representing spatial and temporal aspects of the environment. This representation of the external world is more of an 'allegorical' one than a wholly realistic representation, since what is represented are events and sequences of events which are likely to occur, the 'constantly recurring themes', rather than the details of any actual set of occurrences. Nevertheless the cortical network should have some capacity for prediction—that is for running on ahead to the situation which is likely to obtain at some future time.

However the real cortical network we have to deal with is not completely connected in space and time. Most connections between neurones are likely to be polysynaptic, and each node of convergence is a potential link in a variety of associative pathways. Direct connections between neurones are unlikely to impose a temporal delay of greater than 0·2 s upon signals, so temporal representation is also severely limited. It would appear that the whole cortical network is capable of following somewhat different patterns of activity, even if the major environmental stimuli are the same, because of the intervention of extraneous factors of external or internal origin. This—as noted earlier—is part of the information economy of the brain, allowing multiple associations at each neuronal 'node' in the network, even though this may result in ambiguity of coding. To a greater or lesser extent the representation of reality is thus a 'blurred image'. Even as an 'allegorical' representation it is imperfect. This being so, one cannot expect the network to perform faithful recognition of complex trains of events, or carry out complex goal-directed sequences of behaviour under all circumstances, regardless of extraneous influences. Even less can one expect the network to run ahead very far and predict the future in a complex situation. Thus, the cortico–striatal system, as postulated so far, is not adequately tuned to deal with all the exigencies it may in fact meet. In short another function is required which *focuses* the system in some way, so that in any particular situation the optimal representation of relevant information is available.

Consider this *focusing* analogy in more detail. In many sensory systems, neighbouring elements in the array of neurones display 'lateral inhibition' (Whitfield 1967; Levick 1972; Brown and Gordon 1977). Lower-level nuclei in sensory systems also commonly receive descending inputs from higher-levels (e.g. Brown and Gordon 1977) and it has been suggested that these may serve to focus the ascending sensory information by control of the inhibitory interneurones, so maximizing the information reaching the cortex (Miller 1969).* The precise nature of the information processing required for such focusing is quite uncertain, but one must assume that in the primary sensory nuclei it is accomplished by hard-wired connections. In the cortex there are also a variety of sensory arrays arranged in two dimensions. But the kind of representation we are primarily concerned with here is not so simple: it is a 'cell assembly' or a 'network within a network'. Since the precise form of the network is moulded by the environment during learning, any *focusing* system which served to maximize the information being represented, must also rely upon a learning mechanism—a functional plasticity—otherwise it could not be sufficiently versatile.

One might speculate on the type of 'neuronal arithmetic' likely to be involved. For focusing an 'image' represented in the cortical network one might imagine an operation which integrates or adds together all departures from neutral frequency within the cortical network (i.e. all significant excitations and all inhibitions are added together, but regardless of sign). This integrated signal, or something like it, can be regarded as an indication of the 'quantity of meaning' represented in the cortical network. In other words it is the measure which it is desirable to maximize, and it can therefore be used as the basis of a feedback system during the *focusing* operation.

This is illustrated in Fig. 14. Apart from the major input and output lines of the main cortical network, there is a subsidiary output, itself containing

*Miller, R. (1969). Corticofugal and other influences on primary somaesthetic nuclei in the mammalian brain. B.Sc. thesis, University of Oxford.

many connections. Part of this output passes to the box 'I', in which this integrating operation takes place. The other part passes to the box 'H', in which the omniconnection principle applies, and which contains modifiable synapses of some sort. The output from box 'H' returns by a large number of connections to the main (cortical) network. The role of the integrated signal from 'I' ('the quantity of meaning') is to participate in the selection of the particular connections within 'H' which will enhance the *focus* of the information held within the main network. Simultaneously it will increase the focus of the information in the outflows from this network, including, of course, the subsidiary outflow to 'I'. With such a positive feedback system, the integrated signal within 'I' would increase to a maximum, corresponding to the best focus of information within the main network. The process of

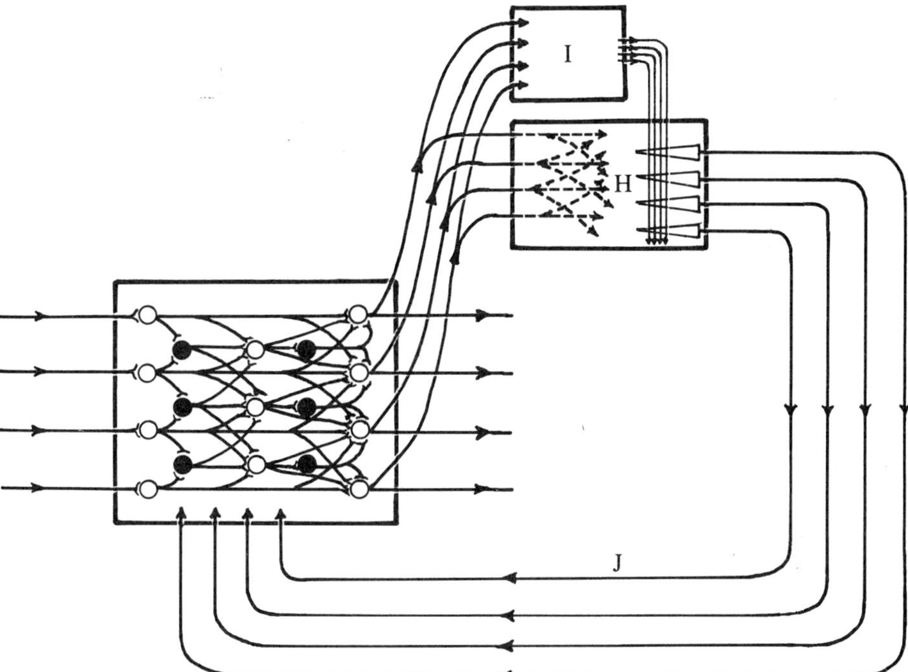

FIG. 14. Diagram to illustrate a positive feedback loop concerned with maximization of information represented in neocortical network. The large box (lower left) represents the neocortex. A part of the output from this passes to the two other boxes. 'I' represents an 'integrator' which can add together all deviations from 'neutral frequency' in the cortical network. 'H' represents an 'omniconnected' structure in which, under the influence of the output from 'I', particular pathways can be selected, for the recurrent pathway 'J'. This pathway conveys contextual signals back to the main network. The mode of operation of the components 'I' and 'H', and the mode of interaction of contextual signals with the main cortical network are not specified. Hypothetically (see p. 156) 'I' corresponds to the dentate gyrus, 'H' to some, or all of the hippocampus proper. Symbols as in Figs. 2 (p. 71) and 6 (p. 82).

selecting connections in 'H' is of course a learning process, in some respects comparable with those considered earlier. It will be considered further in Section 7.2.3.

The signal recurring from 'H' to the main network can be regarded as the 'context' signal. It serves to emphasize the particular aspects of information appropriate to the particular task, or (equivalently) to make decisions about which links and circuits in the potentially ambivalent cortical network, are to be potentiated. If an unfamiliar item of information is presented to the cortex, it will be encoded within the context of the neuronal activity prevailing in the cortex at that time. The learning function postulated also allows that the incongruous item can also be incorporated into, and can modify slightly, the context itself. At the same time, the postulated function is supposed to register the novelty of the situation, and this in turn leads to exploratory activity until the animal is familiar with all novel aspects. Subsequently the initially novel item can be more easily recalled in this context than in any others in which the item might occur. This leads to the possibility of selective attention and that of 'mental blocks' during the retrieval process. The case of an unfamiliar item in a familiar context is thus supposed to trigger new learning; but likewise, so is the case of a familiar item which occurs out of its usual context. In either case there is a 'mismatch' between the item and its context, so information in the cortex is not maximally focused. In the latter case however the result of 'familiarization' is that the item is incorporated into more than one context.

In this scheme it would seem that there should be a mechanism for clear decision between different contexts, when the brain is faced with a range of sensory and motor signals. ('Selective attention' cannot be directed at more than one range of events at once.) Contexts would not therefore be represented in such a versatile fashion as are 'items' in the cortex (which, according to previous arguments, may be interrelated in any imaginable combination in a multidimensional system of cross-classification). Presumably the mechanism for registration of contexts operates in a 'multistable' fashion: by some form of positive feedback, the pattern of contextual activity in the cortex 'gravitates' towards one or another of the contexts which have already been acquired, rather than some intermediate state.

7.2.2. A ROLE FOR THE HIPPOCAMPUS

The main theme of the rest of Section 7.2 is that contexts are registered within a third major element of the forebrain—the hippocampus—and that this structure thus controls the background of activity in the neocortex, upon which details become highlighted as circumstances vary from novelty towards familiarity. It would be impossible not to mention here the recent monograph of O'Keefe and Nadel (1978) which influenced the author considerably in the course of preparing the present work. O'Keefe and Nadel provide a very wide-ranging review of hippocampal function, including anatomical and physiological data, and comprehensive coverage of behavioural findings following hippocampal lesions in man as well as other animals. The whole is integrated within a framework of Kantian philosophy. The fundamental thesis of O'Keefe and Nadel is that the hippocampus serves as a cognitive map in which memories of places are encoded and stored. At first sight this seems a quite different idea of hippocampal function from that to be developed here, but in fact it turns out to be in many ways similar, since the idea of a place is more or less synonymous with a spatial context. Nevertheless, there are significant disparities between the two theories which are more than mere matters of emphasis. In the following pages the role suggested for the hippocampus will be sketched in broad outline, leaving the more detailed consideration of anatomical and other evidence to Section 7.2.3.

The basic tenets of the hypothesis advanced here are as follows.

(i) By virtue of connections projecting to it from widespread areas of the neocortex, the hippocampus can sample all neocortical activity and can thus come under the influence of all inputs to the neocortex. Included in the scope of such sampling are the motor inputs to the cortex, from basal ganglia and elsewhere, as well as the strictly sensory inputs.

(ii) One of the functional outputs from the hippocampus consists of signals about useful contextual information registered in that structure. These signals traverse connections which directly or indirectly relay back to the neocortex, where they influence the precision of representation of sensory and motor information.

(iii) The hippocampus has some form of synaptic plasticity within itself which allows it to register as contexts those overall groupings of information which are most useful in highlighting significant patterns of activity in the cortex (with emphasis on commonly occurring patterns). These contexts are multidimensional rather than simply spatial. Some suggestions have already been made about the positive feedback relationship supposed to exist between neocortex and hippocampus, and about the form of the 'neuronal arithmetic' which must be carried out in order to register such contexts. As part of this arithmetic the hippocampus can also register the degree of novelty or incongruity of an item with respect to its context.

(iv) In addition to output from the hippocampus back to the neocortex (the 'informational' output), there is a second functional output–the 'controlling' output—which can, on the one hand, adjust levels of general locomotor activity, and on the other hand, can modulate some aspect of neocortical function, so that learning processes in that structure occur more readily. If the hippocampus registers incongruity or 'mismatch' between an item and a context, locomotor activity will be increased. Since this will expose the animal to further novel aspects of the environment, a positive feedback situation will inevitably ensue in which the animal focuses its activity particularly around the novel features in the environment. In other words the animal will investigate and explore. If there are no unforeseen interruptions this positive feedback will be broken only when all novel aspects of the environment have been incorporated into the memory stores, and all incongruities have been registered within the (slightly modified) context which was present.

A point which immediately arises from this model is that the hippocampus, in so far as it samples neocortical activity, rather than receives detailed representations of its activity will signify 'match' or 'mismatch' (i.e. familiarity or novelty) without representing all the details contained within the context. We see in this model therefore, a parallel of certain subjective phenomena, in which feelings of familiarity and strangeness may be experienced in isolation, that is, dissociated from the detailed subjective impressions to which these feelings usually apply (e.g. the *déjà vu* phenomenon, or the feelings of strangeness and familiarity elicited in Penfield's temporal lobe stimulation studies (see p. 39).

A second noteworthy point is that the hippocampus is like the striatum in some general features. As one ascends the phylogenetic scale in the mammals the hippocampus increases in size; but (like the striatum) it does not enlarge at a pace comparable with the neocortex as one climbs the ladder of mammalian evolution from small-brained rodents to higher primates (Stephen, Bauchot, and Andy 1970). One suspects, therefore, that the hippocampus, like the striatum, is a region where certain types of information processing take place, though the main site of storage of information, where capacity is important, is in the neocortex. This is compatible with the main idea of this section where the relation of hippocampus to neocortex is one of interdependence, neither structure functioning properly without the other. This relationship, an obvious consequence of the feedback relationship depicted in Fig. 14, is thus similar to the relation proposed between cortex and striatum, which is also one of interdependence.

The chief point of difference between this theory and that of O'Keefe and Nadel (1978) has already been mentioned (p. 146). The word 'context' here refers to multidimensional 'areas' of reference rather than simply to three-dimensional Euclidean space. O'Keefe and Nadel have something to say about representation of non-spatial contexts, particularly the contexts for logical manipulation of words in human linguistics, but clearly the crux of their ideas is that the 'cognitive map' is in essence a spatial one, and any non-spatial mapping is derived from spatial mapping on the basis of formal similarities between the two.

An hypothesis such as that outlined here is far more difficult to investigate than that of O'Keefe and Nadel. For, if it is correct, then the important variables are certainly very remote abstractions from sensory input or motor output. The distinction between a 'portion of information' and a 'context', though necessary on theoretical grounds (see Section 7.2.1) is virtually impossible to make with rigour in a practical situation. A particular cluster of information may be handled satisfactorily by the neocortex alone in one species, or one individual of a species, without requiring additional contextual coding to aid retrieval, whereas in other species or individuals, this cluster overtaxes the capacity of the neocortex for unambiguous registration, so that subsequent recall demands reconstruction of a context as well as the presence of appropriate items of information. Likewise the precise demarcation of familiarity ('match') from strangeness ('mismatch') in any particular context is impossible to make other than by an explicit behaviour test. If these terms have any use at all in a behavioural experiment, they must be employed in quite a flexible fashion, so that generalization can be made between very different situations—different species, different individuals, different inputs to the cerebral cortex, and possibly different ages in the same individual. The whole topic is frighteningly complex. Indeed we are dealing here with one of the psychological functions mentioned in Chapter 1, which are more sophisticated than any man-made device, and which cannot therefore be readily systematized in objective form. It could be suggested that the best machine we have for assessing these variables might well turn out to be the human brain itself, though this immediately makes investigation a prey to all the uncertainties of interpersonal variation in subjective judgement of complex processes. The difficulty reaches its most acute form when one studies hippocampal function in primates (see Crowne and Radcliffe 1975). In such an investigation one is getting close to considering what a human being would regard as 'novel' or 'original' in a particular context. We can never systematize such things as this. Indeed, if we could, there would no longer be any need for original thought by human beings.

There seems to be no sure way out of this dilemma if the main evidence for one's enquiry consists of empirical observations of behaviour (important though such observations are). The hypothesis could however be explored in other ways. Study of the properties of model networks by mathematical or computer simulation techniques might delineate with increased precision the 'weaknesses' inherent in an 'incompletely connected' network, and may suggest a more precise version of the neural arithmetic required to make good this deficit. Furthermore, the experimental investigation of interdependence between neocortex and hippocampus might provide crucial testing evidence (see for instance the discussion of E. R. John's experiments on p. 155). In Section 7.3 evidence relating to the above theory is presented, with emphasis upon anatomical and physiological data rather than behavioural data. To some extent the inner workings of the hippocampus are left unanalysed (as a 'black box'), though it is hoped that pertinent questions are asked. The exact significance of much of this evidence at present eludes the author, though he believes it is so distinctive and intriguing that a comprehensive theory of hippocampal function is now within striking distance.

7.2.3. EVIDENCE ABOUT THE PROPOSED ROLE OF THE HIPPOCAMPUS

In this subsection, evidence of an anatomical and physiological nature will be discussed first, organized in subheadings corresponding to the main components of the hypothesis outlined above (Section 7.2.3(a) to (d)). Following this a brief outline of some of the issues involved in correlating hippocampal function with behaviour will be presented (Section 7.2.3(e) and (f)).

7.2.3(a) Neocortical inputs to the hippocampus. It is necessary that widespread areas of the neocortex should project upon the hippocampus. Substantial inputs to the hippocampus from the entorhinal cortex have in fact been known to exist for a long time (see Chronister and White 1975). This region of cortex has complex and extensive inputs from widespread regions of neocortex, including all lobes (in the primate) and including primary, secondary and association cortical areas (Van Hoesen, Pandya, and Butters 1972, 1975; Van Hoesen and Pandya 1975).

7.2.3(b) Hippocampal output pathways back to the neocortex. A set of connections is required which, directly or indirectly, relays signals back to the neocortex from the hippocampus. The best known pathway from hippocampus back to the neocortex is indirect—that by way of the fornix, mammillary bodies, anterior thalamic nuclei, impinging finally upon the cingulate cortex (see Green 1964). A more direct route, involving projections from the hippocampus straight to anterior thalamic nuclei, also exists (Raisman, Cowan, and Powell 1966; Siegel and Tassoni 1971). In the primate, however, it has been implicit for some time that direct connections, recurrent from hippocampus to neocortex might exist. For instance the mode of spread of seizure activity originating in the hippocampus (Lieb, Walsh, Babb, Walter, and Crandall 1976), the failure of fornix section to mimic the behavioural effects of removal of the hippocampus (Woolsey and Nelson 1975), as well as electrophysiological work (Deadwyler, West, Cotman, and Lynch 1975), all point towards such a direct connection. Recently these direct connections have been demonstrated using neuroanatomical techniques (Rosene and Van Hoesen 1977). The cortical areas to which these re-entrant pathways are directed are similar to those supplied by the indirect pathway from hippocampus to cortex, namely the cingulate and other medial parts of the cortical grey matter. In Chapter 6 the comment was made that these areas, while often classed as 'limbic' in contradistinction to the neocortex, are in fact more like the neocortex than the hippocampus from a structural point of view. Moreover, there are efferent projections from the cingulate cortex to other cortical regions (Powell, Akagi, and Hatton 1974; Airapetyants and Sotnichenko 1976; Mesulam, Van Hoesen, Pandya, and Geschwind 1977). Any information relayed back from the hippocampus to the neocortex will thus be distributed within that structure, in the monkey particularly (as Rosene and Van Hoesen (1977) point out) to 'polysensory' association areas.

There is as yet no direct biological evidence that these connections are concerned with resolving the ambiguities in the cortical network, by provision of a context signal. However, one avenue of investigation which might obtain such evidence is found in the experiments of E. R. John and colleagues (see John 1967; John, Shimococki, and Bartlett 1969; Thatcher and John 1978). These workers trained experimental animals to respond differently to somewhat different stimuli. After the animals were trained, they were presented with an ambiguous stimulus, whose properties were intermediate between the two earlier ones. In such circumstances an animal would respond variably, and its actual response on any occasion served to define how the animal 'interpreted' the stimulus. Records of gross cortical electrical activity were made during performance in both ambiguous and non-ambiguous situations. In such experiments systematic differences of the patterns of activity present during the period of decision were observed, according to whether the animal interpreted the ambiguous stimulus one way or another. Moreover, the different patterns in the ambiguous situation corresponded to one or another of the patterns present in the non-ambiguous situations. If the theory put forward here for the role of the hippocampus is correct, the observed differences which may be present on successive presentations of the identical 'ambiguous' stimulus, should not occur in animals subjected to bilateral removal of the hippocampus: gross electrical activity in such animals should be far more closely defined by the stimulus itself, regardless of its similarity to, or difference from, past stimuli.

7.2.3(c) Intrinsic anatomy and physiology of the hippocampus. The intriguing intrinsic anatomy of the hippocampal formation must owe its special significance to the particular arithmetic operations performed within that structure. Here consideration will be given to the hippocampus proper—including regio inferior ('CA3') and regio superior ('CA1')—and the dentate gyrus. Details of the anatomy of the hippocampal formation may be found in Chronister and White (1979), Andersen (1975), and in O'Keefe and Nadel (1978). The hippocampus proper is a folded sheet, longer than it is wide. The most prominent cell type (and its major output cell) is the hippocampal pyramidal cell. The dentate gyrus forms a cap (a 'bicuspid' tooth in cross section) enclosing one of the longitudinal margins of the hippocampus proper. Its main cell type is the granule cell. The input to the hippocampus from the entorhinal cortex reaches both of these components, by separate pathways. However these pathways do not proceed in parallel very far, since the principal output of the dentate gyrus—the mossy fibres—runs transversely across the width of the hippocampus proper, synapsing with the dendritic trees of CA3 pyramidal cells, as these fibres interlace with them. The CA3 pyramidal cells also send transversely-directed collaterals (the 'Schaffer collaterals') which impinge upon CA1 pyramidal cells in a fashion rather similar to the mossy fibres. There is thus a trineuronal pathway transversely across the hippocampus from granule cells to CA3 pyramidal cells to CA1 pyramidal cells.

Prima facie at least there is some correspondence between this anatomical arrangement and the pattern suggested in Fig. 14 on theoretical grounds: boxes 'I' and 'H' both receive inputs from the same (neocortical) source, and box 'I' then contributes a pathway to influence the principal output neurones in 'H'. Tentatively one can identify the dentate gyrus with the 'integrator' (box 'I'), and the hippocampus proper with the structure in which specific pathways are selected to represent contexts (box 'H').

In the hippocampus proper it would be expected that unit responses would be particularly sensitive *inter alia* to: (i) familiar contexts, and (ii) incongruities or 'mismatches' between items and the prevailing contexts (i.e. to 'novelty'). Vinogradova's work (1975) demonstrates that many CA3 neurones appear to be genuine novelty detectors: with repeated presentation of a stimulus the neuronal response, whether it be an increase or fall in frequency, gradually declines, but it can be reinstated by any perceptible change in intensity, duration, or rhythm of the stimulus. O'Keefe and Nadel (1978) on the other hand, describe hippocampal units which fire selectively when the animal is in a specific place in the experimental maze, or if it is in a specific place and carrying out a particular behaviour (e.g. sniffing). Other units increase their firing rates when the rat goes to a particular place and fails to find there an expected object or other cue. In a third study, that by Ranck (1975), the most selective hippocampal unit responses were mainly of two types: (i) units which increased their firing rate during specific portions of consummatory or appetitive behaviour; (ii) units which fired most rapidly if such a fragment of behaviour was unsuccessful, that is if some expected contingency was omitted. Ranck also mentions a few units which had specific responsiveness to location in the experimental set-up, and one which fired specifically when the rat was near a motivationally significant object—a water bottle.

The experimental conditions in these studies are far from identical. Vinogradova's rabbits were slightly restrained in a confined box, and 'novelty' was thus an easier feature for her to impose on the environment than 'familiarity'. It is not surprising, therefore, that Vinogradova emphasizes the novelty-detection aspect of hippocampal function. O'Keefe and Nadel, and Ranck, on the other hand, used rats freely moving in a complex environment. In such circumstances it would be quite possible for the experimenter to detect consistent correlation between a pattern of neuronal firing and a sensory or motor aspect of the animal's behaviour with which the animal was familiar (i.e. a repeated association). But to monitor fluctuating responsiveness associated with the transient state of novelty would be exceedingly difficult. The latter two studies, therefore, give more emphasis to the representation of familiar contexts by hippocampal neuronal responses. In fact, these two studies also emphasize different aspects of context representation,

O'Keefe and Nadel stressing spatial contexts, Ranck stressing behavioural contexts. In both studies, however, the situation is not clear cut, and it is likely that both are observing different aspects of the same phenomenon. For instance, O'Keefe and Nadel note also that some of their 'place units' discharged only if a particular action was also being performed. These data are therefore compatible with a role for the hippocampus in representing multidimensional sensorimotor contexts. This is also suggested by the recent report of Brown and Horn (1978), in which monkeys were trained to compare successive visual stimuli. Hippocampal units in such animals responded not so much to a particular stimulus, but to the significance which a stimulus had in the context of the particular succession the animal had been presented with. Again we are dealing with a non-spatial context (an order of succession of stimuli). The conclusion from these single unit studies is as follows: just in so far as 'novelty' and 'familiarity', and the concept of a context are inextricably linked together, so one can regard Vinogradova's results as entirely complementary to those of the other workers mentioned.

An interesting additional finding reported by Vinogradova (1975) lends some support to the interpretation of Fig. 14 given above. The response of sensory stimuli in CA3 neurones habituates with repeated presentation of stimuli. In addition, prior electrical stimulation of the dentate gyrus will also abolish the response to sensory stimuli in CA3 pyramidal cells in the same transverse lamella of the hippocampus. Furthermore in animals in which mossy fibres are disrupted by immunological means, the normal process of habituation fails to occur. It thus appears that, in the face of novelty, certain pathways to the hippocampus proper are initially 'open' and as the novel item is assimilated into the prevailing context, the dentate granule cells and their mossy fibres participate in the selective closure of these pathways.

A number of other examples of functional plasticity in the hippocampus have been quite extensively studied. These include frequency potentiation (increased responsiveness to repetitive stimuli, especially in the frequency range 10–15 Hz), and long-lasting post-tetanic potentiation (Andersen 1975; Andersen, Sundberg, Sveen, and Wigström 1978; Lynch, Dunwiddie, and Gribkoff 1978; McNaughton, Douglas, and Goddard 1978). Such phenomena would appear to be examples of synaptic strengthening whereas the 'novelty-detection function' seems to demand some form of 'negative learning' (Vinogradova 1975) or 'inverse contiguity', in which converging inputs upon a neurone are fully effective before information has been fed into the system, and become progressively weakened as particular associations of input are repeated. The role of these phenomena in overall hippocampal function therefore remains enigmatic. Likewise the physiological role of the theta rhythm of the hippocampus—the most regular of all electroencephalographic rhythms—is uncertain. Does it, for instance, serve to 'entrain' incongruous activity in specific connections of the cortical input, so that the incongruities are gradually modified to correspond to theta activity during the transition from 'mismatch' to 'match'? If that were to be so, it would imply that the activity, recorded as a hippocampal theta rhythm would have a high information content (expressed within the neocortex as a context), and when different contexts are being registered, apparently similar EEG signals would convey quite different information to the cortex.

Apart from this, any attempt to construct a full neuronal model of the hippocampus must bear in mind one very striking feature: the hippocampus is non-isotropic, that is, the three spatial dimensions of the (unfolded) hippocampus are not equivalent. (In comparison, one may note that the striatum appears as a homogeneous three dimensional block of tissue; the neocortex as a laminated structure in which the two horizontal dimensions are roughly equivalent, but different from the vertical dimension, while the hippocampus, like the cerebellum, has three quite incomparable spatial dimensions.) What is more, in the hippocampus there is an orderly topographic arrangement of connections from different parts of the entorhinal cortex. The mediolateral dimension in the entorhinal cortex is mapped along the length of the dendrites of dentate granule cells and those of the CA3 pyramidal cells in the hippocampus proper (Hjorth-Simonsen 1972). Likewise the dorsoventral dimension of the entorhinal cortex appears to map along the length of the hippocampal formation, from its dorsal to its temporal end (Hjorth-Simonsen and Jeune 1972). In any region of the brain where there is an orderly topographic representation, without obvious relation to an external sensory or motor field, the question arises: 'What variable is being mapped?' It seems most unlikely that it is as concrete a variable as Euclidean space (as O'Keefe and Nadel suggest).

The transverse dimension is the easiest to answer for: within any transverse lamella of the hippocampal formation, there is a sequential signalling from dentate gyrus to regio inferior (CA3) to regio superior (CA1), the latter two also being regions of hippocampal output. Some indication of the variable mapped along the length of dendritic axes is provided by the results of Stafekhina and Vinogradova (1978). The medial and lateral parts of the entorhinal cortex, which project to different parts of the dendritic shafts also have different preferred stimuli: in the medial entorhinal cortex neurones are especially responsive to distant stimuli (visual and auditory), whereas neurones in the lateral region are more responsive to somatosensory stimuli. As far as the longitudinal dimension of the hippocampus goes, it appears that there may be lateral inhibition between neighbouring transverse lamellae (Vinogradova 1975; Struble, Desmond, and Levy 1978). In connection with this it is relevant to recollect the suggestion made on page 150, that a context representation is a unitary entity, not easily combined with another such representation. Contexts thus form a range where clear decision is necessary between different contextual representations. Possibly some important variable of different types of context is mapped along the length of the hippocampus, contexts represented in neighbouring transverse lamellae being mutually exclusive. Vinogradova (1975) reports that the ventral part of CA3, while in many ways similar to the dorsal part, deals with more extended and longer latency responses. Possibly the variable mapped along the length of the hippocampus is therefore some aspect of scale or generality of contexts.

7.2.3(d) The 'controlling' outputs from the hippocampus. In addition to the 'informational output' from the hippocampus, dealt with above, it is envisaged that there would be additional output pathways by means of which the hippocampus can modulate levels of locomotor activity. In principle this function could be achieved either by a link from hippocampus to the monoaminergic centres which modulate striatal function (e.g. the substantia nigra), or it could involve a set of connections direct to the striatum, so that the background of 'excitatory' input which is available for modulation will be increased in novel situations. Projections from the hippocampus to the striatum are well known (Carman, Cowan, and Powell 1963; Raisman, *et al.* 1966; Siegel and Tassoni 1971; Poletti, Kinnard, and McLean 1973). The principal target of such projections is the limbic striatum (structures such as the septal nuclei and *nucleus accumbens*), and from the electrophysiological study of Poletti *et al.* (1973) it seems that their major influence is excitatory. Until recently, the limbic striatum was regarded as somewhat separate from the neostriatum. However, the sharpness of this separation is now under question, and it seems that nucleus accumbens, in particular, has no sharp identity as distinct from its neighbour, the neostriatum (Nauta *et al.* 1978). It thus seems likely that hippocampal input to this structure will exert an influence which can spread widely through the striatum, and can thus in fluence locomotor activity. The other possible route by which the hippocampus could influence locomotor activity, namely via the monoaminergic nuclei supplying the striatum, has as yet no evidence, either neuroanatomical or electrophysiological, to support it. Though such a route may exist, it is not necessary in view of the direct link to the striatum.

Finally, one might expect there to be hippocampal output pathways to the central brain stem structures which can control neocortical function. Amongst the targets of such an output might be the monoaminergic centres which innervate the neocortex. Such a projection was implicit in the study of Valenstein and Nauta (1959), on the descending connections of the fornix. In all species examined there were direct connections to the rostral part of the central grey matter of the midbrain, and in rodents these connections passed into the caudal midbrain as well. The latter fibres, it should be noted, terminated particularly in *nucleus centralis superior*, or as it is otherwise known, the median raphe nucleus, source of serotonergic fibres to much of the forebrain, including the cerebral neocortex. The physiological influence of descending hippocampal outputs upon 'brain control systems' ascending from the pontine tegmentum was demonstrated at about the same time (Adey, Segundo, and Livingston 1957). In more recent years little information has been added concerning the actual fibre pathways mediating such influences. More detailed physiological accounts of the hippocampal influence upon neurones in the reticular formation have, however, been provided by Grantyn, Margnelli, Mancia, and Grantyn (1973) and by Vinogradova (1975).

Whether these descending influences are also directed to the brainstem monoaminergic pathways which supply the cortex is impossible to say on the basis of available evidence. The ascending pathways which cause electroencephalographic activation of the neocortex (and the production of a hippocampal theta rhythm) rely partly on cholinergic mechanisms, partly on non-cholinergic mechanisms (Kramis, Vanderwolf, and Bland 1975; Robinson, Kramis, and Vanderwolf 1977). Both types of activation survive the depletion of forebrain catecholamines (Robinson, Vanderwolf, and Pappas 1977; Whishaw, Robinson, Schallert, de Ryck, and Ramirez 1978). Serotonergic mechanisms appear to play a part in the change from an activated to a drowsy EEG pattern: stimulation of the median raphe nucleus produces a drowsy EEG, lesions in this nucleus results in an aroused EEG, and subsequent injections of 5-hydroxytryptophan reinstate the drowsy EEG pattern (Yamamoto, Watanabe, Oishi, and Ueki 1979). Control of cerebral activation thus probably involves several parallel processes, which are not spatially separable in the brainstem (see for example Robinson and Vanderwolf 1978). Destruction of one component of these controls does not therefore abolish all control of cerebral EEG. The relation between ascending pathways which control the EEG and the aminergic mechanisms which supposedly mediate synaptic changes during learning is far from clear. The two are certainly not identical though there may be some overlap between the two functions. In any case, it is likely that both functions vary concomitantly in the intact brain. For instance, an intimate reciprocal relationship between one aminergic nucleus—the *locus coeruleus*—and neurones in the adjacent reticular formation has been shown during various phases of sleep and waking (Hobson, McCarley, and Wyzinski 1975).

7.2.3(e) Behavioural correlates of the hippocampal theta rhythm. There is a wealth of information available about behavioural correlates of hippocampal EEG activity (Bennett 1975; Vanderwolf, Kramis, Gillespie, and Bland 1976; Klemm 1976; O'Keefe and Nadel 1978), which can be discussed only very briefly here. The particular aspect of hippocampal EEG activity which has aroused most curiosity is the strikingly regular 'rhythmic slow activity'—the theta rhythm (4–7 Hz in cat; 5–10 Hz in rat). Information on the theta rhythm is very complex and it is possible that there are important species differences in its behavioural correlates. The ultimate goal of experimentation here would be to discover an abstraction from the various behaviours described which applied, with appropriate qualifications, to all mammalian species, and under which all behavioural correlates of hippocampal theta activity could be subsumed.

Theta activity dominates the hippocampal EEG during behaviour involving exploratory investigation of a new environment (O'Keefe and Nadel 1978), though this is not the only circumstance in which theta activity occurs. It also occurs commonly in association with orienting—the so-called reflex, in which an animal appears to 'focus' its sensory systems upon a significant or 'attractive' stimulus (Grastyán, Lissák, Mádarász, and Donhoffer 1959; Bennett 1975; O'Keefe and Nadel 1978). This correlation is particularly prominent in the cat, whereas in the rat theta activity occurs in a much wider variety of circumstances (Bennett 1975). Orienting is in part a variety of exploratory activity, though orienting also occurs at times when an animal performs a quite familiar behaviour, which is cued by a distinctive stimulus, for which the animal waits. Bennett (1975) found that performance of a familiar task involving a delay was accompanied by hippocampal theta activity only if a cue was used to signal the end of the delay, corresponding to the time after which a response would be rewarded. Some of the evidence, particularly in the rabbit, suggests that theta activity can be initiated by distinctive sensory stimuli, without overt motor signs of orientation (Klemm 1971; Harper 1971; Kramis, Vanderwolf, and Bland 1975). In rats, sensory stimuli do not induce theta activity unless there is concomitant orienting (Whishaw 1972). On the other hand, in immobile rats preparing to jump, theta activity is present. It is, of course, difficult to rule out all motor movements in an attentive animal, such as in a cat, where visual attention is accompanied by eye movements.

Many investigators believe that a principal correlate of hippocampal theta activity is bodily movement, or at least some types of bodily movement (Vanderwolf *et al.* 1975; Black 1975; O'Keefe and Nadel 1978) and a good deal of evidence can be amassed to support this view. Amongst this evidence are instances in which it is unlikely that new information is being acquired, e.g. during walking (Black 1975), or continuous lever pressing (O'Keefe and Nadel 1978, p. 175). The apparent exceptions to the association between theta activity and motor movements are certain motor acts, which as a rough generalization could be described as automatic (e.g. licking, chewing, chattering of teeth, defaecating, pelvic thrusting, etc.) rather than voluntary (see Vanderwolf *et al.* 1975). The relationship between theta activity and types of motor performance is more complex than this, however. Theta activity can vary in frequency, and high frequency theta activity is more likely to occur during certain types of behaviour (e.g. the more vigorous types of movement). Vanderwolf *et al.* (1975) have also obtained evidence that high frequency theta activity is generated by different mechanisms from low frequency theta activity, since it is not abolished by centrally acting muscarinic blockers, whereas low frequency theta activity is. High-frequency theta activity is, however, not uniquely associated with vigorous bodily movement: it occurs during paradoxical sleep at times when phasic muscular twitches also occur (Robinson, Kramis, and Vanderwolf 1977) and it has also been claimed that it occurs during waiting periods, in operant schedules involving a delay (Bennett, Hébert, and Moss 1973).

A number of studies have attempted to correlate hippocampal theta activity with actual learning processes. Powell and Joseph (1974) established a differential conditioned reflex in rabbits, in which one stimulus (CS+) was associated with a subsequent shock (US) to the eye, while a second (CS−) was associated with no shock. During the early stages of learning either CS+ or CS− was accompanied by theta activity. In the later stages when the conditioned response occurred only to CS+, only the latter conditioning stimulus was accompanied by theta activity. Elazar and Adey (1967) trained cats in a Y-maze discrimination task, and found that theta activity occurred during the passage down the runway only on those occasions when the subsequent choice was correct, but not if it was incorrect.

In O'Keefe and Nadel's monograph, the authors unify this complex data by postulating firstly that theta activity occurs both during acquisition and during readout of memory. The information provided above shows that there is a good case to be made along these lines. Examples of the occurrence of theta activity during acquisition are numerous in the evidence quoted. Examples of its occurrence during readout include: orienting during performance of a familiar task involving cueing; in preparation for a jump; in association with significant cues in a differential conditioned reflex, after the response has been learned; in association with correct (but not incorrect) behaviour in a Y-maze discrimination task; and possibly during performance of routine voluntary (i.e. learned) bodily movements.

O'Keefe and Nadel's specific proposal is that acquisition and readout by the hippocampus is synonymous with construction (or modification) of spatial maps, on the one hand, and their use for predictive purposes, on the other. In association with this, they present a tentative model in which the theta rhythm actually is the travelling wave which reads out environmental space from its hippocampal representation. In particular they cite three points in favour of this: (i) the fact that phase relationships of theta activity in different parts of the hippocampus remain the same even when frequency of theta activity changes; (ii) the fact that theta activity is prominent during movements involving spatial translation of an animal; (iii) their own evidence that theta frequency for jumping rats is systematically related to the height of the jump (and therefore either to velocity or displacement resulting from the jump).

This tentative model seems implausible. Firstly, there is no decisive evidence that high frequency theta activity really does 'shift the focus of excitation from the place representation corresponding to the animal's position at the start of movement, to one whose co-ordinates fit the distance covered by the movement'. More importantly however, even if one accepts the premise that phasing of the theta rhythm is crucial in registration and read-out along a quasi-spatial dimension in the hippocampus, it is difficult to see how a travelling wave of activity, of variable frequency, can register and read-out in more than one dimension. But, in reality, the mapping of movements in space involves three dimensions at least, and probably more than this to cope with additional variables of velocity, acceleration, rotation, friction at contact surfaces, wind speed, etc. O'Keefe and Nadel scarcely recognize that a problem exists here.

Although these specific proposals seem unconvincing, the general statement that hippocampal theta activity is generated during construction of a contextual representation and is regenerated to reconstruct this representation during memory retrieval has the potentiality of providing a coherent interpretation of the evidence. If the notion of a context is taken in a multidimensional sense, applying to motor as well as sensory information—that is to all major inputs to the neocortex—then a parsimonious explanation of the overlapping behavioural correlates of theta activity—sensory, motor, exploratory, attentional, and learning-related—may be within reach. Generation of theta activity would then be involved in reconstruction of a context during recognition of a sensory stimulus, and also in reconstruction of the context in which performance of a difficult or skilled motor task was previously accomplished (e.g. in rats preparing to make a jump). The absence of theta activity during activities roughly classified as automatic is compatible with this notion, since these probably do not require use of the recurrent input pathway to the neocortex from the basal ganglia and cerebellum. On the other hand, the occurrence of theta activity during learning situations involving slight or no spatial movement indicates that theta activity is not simply related to formation of spatial contextual representations (as O'Keefe and Nadel suggest).

In different species of animals the importance of different sensory inputs to the cortex, and of the motor input from basal ganglia and cerebellum may be expected to vary. Thus, the types of context which are most likely to correlate with hippocampal theta activity can be expected to show important species variation. The contrast between the cat, in which theta activity correlates with orienting behaviour, and the rat in which correlation with motor movements is prominent, is an example of this. To argue this particular case in detail is well beyond the scope of this section. Indeed, the approach required—that of comparative neuro-ethology—is, in the main, a task beyond present day brain research.

7.2.3(f) Hippocampal lesion studies. In their monograph, O'Keefe and Nadel review studies of the behavioural effects of hippocampal lesions in impressive detail. The more straightforward parts of their review constitute a strong case for the authors' contention that the hippocampus is involved in forming representations of places. However, other parts of the evidence discussed seem to have a more parsimonious explanation if it is assumed that 'places' are only one of a variety of types of context, the latter being the important abstraction with which the hippocampus deals. For reasons already given it is not proposed to give a precise definition to the concept of a context for use in interpreting behavioural evidence. The points made below are thus intended to show merely that the evidence presented by O'Keefe and Nadel is compatible with an interpretation alternative to theirs, though much of the evidence is sufficiently ambiguous to prevent clear proof one way or the other (if behavioural evidence alone is to be the test). In the paragraphs below animals with hippocampal lesions are referred to as 'hippocampal animals'. Page numbers refer to the relevant parts of O'Keefe and Nadel (1978) where details of literature may be found.

O'Keefe and Nadel cite various experiments showing that animals with hippocampal lesions have difficulty in learning and performing tasks where a response has to be made in a particular context (usually a place context). On the other hand, if a response is to be made to a particular object or cue (regardless of context) no difficulty is experienced (p. 269). For instance lesioned rats have great difficulty in a water-finding task when water is always located at a certain place, but not when it is marked by a bright light as a cue (p. 274). Similarly, in maze learning tasks, hippocampus-lesioned rats show deficits because they cannot utilize information about place. Instead they make use of less effective strategies, such as patterns of individual responses which in themselves are simple enough to be regarded as items of motor behaviour rather than as contexts (p. 290). In aversively conditioned behaviour, hippocampal animals perform without deficit, provided the aversive stimulus is associated with a discrete item from the experimental environment. But when the aversive stimulus is associated with a particular place, lesioned animals show deficits. For instance, in a one-way active avoidance task—a task where a particular place must be avoided—some studies have clearly shown a deficit in hippocampal animals. In those that did not, a discrete conditioning stimulus was used as a cue to signal the impending aversive stimulus (p. 306), so that the animal was not using 'place' as a context in which the avoidance behaviour was recalled. In experiments where animals learn to avoid an aversive stimulus by a discrete operant act (e.g. lever-pressing), no deficits have been noticed in hippocampal animals, except in one study where learning the lever-pressing task involved suppressing a previously acquired lever-holding task (p. 311). Presumably contextual information was needed in the comparison of the two similar contingencies, which would not have been needed if no comparisons had to be made. In tasks where animals are rewarded for alternation between two spatially different responses, hippocampal animals show deficits if the alternation is between two arms of a T- or Y-maze, but when alternation is between different levers in an operant chamber deficits are neither so profound, nor so consistently reported (p. 329). When rats were rewarded for traversing a runway at slower speeds than they would do spontaneously, normal rats acquired the task by delay at the start of the runway, that is they recognized the context in which delay was required. Hippocampal rats, on the other hand, delayed only when they were in sight of the goal, that is, they could only form associations between the goal and an item (p. 350). Kimble (1969) trained rats on a brightness discrimination task in a Y-maze for water reward. Normal rats stopped running the maze at the same time as they stopped drinking, but hippocampal animals continued to run the maze when they had satisfied their thirst. Clearly, they did not properly associate their behaviour with the context in which it had been acquired—the need to obtain water reinforcement.

The experiments cited in the previous paragraph are examples of animals using familiar contexts as guides to behaviour, and most of those contexts were places. However, a normal animal does not spontaneously choose what is familiar. Studies of an animal's response to novelty provides further evidence of the role of the hippocampus, and here much of the evidence clearly relates to contexts other than places. Observation of the spontaneous activity of normal animals in an unfamiliar environment shows that they are curious, unpredictable and seek out novel aspects of the environment for investigation. Hippocampal animals, on the other hand, while still very active (usually hyperactive) tend to engage in predictable, stereotyped, repetitive activity. They are not sensitive to the novel aspects of the environment, nor to the novel aspects of their own behaviour (p. 255). A particular example of this is the phenomenon of spontaneous alternation. Normal animals tested in a Y-maze usually tend spontaneously to choose the arm opposite to that chosen on the immediately preceding trial. In hippocampal animals, however, there is a tendency to repeat the same arm of the Y-maze for many trials, or to choose randomly (p. 263). The tendency of hippocampal animals to behave more predictably and less flexibly is seen also in extinction trials: rates of extinction are very much slower in hippocampal animals, though not so strikingly in the case of tasks involving discrete operant acts such as lever-pressing (p. 343). Persistence of response habits can explain a number of other abnormalities in hippocampal animals—such as the persisting running by animals (after thirst has been satisfied) in the experiment of Kimble (1969) mentioned above, deficits in non-spatial reversal tasks (p. 281), and the increased responding seen with continuous or fixed-ratio reinforcement schedules (p. 323). Persistence of responding must be seen as an inability of the animal to notice the familiarity of a succession of identical behaviours, which in the normal animal would lead to decreased use of the behaviour (habituation).

The response of an animal to strictly sensory novelty can be assessed as 'distractibility'—the ease with which an intruding stimulus can divert an animal from performance of a task it is engaged in. Generally, hippocampal animals are less distractable than controls (p. 251), indicating that out-of-context stimuli do not register a 'mismatch' in the lesioned animals. As further evidence of the role of the hippocampus in representing non-place contexts, the evidence (pp. 349–50) of response to changes in reward intensity can be cited: whereas in normal animals increases and decreases in quantity of reward (e.g. concentration of a sucrose solution) will hasten or slow runway speeds, in hippocampal animals these differences are not observed.

The temporal aspects of information processing become relevant in two ways when considering contextual coding by the hippocampus. *Firstly*, for behavioural tasks involving sequences of sensory or motor representations, ambiguity is likely to arise unless the chain of items of information is matched to a corresponding chain of contextual information. Animals with hippocampal lesions are thus likely to show greater deficits in sequential tasks than in tasks where a single discrete response to a stimulus has to be made. The majority of studies of learning of response sequences cited by O'Keefe and Nadel (p. 326) do in fact show this, though with some discrepancies. Likewise, one may refer to studies of learning involving complex reinforcement contingencies, such as the higher fixed-ratio schedules, or the 'differential reinforcement of low rates' (pp. 322–33). Such behaviours are usually taught by initial training on continuous reinforcement schedules, followed by transition to the more complex schedules. Hippocampal rats have difficulty in acquiring such behaviours, particularly if the transition (in fixed-ratio experiments) occurs too abruptly. *Secondly*, it may be remembered from Section 4.4 that the immediate change occurring in cortical synapses during learning is probably of brief duration, corresponding to the short-term memory interval (5–20 s) and is prolonged only if repetition of the information pattern occurs during that interval. In learning trials where inter-trial intervals are brief, contextual reconstruction at each trial will not therefore be required, because the cortical synapses representing a particular context will still be in an active state when the next trial occurs. If, however, inter-trial intervals (ITIs) are longer, contextual information is likely to have changed, and previous contexts will not persist between trials, so reconstruction of the correct context may be necessary to interpret an item or cue without ambiguity. Hence hippocampal animals may show particular deficits if ITIs are long. A number of examples of such phenomena are cited by O'Keefe and Nadel. In a spatial reversal task hippocampal animals can perform as well as controls if ITI is 5 s, but show deficits when ITI is 4 min (p. 282). In a task where alternate lever-presses were rewarded and not rewarded, hippocampal rats learned normally provided that ITIs of 10 s were used, but were deficient with larger ITIs (p. 334). Extinction of a lever-pressing task, where spontaneous ITIs are likely to be short, proceeds without deficit in hippocampal animals, but in a complex maze where the repetition rate for a particular response is likely to be slow, deficits are present in hippocampal animals (p. 344).

7.2.4 COMMENT

What then are we to make of O'Keefe and Nadel's philosophical objective – that is to demonstrate that innate *a priori* knowledge of Euclidean space is represented within the brain (the philosophical position adopted by Kant) and mapped specifically in the hippocampus? Six points will suffice to summarize the outcome of the above discussion.

(i) Innate *a priori* representation of space, as a context within which spatial learning processes may operate is not proven. On the other hand, certain well-known physiological findings, relating to lower levels of the nervous system than those thought to be chiefly concerned with learning, do show innate representation of the structure of space. The phenomenon of surround inhibition (Levick 1972; Brown and Gordon 1977), seen in the lower parts of several sensory systems, is essentially a device for heightening the contrast possible between adjacent regions of a two-dimensional Euclidean surface, and it is thus an innate adaptation to the structure of the space we live in.

(ii) It is highly likely that the hippocampus can acquire information about places and other contexts, and that this can aid in retrieval in circumstances where neural activity impinging upon the neocortex is ambiguous.

(iii) The concept of a context, and those of 'novelty within a context' and 'familiarity within a context' are such high-level abstractions, and are likely to apply in such flexible ways in different species, at different times, and with different sensory inputs, that they cannot be given a rigorous objective definition. In this area of brain research we are therefore approaching the limits of what the scientific method can grapple with. To some extent, however, we may rely on our own subjective and idiosyncratic assessments of what constitutes a context, or novelty and familiarity within a context. Though this is obviously far from satisfactory it has some validity, for we too have hippocampi, which allow us to assess these variables subjectively, when no mechanical device can do so.

(iv) There is, in the organization of the brain, a form of spatial representation which genuinely is *a priori* in the Kantian sense. This is a 'multidimensional space', and its neural substrate is a more or less complete omniconnected network. This network does not give us innate knowledge of Euclidean space, but it does endow us with an innate capacity for performing operations in inductive logic. The conclusion of such operations are delivered direct to consciousness. It will be argued in the final chapter that we ignore such conclusions at our peril.

(v) 'Space' as an abstraction is a most important example of the contexts with which the hippocampus can deal. Indeed, it may be unique, in so far as lower levels of the nervous system are innate analysers of spatial arrays (see above). It is so deeply embedded within our cerebral structure and function that as adults we can use this context to solve certain logical problems which otherwise would defy solution. These problems – for instance, that of predicting a short-cut route between two familiar regions of the environment – are also soluble by mammals in general. However, there is no compelling reason to suppose that this most important context is innately represented in the hippocampus. It is more likely that it is acquired after the time that an animal, or human, is exposed to the variables that are possible in Euclidean space. If it is asked how we acquire such knowledge (as do O'Keefe and Nadel, on their p. 60) the answer must be 'by formation of a multiplicity of associations, which, taken together, define the spatial context'. For instance, the capacity to solve short-cut problems may develop from chance instances when, having traversed three sides of a square, we just happen to traverse the fourth side, and then find ourselves back at our starting point. Repeated experiences of this sort will allow us to form a general representation of two-dimensional Euclidean space. Evidence that information about the structure of space can be acquired, is the demonstration that, if a subject is required to wear distorting spectacles, his distorted perception of the world does not hamper him for long. A subject soon learns to reinterpret visual messages so that they can serve the same functions as before. The experiments of Blakemore and Mitchell (1973) also indicate that the ability to perceive fundamental aspects of space, such as straight lines, is subject to influence by environmental stimuli, at least in immature animals. These findings, originally made in kittens, are now believed to apply to many other mammalian species, including man.

(vi) Just as short-cut problems cannot be solved without a representation of space, as a context for logical operations, so many other logical problems cannot be solved without the corresponding context in which the terms used are defined. For instance deductions about arithmetic, or genetics, cannot be solved unless we have representations of the context of number, or of the principles of Mendelian inheritance, respectively. This argument is expanded in Sections 7.4 and 8.2.

7.3. Introspection and the influence of internal states upon consciousness

In Chapter 1 our capacity for introspection was seen as a fundamental fact which shaped the philosophical position outlined in that chapter. In Section 2.7, however, it was argued that, at a less abstract level, introspection is a scientific question in its own right. It was argued that introspection is the accessibility of information about internal states to the mechanism of learning. Learning is an investigable phenomenon, and it is also possible to control internal states in behavioural experiments. Introspection thus becomes a realistic subject for experimentation, both in animals and in man.

The term 'internal state' refers to an imposed change in the brain which may be either localized (e.g. electrical stimulation) or diffuse. The former alterations are of less theoretical interest than the latter, because their influence in behavioural tests could be explained in terms of altered impulse activity in a small proportion of connections, which can be registered by the learning mechanisms considered in earlier chapters. In the case of a diffuse influence, however, one has to explain how a disturbance which probably affects all regions of the brain can register upon a brain which is in an abnormal state. The most widely studied of such internal states are those imposed by systemic injection of centrally-acting drugs (Overton 1971, 1978), although other diffuse states, such as that following electroconvulsive shock, have also been investigated (Overton, Ercole, and Dutta 1976).

Alteration of state, such as is achieved by administration of a centrally-acting drug, may abolish all learning ability. There are two more interesting situations which may be achieved with lower doses of a drug. (i) In state-dependent learning, memories acquired in one drug state cannot be recalled unless the same drug state is repeated (dissociation of memory). This situation bears some resemblance to the dependence of memory retrieval upon contextual reconstruction, discussed in the previous section. (ii) The drug state itself may acquire the ability to act as a cue in learning (just as would a sensory stimulus), but does not cause dissociation of memory. This second situation—drug discrimination—differs from state dependent learning in that control of behaviour by a drug state is acquired gradually over a number of trials.

Overton (1971) regards state-dependent learning and drug discrimination effects as different aspects of the same phenomenon, the former occurring with high drug dosages, the latter with lower dosages. From the point cf view of experimental investigation of introspection we may equate state-dependent learning with a disturbance of internal state so profound that the experimental subject has lost insight into the relationship between the new state and the normal state, whereas examples of drug discrimination (or discrimination of any other internal state) are equivalent to acts of introspection.

There are many examples known in animals in which memory can be dissociated by change of state, including drug effects, post-seizure states, after inactivation of the septal nuclei with local anaesthetic, or even according to the time of the day (Overton 1978). In humans, various pathological phenomena fall in the same general category—multiple personality, lack of insight during or after a psychotic episode, alcoholic blackouts (Overton 1978), possibly also the confabulatory denial occurring after certain cerebral lesions (see Geschwind 1965b). In fact, the lack of insight (in psychotic illnesses, etc.) could well be regarded as one of the more severe aspects of the pathology in these cases.

The less profound disturbances—awareness of which *is* available to introspection—have been documented in many studies of centrally-acting drugs. Almost all groups of centrally-acting drugs are discriminable in learning tests (Overton 1971, 1978). It appears unlikely that this discriminability is a function of direct or indirect actions of these drugs on sensory systems. Furthermore, it seems unlikely that performance of the required response is restricted to the drugged state on account of amnesic effects in other states: the dosages of drugs required to achieve dissociation of memory are much larger than the minimal doses which can be discriminated. It is also unlikely that performance is linked to specific pharmacological properties of a drug which might encourage certain types of behaviour. For instance, rats can be taught to perform on a 'differential reinforcement of low rates' schedule of reinforcement, cued by an injection of amphetamine (Harris and Balster 1971). Initial acquisition of this task is achieved in the non-drugged state before introducing the drug state as a cue, and in fact the action of a stimulant such as amphetamine is, in itself, likely to adversely affect performance on this schedule, though the drug can cue such behaviour after appropriate training.

What explanations can be offered for phenomena of this sort? A definite answer to this question cannot be given. In general terms, however, the answer must be a combination of two mechanisms, which correspond to the two ways considered earlier by means of which information may be represented in the brain.

Firstly, information about internal states may be represented as activity in patterns of connections. For instance, Edelman (1978) has proposed that 'phased re-entry' of signals leaving a brain structure along defined pathways, could account for some of the attributes of a self-aware organism. A development of this concept, which is readily compatible with the argument presented here, is that the hippocampus is part of the circuitry by which re-entry is achieved, so that somehow knowledge of an internal state, such as a drug-state is encoded as a form of context. The obvious objection to this is that centrally-acting drugs will influence the hippocampus as much as anywhere else, so the hippocampus is not itself a stable machine unaffected by the state it is attempting to monitor. There is a certain truth in this argument, but in practical terms it is difficult to ignore the possibility that low-dose drug states could be registered as contexts.

Secondly, it is possible that internal states bring about corresponding specific alterations in activity of the diffusely-acting neurotransmitters. For instance, it may be that a particular drug is discriminable because it sets up distinctive patterns of drive stimuli. Direct evidence for this is lacking, but it is clear from the experiments of Kendler (1946) that different drive stimuli are discriminable from one another. Kendler's finding may be thought of as a special case of internal state discrimination, so that if it is to be explained as discrimination of pharmacological activity of diffusely acting neurotransmitters, then any other agent which influences the activity of these transmitters will also be discriminable. It is also possible that differential influence of drugs upon reinforcement systems also helps in drug-state discrimination. For instance, Stutz, Butcher, and Rossi (1969) showed that electrical stimulation of the brain in different regions could easily be discriminated if the stimulations differed in rewarding propensity, but if they were matched in this respect they could be discriminated only with difficulty. How such effects are achieved is uncertain. No explanation is offered for direct discrimination of different levels of reinforcement, but since reinforcement inevitably influences widespread regions of neocortex, the reinforcing intensity of brain stimulation might be indirectly registered as a context, by the hippocampus.

To what extent either or both of these two ways of representing information actually contributes to discrimination of internal states is mainly a matter of conjecture. The matter is of formidable complexity. However, there seems to be no convincing reason to go beyond the two basic methods of representation of information to explain these phenomena.

7.4. The ontogeny of human intelligence: sensorimotor modelling, imitation, and language

The basic processes so far dealt with have been sensorimotor associations in the cognitive and operant modes, together with the further composite process—novelty detection and contextual representation. Although these processes, acting in concert, can account for a number of the most important features of mammalian learning, it is not immediately clear that they also underlie the psychological functions which distinguish man from most other mammals. In this section three functions will be considered, which, while not unique to man (or even to mammals for that matter), are regarded as closely related to one another, and to the gradual emergence, in the evolution of the higher primates, of what is regarded as characteristically human intelligence.

These three functions are:

(i) the capacity to build up internal models of action in advance of, and in preparation for the action itself, that is, the capacity for thought;

(ii) the capacity for imitation;

(iii) the linguistic faculty. Descriptions of such functions usually employ a conceptual language very different from that which has been employed so far in this book (exemplified in the writings of J. Piaget, to take one instance). The present section is thus an essay in translation, and aims to show that at least the early steps in development of human intelligence (as Piaget might describe them) can be given equivalent descriptions in the biological terms used here. The functions we are to deal with are thus not to be regarded as radically different from those already considered, but are the properties which emerge unpredictably, when the size of the brain, and especially the size of the areas of association cortex, is greatly increased, as it is in the higher primates.

7.4.1. SENSORIMOTOR MODELLING

The first of these functions becomes clear when we compare the schema proposed for integrated operation of cortex and striatum (Figs. 10 and 12) with what is known of the behaviour of the higher primates. Consider a classic example of a problem: a bunch of bananas is visible high up in a chimpanzee's cage, but out of reach, and around the cage are the various means by which the chimpanzee can reach the bananas—a couple of boxes and a long stick. Simple problems of this nature can be solved by an adult chimpanzee, on first exposure to it (Köhler 1927) and without the simplistic trial and error learning supposed to operate in acquisition of simpler tasks by simpler animals. In more complex examples, the chimpanzee may manipulate the various useful objects into various combinations before the solution is reached, but again, the first correct performance of the task is not a simple function of random behaviour: the preliminary manipulations are obviously attempts to find a means to a predetermined end. There may be a considerable delay between presentation of the problem and finding the solution. It is therefore apparent that there is a clear separation between formulation of the ends or goals, and deriving the means which can best serve those ends (a distinction which Piaget also recognizes in infants beyond the age of about nine months). It is also apparent that internal computation ('thinking') is a necessary preliminary to solution of such problem. We seem to have a sympathetic understanding of the chimpanzee's approach to solving similar problems. On the basis of this we may hazard a guess that the internal computations in the example above amount to internalized combinations of representations of the various means to the end, in various permutations, until the point of insight is reached, where the correct solution is realized. Only after this is performance initiated.

These features have no representation in the schema of Figs. 10 and 12. If, however, allowance is made for a greater amount of information processing in the cortical network, a plausible account of such problem solving behaviour can be offered. This is illustrated in Fig. 15.

The key to understanding Fig. 15 is the role of the class of neurones, labelled X, contained within the enclosure (broken rectangle) which is part of the cortical network. These neurones encode the relationships of contiguity which occur between two sources of input to the cortex: (i) the motor programmes relayed to the cortex, from basal ganglia and elsewhere, which define particular acts; (ii) the sensory circumstances in which an act is performed and the changes in sensory circumstances—the 'consequences'—resulting from the act.* Neurones such as X, therefore, come to represent the associations which exist between possible means and possible ends. These neurones, for short, will be referred to as 'command neurones'. This is a terminology used in various ways by neurobiologists. Its usage here

*The term 'consequence' is used here, rather than 'effect', because the latter term has been reserved for influences of significance for primary motives of an animal. The term 'consequence' is used in a wider sense, covering influences of the animal upon the environment regardless of their bearing on basic motivational systems.

corresponds most closely to that of Mountcastle *et al.* (1975) who refer to command functions for some of the neurones in monkey parietal cortex. These neurones responded most specifically during acts of reaching for objects of apparent interest. However, according to Rolls, Perrett, Thorpe, Puerto, Roper-Hall, and Maddison (1979) responses of neurones in this area are not specifically linked to stimuli of primary motivational significance. These neurones may well be the true counterpart of those suggested here on theoretical grounds.

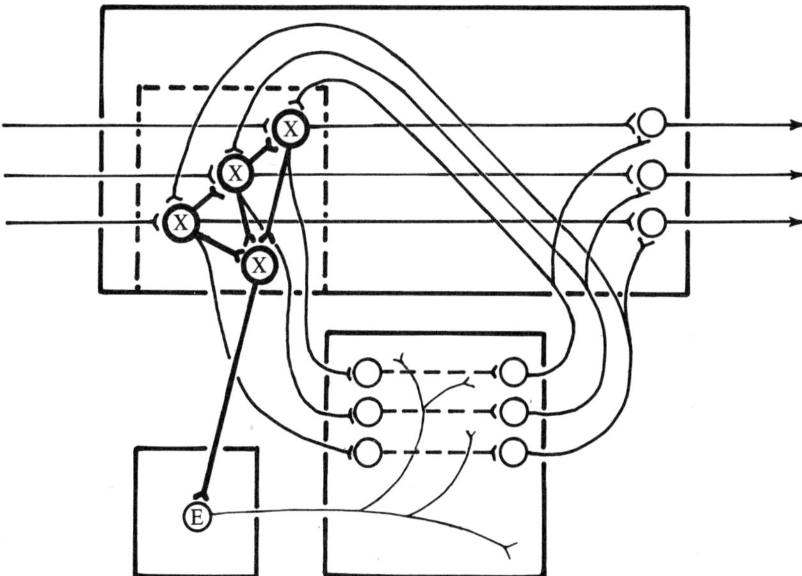

FIG. 15. See text p. 172. Diagram to illustrate the network of connections required for sensorimotor modelling. The upper rectangle represents the neocortex; the lower squares the striatum (large) and the reinforcement system (small). The enclosure in the upper rectangle contains neurones ((X)——) called 'command neurones' (p. 172) whose interconnections can perform sensorimotor modelling functions, in advance of actual initiation of any action. They receive inputs from sensory systems (upper left) and from motor systems (recurrent connections from striatum). They thus link means with ends. They can influence the reinforcement systems, and the striatum. Once the correct model of action has been discovered, they can thus 'open' pathways which can lead to initiation of this action.

In so far as any one means can serve various ends, and any one end can be met by various means, as circumstances dictate, so the connections within the enclosure in Fig. 15 will not be simply 'one to one' links, but will constitute a complex network of inhibitory and excitatory relationships, encoding a cross-classification of generalizations and discriminations, as elsewhere in the cortical network. Thus, just as the cortex in its sensory associative role comes to form a 'model' of the external world as viewed by a 'passive observer', so this particular set of cortical neurones comes to form a model of the external world as viewed by an 'active observant agent' or 'experimenter'.

With this concept of command neurones in mind, we are in a position to reconsider the chimpanzee's problem. Four classes of command neurone seem to be relevant to this problem: (i) command neurones which link together the act of stacking boxes with the possible consequences of this act; (ii) those linking the act of standing on something with its consequences; (iii) those linking the act of waving a stick in the air, with its consequences; (iv) those linking the act of reaching upwards, and its consequences. It must be assumed that the synapses which define the functions of each of these four classes of neurone have already attained their strengthened form, as a result of prior exposure to many circumstances in which each of the above acts might have been used. In the problem we are considering each of the first three classes of neurone would to some degree be activated by the corresponding objects in the environment. The fourth one may also be activated if an object well out of reach happens to be included in the same generalization as 'interesting objects within reach' with which the fourth class of neurones is likely to be concerned. In any event, none of the four classes of command neurones by itself represents a sensorimotor program which can acquire for the chimpanzee the bunch of bananas. Yet the animal, whom we assume to be hungry, recognizes, on the basis of past associations, that there are bananas to be had which can satisfy its hunger.

The key steps in the argument are as follows. 'Stacking boxes', and 'standing upon something' may be regarded as examples of a generalization —'moving nearer the ceiling'. These two, combined with the third class of actions—'waving a stick in the air'—may be regarded as examples of a further generalization—'reaching upwards for an inaccessible but interesting object'—which is subsumed in the generalization with which the fourth class of command neurones deals. Thus, if by chance the first three classes of command neurones happen to be activated in the sequence just mentioned, there will inevitably be a tendency for the fourth class of neurones to be activated finally. To put this in another way, one may say that if the cognitive modelling of each of the three subsidiary classes of command neurones is an accurate and fairly complete representation of its sensorimotor scheme, then the combined sequential activation of these three classes will inevitably tend to activate the fourth class. The reliability with which this actually occurs will depend on exactly what the general context of cerebral activity is at the time. More reliable model building will be possible if a context is present suitable for 'spatial operations in the vertical dimension', than if some other contextual representation is activated. If the model can be constructed as far as this, the next step would be the jump from 'reaching upwards for an inaccessible but interesting object' to 'obtaining food'. In previous experience of a chimpanzee, the former must very often have preceded the latter, so it also is a likely further consequence of continued neural activity.

Once the representation of 'obtaining food' has been activated, the positive reinforcement system is also likely to be activated, even though no food has been obtained yet, and no coherent action performed (just as in Fig. 12). Any striatal synapses which have been put in a 'state of readiness' as a result of command neurones firing, and any tendency to initiate actions, will thus be encouraged. The final decision to initiate action would probably depend on convergent activation of motor cortical neurones, partly from associated command neurones in the cortex, partly by input from the striatum. This cannot however occur until the right combination and sequence of activation of command neurones has occurred, for without this the internal triggering of the positive reinforcement system would not occur.

Activation of the correct combination of command neurones, in the correct sequence, does not occur automatically. It has to await the moment of coincidence, when the right context is present, and the right timing of activity in the different classes of neurones actually occurs. This may take some time, and be accompanied by a variety of abortive attempts at action (as actually described by Köhler, 1927). However, in so far as problem solving can occur without such trial and error behaviour, one may regard it as a function of internalized trial and error processes, possible only in an already well constructed model, after prior learning of the types of achievement that can be expected of a large range of possible acts. In this limited sense there can be no problem solving which is genuinely creative.

The real achievement in such behaviour is not a magical sort of foreknowledge, but a skilled employment of a variety of internalized combinations. Other examples of the same process will be considered shortly, when discussing imitative and liguistic functions. Correct modelling and prediction by such internalized combination does not occur of necessity. In any particular example of correct modelling, the internalized operations (or thoughts) are valid only in so far as the right rules of combination are used in any one circumstance, and these rules must have been acquired in past experience of similar circumstances. To put this in biological language, combinations of neurones have no power to predict unambiguously, unless the general context of neural activity is appropriate. Thus one might need a different context of activity for spatial operations (such as the chimpanzee's problem above) compared with that needed in imitation. Even though similar groupings of command neurones were employed in both circumstances, the act which is modelled, as the culmination of these combinations, would be quite different according to the context which was present. In thinking up a complex new strategy of action a far more powerful act of insight is required if a large number of acts are to be co-ordinated than if a small number of acts are to be used in concert. These more powerful acts of insight will require either longer periods of unexpressed neural activity, or alternatively will require far more precise definition of the context in which modelling operations are to be performed. The necessity of having the correct context for any sensorimotor modelling seems to correspond well with the common human experience that thoughts follow one another along certain lines, but that it is easy to interrupt a train of thought with distracting stimuli.

The question may well be raised whether sensorimotor modelling has any learning component included in it, rather than being merely a function displayed by a well-formed neural network, without modification of connections therein. Probably, learning (i.e. synaptic modification) *is* involved, for as we have seen (p. 112) the neural representation is never static, but is always in a state of flux; a particular example of sensorimotor modelling can be regarded as part of the more general and continuous remodelling of cortical connections referred to earlier. Thus, we can still preserve the notion that learning is the most fundamental of the processes occurring within consciousness, because thought has a component of learning.

7.4.2. IMITATION

With the above schema in mind for the prior modelling in thought of an untried strategy of action we can move on to another related component of human intelligence, the capacity to imitate. The importance of this faculty is indicated by the fact that a large component of what an adult has learnt, especially in the linguistic area, is learnt by imitation. This begs the question 'by what logical processes is imitation itself possible?' Piaget and Inhelder (1969) addressed themselves to this problem, and more recently others have also considered it (for a review, see Parton 1976). As a developmental sequence, three stages can be recognized. (i) The infant 'imitates himself', matching his own responses in simple interactive actions. Infant babbling, or the games an infant may play whilst watching his own fingers or toes, are examples of this process. (ii) The infant matches the responses of another person when these responses are ones the infant has seen himself perform. (iii) The infant matches the responses of another when these responses are not in the infant's own repertoire of actions.

To explain the first of these stages, two premises need to be combined. We need, on the one hand, the command neurone function, which, in this case, links together representation of an act with that of the most immediate consequences of the act—the sight of fingers and limbs actually set in motion, or the sound produced by vocal acts. On the other hand, we require the functions of novelty detection and exploration, discussed in Section 7.2. Given these two premises, an infant will inevitably tend to reiterate an act, as a form of exploratory behaviour, in order to familiarize himself with all new aspects of what he can see or hear of his own behaviour. Parton (1976) has summarized some evidence consistent with this explanation. In infants who are blind at birth, iterative motor responses which are easily visible to a normal infant (e.g. finger games) were not present. Likewise in infants deaf from birth, iterative babbling fades very rapidly during development, compared with normal infants.

The extension from here to the second stage depends on the circumstance of someone performing, in front of a child, a gesture which the child has just made (see Piaget and Inhelder 1969). The infant perceives that there are elements of similarity between his view of his own responses, and his view of the other person's. Even though these two views are far from identical, the other person's gesture will be subsumed in one of the generalizations represented in the child's network of command neurones pertaining to the child's own acts. Performance of a simple act by another person will therefore tend to elicit roughly comparable acts from the child. Consistent with such an explanation is Piaget's observation that imitative acts of a child involving the parts of the child's body which the child can actually see, or vocal imitation (which is also within the scope of direct perception) are acquired earlier than imitation involving facial expression. Facial musculature, being invisible to the child, cannot be controlled for imitative purposes until far more powerful schemes of generalization are available to the child than those directly dependent upon perception. It should be pointed out that Piaget's evidence has been questioned by some (see Parton 1976). In part, this may result from a study of facial movements which are specifically linguistic in function, since vocal and linguistic imitation is, according to Piaget's idea, likely to develop early.

The third category of imitation (involving acts that have not hitherto been in the child's repertoire) has a rather similar explanation to the problem solving test considered earlier, in that it involves combinatorial skills of the infant. For instance, to imitate a certain word pronunciation a child has to find the right combination of already-present vocal command neurones to model the new sound. If the child already has a wide range of vocal command neurones, there is a possibility that a combination might be selected, which on first trial, is a fairly good imitation of the pronunciation required. The more likely possibility, however, is that there will initially be substantial discrepancy. The child will perceive this discrepancy, and as in other examples where sensory input is in some respects discrepant with past experience, will engage in exploratory activity, until all the discrepant features are no longer discrepant. In this case the exploratory activity will consist of repeated attempts to find increasingly accurate ways of producing the required sound.

7.4.3. LINGUISTIC FUNCTIONS

The psychological faculty which is most distinctively human is, of course, language. The close relationship between language and imitation is clear from the fact that acquisition of a particular language can come about only by contact with that language, almost always in its spoken form. In a language, particular vocal acts or written markings perform the function of signs, signifying something else that is not actually present at the time the sign is used. Piaget and Inhelder (1969) have described a sequence of steps, in which imitation becomes gradually divorced from the feature to be imitated. In the early stages of this process ('symbolic play') a child's acts are still detectable as representations of other events, though in a more or less symbolic form. The child's acts are so to speak response generalizations of the true imitative act. Eventually, acts can come to have the role of signifiers, even when there is no detectable similarity between an act and the events it represents, provided the linkage between the two happens to be an accepted convention amongst the group of individuals who use the particular signifier in a particular way. This is presumably one of the processes which led to the birth of language. However, there is no sharp distinction between symbol and sign functions in language, and present day languages contain some components with a symbolic as well as just a significatory role (e.g. onomatopoeic words, or certain chinese characters which, in origin, are known to be symbolic representations of what they signify).

Linguistic signs are no respectors of the divisions between different channels of sensory input, or of motor output. The meaning of a word may require information from any of these diverse channels for its definition. Moreover, diverse channels may be required for the processes of receiving linguistic messages (understanding speech, reading) and for producing them (speaking, writing). It is clear, therefore, that the cerebral representation of linguistic signs must be in a structure where all types of input (visual, auditory, tactile and so on) converge, and where outputs can influence both bodily motor functions and verbal motor functions. Without this, the associations between a sign and what it is intended to signify could not be established.

Much of the present book has been concerned with formulating 'the omniconnection principle' and discussing its potentialities, its degrees of correspondence to real neural networks, and therefore the shortcomings of such networks. Geschwind (1965*a*) has pointed out that in mammalian species other than primates it is only in the limbic cortex that all sensory inputs converge. The role of such convergence within the hippocampus, in overcoming some of the deficiencies of the neocortical network, was discussed in Section 7.2. Geschwind also points out that in higher primates areas of association cortex also exist in which these multiple convergences of pathways are present, and he speculates that the emergence of linguistic function is closely linked to the development of such areas. In such regions of cortex, particularly in the human cortex, we find another mechanism for overcoming the shortcomings of actual neural networks, compared with the idealized omniconnected network. In these regions, one may imagine that all memories have the potentiality of being re-coded in linguistic form. Although many individual memories themselves may be incapable of interacting and associating with other such memories, nevertheless, after re-coding in linguistic form, the possibilities of thorough intermingling implied by the idealized omniconnection principle will be approached far more closely.

It is not surprising that some students of consciousness regard linguistic ability and consciousness as practically different aspects of the same thing. In particular, Eccles (see Popper and Eccles 1977) regards the left hemisphere, with its specialized language function, as the seat of consciousness, whereas the right is not involved in mediation of consciousness. It should be made clear that this subdivision of function is fitted into a philosophical framework quite different from that adopted in the present work. Here, it seems unnecessary to use the word consciousness in such a restricted sense. If it is acknowledged that the word refers to an ideal which can never be met with in actual practice, then arguments about the precise demarcations of brain regions which do and do not subserve consciousness would appear to be merely semantic in nature.

The ways in which the left hemisphere differs from the right, in order that it can have a special linguistic function, are at present largely a matter of conjecture, though it is expected that many further advances may be made in this field. It is now clear that certain parts of the temporal lobe (planum temporale) are larger on the left side than the right, in most people, and that this difference exists before the age of acquisition of language (Witelson 1977). It has also been reported that there are biochemical asymmetries in the human thalamus, noradrenaline levels being higher on the left than on the right in some nuclei (Oke, Keller, Mefford, and Adams 1978).

At the psychological level there is also plenty of evidence of asymmetrical processing of linguistic information in the two hemispheres. Children subjected to hemidecortication before the age of language acquisition (as a measure to prevent intractable epilepsy of unilateral origin) subsequently can acquire many language functions. In analysis of phonemes, and in apprehension of the meaning of words, there appears to be little difference between right- and left-decorticate children. However, the left-hemidecorticate children are significantly impaired in linguistic functions involving complex syntactic structuring (Dennis and Whitaker 1976). It would appear that the left hemisphere, in some mysterious way, is inherently specialized for syntactic linguistic function, a viewpoint reminiscent of Chomsky's ideas on synactic information processing (Chomsky 1971).

Flexible use of syntax for operations in verbal logic is another example of internal combinational skills. We have already seen that this sort of mental operation can work satisfactorily only if the correct context for these operations has been defined, and its representation set up in the cortical network. It may be, as O'Keefe and Nadel (1978) suggest, that the left hippocampus has a specialized role in establishing the correct semantic context, just as the hippocampus in general seems to be concerned with contexts of other kinds. Such a specialization could underly the radically new form of information processing which develops in humans; the capacity for deductive logic using verbal and other signifiers.

Evidence also exists that the left hemisphere is specialized for linguistic function at a much more basic level than this—namely in analysis of phonemes (as opposed to other non-vocal sound patterns). The particular feature which appears to be important in distinguishing phonemes from other sounds is 'voice onset time'—the interval between an initial consonant and the later initiation of laryngeal vibrations (Eimas, Siqueland, Jusczyk, and Vigorito 1971)—and the ability to make such distinctions exists before the acquisition of language. In dichotic listening tests, it has been found that the right ear possesses significant advantages over the left in perceiving initial and final stop consonants, but not for perception of vowels (Studdert-Kennedy and Shankweiler 1969). Exactly what biological specialization this difference might reflect is unclear. Possibly it could depend upon a preponderance of certain ranges of conduction velocity in the axons connecting with the cortical region performing auditory analysis of phonemes, so that more accurate temporal analysis is possible on one side than on the other. However, it has also been claimed that, in direct assessment of temporal analysis, there is no difference detectable for left- and right-sided stimuli. No doubt other examples of hemispheric specialization await discovery, both at the biological and the psychological level. An integrated account of hemispheric specialization and language function cannot be expected to emerge until more evidence exists than is currently available.

8. Summary and philosophical epilogue

THE final chapter has two aims: firstly, to summarize the main points of the theory constructed in Chapters 2–7, concerning the biological and psychological processes which make up consciousness; and secondly, to reconsider the philosophical issues, initially raised in Chapter 1, in the light of the theory presented in the later chapters.

8.1. Summary of main points of the theory

1. From consideration of the evidence about cerebral localization of function, it is concluded that in a large part of the cerebral hemisphere, particularly the large areas of association cortex and the caudate–putamen, the concept of punctate localization of function does not apply: it appears that the function of such regions can be understood only if large masses of grey matter are considered as integral wholes.
2. Experimental and theoretical considerations suggest that information is represented in these cerebral structures in a distributed holographic fashion. An alternative viewpoint—that discrete portions of information are stored within single neurones—seems untenable.
3. The astronomic number of neuronal connections in the mammalian brain suggests that a major aspect of information storage in the cerebrum involves coding of information in terms of patterns of connections. It seems less likely that 'fields' of electrical activity or sequences of bases in macromolecules can represent information derived from the environment.
4. The notion of meaning, in its most general sense, implies a complex information network of internal relationships between component parts (a Gestalt). If such an information structure is to be represented in connectionist terms, it implies the existence within the brain of diffusely connected neural networks, in which every neurone has the potentiality of influencing every other. Such a network is called an *omniconnected network* here.
5. This omniconnection principle is a simplified, idealized statement of the connectionist basis of conscious processes. In real brain structures direct connection of every neurone with every other is not found. The majority of connections between neurones in a brain structure capable of representing meaning will thus be polysynaptic.
6. On account of the presumed random nature of the omniconnected network which underlies conscious processes, there is no precise theoretical limit to the associations of sensory input which can be represented therein.

Hence information stored in such a structure may represent any of the statistically significant correlations of sensory input relayed to it following environmental stimuli.

7. The actual stable anatomical connections in the forebrain regions mentioned in 1 (above) represent the potential for formation of associative links. Physiological (probably neurochemical) processes are involved in converting potentiality into actuality, in response to environmental stimuli, thus laying down the memory trace as functionally secure connections. There must therefore be mechanisms for modifying security of transmission at synapses in response to the sensory stimuli which are required to be remembered.

8. Modifiability of synaptic connections must apply to inhibitory as well as to excitatory synapses, if the psychological phenomenon of discrimination is to be explained.

9. In any omniconnected structure, the electrophysiological representation of meaning at the neuronal level is a significant change of impulse frequency (either a rise or a fall) which is considerably longer in duration than the 'synaptic millisecond'. The single action potential cannot be distinguished from background noise by the mechanism which triggers alterations in synaptic security. More complex temporal codes in single axons are not involved in the representation of meaning.

10. In attempting to explain learning processes a crucial distinction is made between *cognitive learning* (dependent on sensory input alone) and *operant learning* (which additionally requires feedback of the effects of behaviour).

11. In the context of an omniconnected holographic structure, cognitive learning can be adequately explained if it is assumed: (i) that when activation of an excitatory synapse is contiguous with a significant elevation of activity in the post-synaptic neurone then that synapse will be strengthened; and (ii) when activation of an inhibitory synapse is contiguous with a significant fall in the post-synaptic activity, that synapse will also be strengthened.

12. Operant learning requires a substrate of random behavioural activity from which favourable portions of behaviour can be selected.

13. In operant learning, contiguous activation of pre- and post-synaptic elements (at the microscopic level) cannot explain the selection of portions of behaviour which subsequently have a favourable effect. Feedback of a neural signal (at the macroscopic level), dependent on the effect of a portion of behaviour, cannot specify the synapses whose activation defines that portion of behaviour. If, however, both the microscopic and the macroscopic mechanisms operate together, the former to make a preliminary selection of active synapses (of either sign) on active neurones, the latter to selectively reinforce those of appropriate sign (excitatory or inhibitory), then operant learning can be explained.

14. It is therefore necessary to have independent positive and negative reinforcing systems, capable of influencing excitatory and inhibitory synapses

respectively, plus a sensory analyser which can assess the motivational significance of a portion of behaviour.

15. The major postulates concerning connectivity (see 3, 4, and 5 above) and change in effectiveness of synaptic transmission (see 7, 8, 9, 11, and 13 above), are adequate, when combined, to explain many of the phenomena of discrimination and generalization observed in operant and cognitive learning in mammals. However, these phenomena have somewhat different explanations in the two types of learning.

16. An efficient and plausible way in which cognitive learning could be controlled is by means of one or more diffusely acting chemical mediators, which can exert influence on large numbers of modifiable synapses within a diffuse network.

17. Likewise, it is probable that the twin reinforcement signals must be capable of spreading their influence diffusely in the relevant brain structures, rather than by specific connections, since they may be required to impose their reinforcing influence on any of the synapses of a particular sign within the structure concerned.

18. The two proposed mechanisms involved in modifying synaptic security in sensory and in operant learning are so different from one another that they cannot both occur in the same gross brain structures. Reciprocal excitatory and inhibitory connections necessary for specification of the internal relationships within any Gestalt cannot be formed in the structure in which operant learning takes place.

19. Arguments are presented to suggest that the associative steps taking place in operant learning occur in the caudate–putamen, whose random neuronal activity generates the unspecialized behavioural activity referred to in 12 (above). Synapses in the caudate–putamen are thus supposed to be modulated according to the rules proposed in 13 (above), relying both on contiguity and the law of effect.

20. The cerebral neocortex is supposed to operate on the basis of contiguity alone, as in 11 (above), thus serving the function of cognitive learning.

21. Different regions of cerebral neocortex encode different categories of contiguity based association, in so far as the different regions have different categories of information afferent to them. In addition to forming associations within the sensory inflow, the motor area of the neocortex is capable of forming a permanent record closely related to the operant behaviour acquired in the basal ganglia. Other regions of neocortex are capable of encoding higher-level contiguities between re-entrant signals, representing information which has already been processed to a considerable degree.

22. With such a scheme an animal has a behavioural repertoire which may include a variety of response strategies to any one sensory situation. The role of the striatum in the adult is thus threefold: (i) the detection of correlations

between a response and its effect; (ii) the transference of a representation from striatum to neoçortex; and (iii) the selection of cortical programmes for temporary use, as they become appropriate.

23. In the mammal, the concept of 'consolidation' of a memory has no simple biological substrate, because it is a product of a variety of processes, some related to properties of synapses, others to shifting localization of a memory trace.

24. Temporal aspects of memory coding are discussed. It is suggested that the substantial delays involved in axonal conduction in the slower-conducting intra-cerebral axons can, when combined with the above mentioned mechanisms for modulating synaptic security, account for the encoding into the mnemonic imprint of some of the real-time relationships of sensory and motor sequences.

25. This concept of the representation of temporal information can account for a number of macroscopic (behavioural) features of temporal information processing. In particular, it can explain the 'psychological moment' (the time interval over which elementary integrations of information are carried out) and the pre-integration 'buffer delays'.

26. Short-term memory—the holding of information for fractions of a minute—probably corresponds, in part, to a transient biochemical activation of synapses. Only if activation is repeated within the short-term memory interval will it give rise to cumulative modification of synapses.

27. It is proposed that the diffusely acting modulators required in control of cognitive learning, and in the reinforcement of operant behaviour, are the various monoamine neurotransmitters—noradrenaline, dopamine and serotonin. Evidence is reviewed supporting this idea, in particular that these transmitters act diffusely.

28. Tentative suggestions are made about how the co-operative action of changes in neural activity (resulting in changes in intracellular concentration of various ions), and of monoaminergic influence (resulting in changes in concentration of intracellular cyclic neocleotides), might bring about alterations in synaptic efficacy in the different types of learning.

29. It is proposed that striatal dopamine and 5-hydroxytryptamine are the positive and negative reinforcement systems involved respectively in strengthening excitatory and inhibitory synapses. The most direct evidence in favour of these postulates concerns acquisition of active and passive operant responses, and intracranial self-stimulation and avoidance phenomena. In so far as the evidence currently available is incomplete, predictions are made. The role of these two monoamines in several other related types of behaviour is also discussed.

30. In the scheme proposed for operant learning it is essential that the pathways carrying the twin reinforcement signals carry a temporal pattern of reinforcement. Emphasis is therefore placed on the difference between directly and indirectly acting agonists of the transmitters involved, since only

the latter would be able to mimic or enhance normal processes of reinforcement involved in operant learning.

31. The role of neocortical monoamines in control of the level of consciousness, and in other cognitive and quasi-cognitive functions is discussed. The tentative suggestion is made that neocortical catecholamines and serotonin are necessary neurohumors for modulation of excitatory and inhibitory synapses in the cortex. If this is so, it is argued that neocortical catecholamine depletion will result in partial deficits in learning ability (applying particularly to long-term storage processes rather than initial acquisition), and in a reduction of the flexibility by which a sensorimotor programme already established in the cortex can be overridden during subsequent learning. Much evidence is compatible with these inferences.

32. Certain features of Parkinson's disease, and of psychotic disturbances of thinking, can be explained in the context of this discussion of the relations of monoamines to behaviour. Suggestions are made of theoretical limitations which are likely to apply to therapy of neurological and psychiatric disturbances resulting from deficiencies of central neurotransmitters.

33. Consideration is given to the acquisition of sequences of behaviour, where goal-fulfilment occurs only at the end of the sequence. In part, this faculty can be explained by sequential association ('chaining') applying simultaneously in the cognitive and the operant mode, that is, as a by-product of the interaction of neocortex and striatum. In this process, the response which is learned last is that which is least directly related to goal-fulfilment.

34. An additional concept required for many instances of acquisition of sequences of behaviour, is that of a 'drive'. The biological representation of a drive seems to be a slowly developing, and slowly dissipating signal which acts diffusely, and can form associations with other signals concurrently represented in connectionist form. The drive signals, being simple but pervasive, may be mediated by diffusely acting chemical transmitters—possibly by some of the various neuropeptides.

35. The overall form envisaged for the neural networks in which learning occurs is such that each neurone may be the site at which a variety of separate associations are coded. Moreover, each identifiable associative group is represented in a variety of neurones. These features confer greater stability upon the network, and increase its total information capacity. However, they limit the rate at which information can be acquired without confusion in coding.

36. The multiple roles of each neurone in the network implies that retrieval of memories cannot always be accomplished unambiguously, unless the overall spatio–temporal pattern of activity established in the network is similar to that which was present during acquisition.

37. To allow unambiguous retrieval of information it is therefore necessary to acquire representations of global contexts in which portions of information are gained, so that with the aid of this representation the spatio–temporal

pattern of activity present during acquisition may be reconstructed during retrieval.

38. From consideration of connections, gross electrical activity, single unit studies, and lesion studies of the *hippocampus*, it seems probable that this structure can construct contextual representations and can reconstruct them given adequate cues.

39. It is not yet possible to construct a neuronal model of the hippocampus, except in rather general terms. The basic logical functions of this structure have not yet been defined with sufficient precision for this to be accomplished.

40. The faculty of introspection is viewed as a potentially investigable phenomenon, both in man and animals. In scientific terms this faculty corresponds to the fact that some, but not all, internal states of the central nervous system can come to act as cues for behaviour, just as external stimuli can.

41. Some of these internal states may be discriminable because they specifically activate certain drive systems. Others may be discriminable because the hippocampus can register them as contexts.

42. The combined operation of neocortex, striatum and hippocampus allows, within the cortex, a certain degree of sensorimotor modelling of the way in which parts of the environment may be expected to behave. This depends particularly on the existence of neocortical neurones which can establish associations between the means and the ends involved in a particular behaviour. (These are called 'command' neurones here.) Provided the appropriate context of cerebral activity is established, such models can be used for predictive (deductive) purposes. The operation of these modelling functions corresponds to our thoughts. They can be used to trigger behavioural actions, whose programme has been established without the trial and error strategy of simple operant learning.

43. The development of imitative abilities in higher primates is a faculty which emerges out of sensorimotor modelling processes. Linguistic ability emerges likewise from imitative skills. Neither of these demands radically different modes of cerebral information processing from those considered earlier.

44. Information, for processing in the brain, is represented in three ways. (i) As trains of impulses in neural networks, in which the category of information is specified by the particular connections the impulse invades. (ii) As trains of impulses in fibre systems which release diffusely acting transmitters, whose pharmacological activity after release is short-lived. Such signals can convey temporal patterns, but not spatial patterns. (iii) As trains of impulses releasing long-lived neuromodulators. Such substances are capable of signalling neither spatial nor temporal patterns, but on account of their chemical diversity and the specialization of corresponding pharmacological receptors, they can perform vital and specific functions within the brain.

45. It is possible to identify some of the features of brain organization giving

rise to the subjective fact of the unity of consciousness. (i) Diffuse networks of connections, approximating to the idealized omniconnected network. (ii) Diffusely acting neurotransmitters. (iii) Information processing by the hippocampus which forms a global representation of all information impinging upon the cerebral cortex, though one in which detailed representations are lacking. (iv) In *man*, the acquisition of linguistic functions. The last two of these four constitute ways of overcoming the inadequacies of real neural networks compared with the idealized form of an omniconnected network.

8.2. Varieties of inference and brain mechanisms

In Chapter 1, attention was drawn to the fundamental difference between two ways of deriving conclusions from premises, namely, inductive and deductive inference. *Inductive inference* is argument from a number of *particular* data to a *general* statement which subsumes all these data and leads us to expect further instances of this general statement. Typically, if a pattern of events has occurred sufficiently often in the past we come to believe it will recur in the future in the same way. Many of the learning paradigms which have been considered in earlier chapters are formally equivalent to inductive inference. In classical conditioning, repeated particular instances of pairing a conditioning stimulus with an unconditioned stimulus cause the animal to acquire the general propensity to respond to the conditioning stimulus as it does to the unconditioned stimulus. Learning to recognize patterns (both spatial and temporal) is a form of inductive inference, for a pattern is a generality formed by repeated association of the components of the pattern, in previous experience. Formulation, and verbal labelling of concepts, in man, appears to be a sophisticated example of the same faculty. Many examples of goal-seeking behaviour in animals reflect a capacity for a form of inductive inference, for, at least in lower mammals, such behaviour is commonly acquired as a result of repeated examples in which a particular action has been followed by reward or punishments. In the above types of learning, the requirement for overt instances of repetition is not a rigid one. The time scale in which a 'single instance' of a learning situation is likely to occur is usually sufficiently prolonged for hidden repetitions of neural activation to take place. It is thus common to find examples of single-trial learning, especially if intense or distinctive stimuli are used.

Statements resulting from inductive inference were labelled 'synthetic statements' by Kant, as in his example: 'All bodies are heavy'. Statements based on recurrent observations, that is empirical statements, are always of this type (though as we see below, Kant argued against the converse proposition, that all synthetic statements are necessarily empirical). For statements based on inductive inference, the conclusion is not guaranteed by the individual premises, but only made to greater or lesser extent probable, depending on the number of instances included in the premises.

Deductive inference is the derivation of one or more *particular* conclusions from a given *general* premise. In its simplest form, deduction merely involves transferring to the conclusion something that it already stated in a premise, or in the definition of one of the terms used in the premise. Elementary syllogisms are of this form. Such arguments adhere merely to two rules: (i) that conclusion and premise should not be in contradiction; (ii) the conclusion requires no other premises than the stated one to establish its veracity. In animal behaviour one can see a formal similarity between such simple deductive inferences and *performances* of an act based on internal programs —whether hereditary, or acquired by learning—in which a generalization about sensorimotor relationships can give rise to a variety of particular instances of behaviour.

Statements resulting from deductive inferences were labelled 'analytic statements' by Kant, as in his statement: 'All bodies are extended'. Statements based on deductive inference require no input of external information, though to perform deductive inference, information from the environment may have been stored in the past. Considered simply as a form of inference, therefore, deduction is non-empirical, or (as Kant called it) *a priori*. In the simple classes of deductive inference mentioned so far, none of the conclusions are very different from the premises. However, the premises guarantee the conclusion absolutely. If the former are correct the latter *must* be correct, and probability and degrees of correctness are not involved.

A more impressive form of inference than the simple syllogism arises when complex combinations of premises are used to frame a deductive argument, in which case the possible conclusions are not so obvious as in the typical syllogisms. For instance, I might have reason to believe the following premises:

about cats: they have four legs; they have whiskers; they make a purring noise; they like cream; etc.

about cream: it is tasty with apricots; it floats at the top of the milk; it costs 30 cents a bottle; etc.

about the contents of my pocket: it contains 30 cents; a penknife; a handkerchief; etc.

about the next street: it has a dairy; a church; a hairdresser; etc.

By choosing the appropriate combination of premises here, I can arrive at a much more substantial conclusion than is possible in a simple syllogism. For instance I might conclude that 'I can buy a bottle of cream at the dairy to feed the cat'. To establish the veracity of any of the premises in such an argument, empirical observations may be needed. However in the argument itself, all individual steps are deductive, constrained solely by the rule of contradiction, so the argument is non-empirical. The argument as a whole brings together a number of particular premises to reach a conclusion, and therefore, in terms of our definition, it also has an inductive element. Likewise, referring to Kant's definition of a synthetic statement, the conclusion is not implicit in any of the premises, and so this statement must be classed as synthetic. However, unlike synthetic statements arrived at empirically, the premises in the above argument guarantee the conclusions absolutely.

The examples given by Kant of 'synthetic *a priori*' statements are rather different from that given above, and generally refer to mathematical statements about spatial or numerical relationships. For instance, statements such as '$7+5=12$' or 'A straight line between two points is the shortest' are classed by Kant as 'synthetic *a priori*.' He writes: 'For my conception of "straight" contains no notion of quantity but is merely qualitative. The conception of the *shortest* is therefore wholly an addition, and by no analysis can it be extracted from our conception of a straight line.' (*Critique of Pure Reason*.) Despite their different appearance there is some merit in placing these examples in the same class as that given above. They are, in reality, statements derived by complex arguments, in which a number of hidden premises are contained in a single word, number, or phrase, so that combinatorial processes must be used to infer the predicate of a statement from the subject(s). For instance, the concept of a line cannot be defined without the concept of space, and implicit in this is the notion that lines may be compared in length.

To relate this discussion to hypothetical brain mechanisms, it may be noted that logical operations involving internal combinations cannot be accomplished, unless the context of cerebral activity in which representation of items of information are 'located', is the appropriate one for the task in hand. A single word, or number, can act as a cue to this context and can thus draw upon far more information than is overtly specified in the word itself. The context thus defines the rules of operation permitted between items. Conclusion of such combinatorial arguments may make use of a wide range of assumptions contained within the context, as well as the overt premises of the argument. Kant's class of 'synthetic *a priori*' statements thus appears to be a valid one, if regarded as a psychological category, if not as a category necessary in pure mathematical logic.

Animals display a limited capacity for logical operations of this combinatorial, or context-dependent type. A simple example is the ability of animals to solve short-cut problems. Other examples are the chimpanzee's ability to solve the problem (p. 172) in which tools had to be used to gain access to an out of reach bunch of bananas. Likewise McGonigle and Chalmers (1977) showed that monkeys could solve a problem in which the correct response depended on understanding the abstract concept of a sequence. The faculty for combinatorial deductive inference appears to emerge as a high-order property, dependent upon the more basic features of mammalian intelligence —the capacity for inductive inference.

The most sophisticated use of combinations and chains of deductive reasoning undoubtedly is that displayed by human beings. Their use of formalized techniques in mathematics and philosophy has developed within historical time, and is largely connected with the development of signs for linguistic communication. The explicit recognition of the difference between inductive and deductive inferences goes back to the ancient Greeks, who were perhaps the first to use long chains of deductive reasoning. In fact, to this day, the degree to which such reasoning is habitually used probably varies a good deal from one human culture to another. For instance, Russell (1946) comments that since Pythagoras, Western philosophy has adopted a different attitude to reasoning from Eastern philosophy.

After the Renaissance a critical approach was adopted to what had been accepted doctrines, and strict deductive inference was one of the methods used in this approach. To illustrate this one can do no better than quote Descartes, the first modern philosopher:

> From noticing many things that seem . . . extravagant and ridiculous, but are none the less commonly accepted and approved . . . I learnt not to believe too firmly anything that I had been convinced of only by example and custom. . . . I thought I must reject as absolutely false anything as to which I could imagine the least doubt, in order to see if I should not be left at the end believing something that was absolutely indubitable . . . Those long chains of perfectly simple and easy reasonings by means of which geometers are accustomed to carry out their most difficult demonstrations has led me to fancy that everything that can fall under human knowledge forms a similar sequence; and that so long as we avoid accepting as true what is not so, and always preserve the right order for deduction of one thing from another, there can be nothing too remote to be reached in the end, or too well hidden to be discovered. (*Discours de la Méthode, 1637.*)

A hundred years later Hume applied Descartes' method with devastating consequences. Using deductive reasoning alone he argued that every conclusion based on inductive inference is suspect. From this argument, we have no right to expect the sun to rise tomorrow in its usual place, or that sugar will always taste sweet. The profound influence he has had right up to the present century is illustrated well by Bertrand Russell's (1946) comments:

> He [Hume] represents in a certain sense a dead end: in his direction it is impossible to go further. To refute him has been, ever since, a favourite pastime amongst metaphysicians. For my part, I find none of their refutations convincing: nevertheless I cannot but hope that something less sceptical than Hume's system may be discoverable.

It is unlikely that Russell's hope will ever be fulfilled if we remain firmly convinced of the critical method which major philosophers have adopted since the time of Descartes. Deductive reasoning has never been able to, nor intended to produce infallible conclusions starting from nothing. The Geometers, who so impressed Descartes, always started from assumed statements, or axioms. The conclusions of any such argument could always be undermined by questioning the axioms. Thus, if the goal we set ourselves is nothing less than to derive perfectly infallible knowledge, deductive inference, by itself, has an inherent paradox just as deep as that inherent in inductive inference.

In the face of this, we might decide to abandon this lofty goal, and adopt a more mundane one—to provide for ourselves a credible and useful set of beliefs, in the awareness that such beliefs are potentially refutable. With such an approach we find that inductive and deductive inference can work harmoniously together towards our goal. Our preliminary beliefs (or hypotheses) are formulated using inductive methods, and can then be subsequently tested against further items of information using deductive methods. Sometimes these further items of information may be incompatible with our beliefs, and yet not be sufficient to force us to change them, since these items themselves may involve many questionable assumptions and may involve inductive inference in their discovery. (This comment has especial relevance when we study an entity as complex as the brain, where any experimental finding rests upon many subsidiary findings for its significance.) In other instances the weight of contradictory items of evidence may be sufficient to warrant overthrowing a previously cherished set of ideas. However, the point at which this happens cannot be formalized rigorously. In the first instance, it depends on a subjective assessment of all available evidence, by someone who is capable of grasping it all simultaneously. His or her belief comes prior to any testing, verification, or refutation.

Thus, deduction and induction should interact in a subtle and delicate balance. If we accept conclusions based on inductive inference too easily, without checking against sufficient relevant data, we will make fatal mistakes. If deductive reasoning becomes overprominent, our system of beliefs collapses into meaninglessness. In the end the decision as to what we believe must be a personal one, and infallible public demonstration of 'the correct beliefs' is logically unattainable.

All this is no more than a dissection of common sense. But there is nevertheless in present times a profound equivocation about the right approach to formulation and testing of beliefs. Polanyi (1958) in a chapter entitled 'Critique of Doubt' wrote:

> It remains deeply ingrained on the modern mind—as I find even in my own mind—that though doubt may become nihilistic and imperil thereby all freedom of thought, to refrain from belief is always an act of intellectual probity as compared with the resolve to hold a belief which we could abandon if we decided to do so.

Inductive inference, the prime method by which we formulate beliefs, is always suspect because it does not provide absolutely certain knowledge; whereas deduction is always looked upon more favourably, because, though it can never provide us with anything to believe, it can always prevent us from holding false beliefs. Many of us have a psychological block against expressing belief. We are afraid of the risks involved.

The two themes forming the background for the earlier chapters of this book were: (i) to provide a possible biological parallel of the subjective fact of the unity of consciousness; (ii) to suggest a mechanism whereby associative learning in both the operant and cognitive modes might be possible, that is to show how we may apprehend meanings and formulate purposive behaviour. (Such processes may now be included under the general category of 'inductive inference'.) It turns out that all the major premises which have been put forward in answer to the first of these two conundrums also happen to be part of the answer put forward for the second of these two. It is evident that the capacity for inductive inference is an integral and necessary part of the notion of a unified consciousness. Any alternative mechanism which could perform the same logical functions could be said to possess consciousness, though it might approximate the idealized condition of consciousness in a rather different way from our own minds.

The capacity for inductive inference depends crucially on the existence of large random neural networks, and therefore also depends on the remarkable anatomical complexity of a typical nerve cell. As a result of this any conclusion derived by this inductive machinery cannot be discovered at any particular locus, but is a property of the whole. It is also clear from the discussion in Section 7.4 that combinatorial deductive inference also demands a random neural network. On the other hand, the simple examples of deduction, such as syllogisms (Kant's analytic statements) do not demand such a network, though the connections by which such an inference is made may be 'embedded within' such a network. Thus, Kant's 'synthetic *a priori*' category appears to be comparable with other examples of synthetic statements, in terms of its necessary biological basis, even though, on the grounds of the certainty of the conclusion in relation to the premises, it can be classed as deductive.

The theory of brain mechanisms put forward here is, as has been stated earlier, no more than a mental construct, though it was constructed as a model of reality. Imagine, however, that some colossal machine intelligence whose mode of operation was beyond our comprehension arrived on this planet, and commenced investigation of the human species. It might eventually form some sort of representation of the way our brains operated, and included in this representation might be the two very curious properties of human mentality—the integration of the *self*, and the capacity for inductive inference. Thus, we may imagine that these properties could be given a completely objective description. In fact, however, for us these aspects of human nature are presented in a totally different way. We do not derive these macroscopic properties by first considering how all the elements of our nervous system are put together and interact as a mechanism. We *are* that mechanism, and we *are* the whole within which induced conclusions can come to dwell. We apprehend these aspects of our nature in a truly *a priori* sense. Some of us may be equivocal about them when faced with the complex task of understanding how they could be possible. But to deny the existence of these things, and our capacity to form beliefs on the basis of induction, is to deny a major aspect of our consciousness. Such a denial seems to rest on the assumption, far more remarkable than the acceptance of inductive inference, that we as individuals, or as a species, are capable of evaluating our own brain mechanisms and of comparing them with something we suppose to be a more effective intelligence. In so far as induction is fallible we are driven to conclude that the Designer of Brains had clearly in mind, when he designed human nature, the old warning: 'He who never makes a mistake never makes anything else.'

What factors can or should determine whether we believe or distrust a potentially fallible statement? In Chapter 6 (p. 142), mention was made of the concept of a 'set point', a property of brain mechanisms for associative inference, which determines whether a particular associative link should be accepted as a valid indicator of linkage of entities in the environment, or rejected as mere coincidence. We do not have to be very observant about human nature to know that such an hypothetical 'set point' seems to be set at many different positions in different human beings—ranging from the melancholy sceptic to the credulous dupe, from the obsessively fastidious to the artist who cannot escape from the flight of his own ideas. The position of this set point determines all acts of human belief, including our allegiance to scientific theories, or our decision to change allegiance. Shift the set point in one direction and we will prevent all change in scientific ideas. Shift it in the other and we will be overwhelmed with new ideas, some brilliant, some hare-brained nonsense. In Chapter 6 a number of ideas were suggested as to what might be the biological basis of this set point. However, the question posed above concerns the *functional significance* of this set point rather than its biological basis. Is the position of the set point arbitrary, or are some positions more useful than others, and if so, can we determine the optimum position?

When Hume first advanced his sceptical philosophy modern science was in its infancy. Although many of the leading thinkers of the day believed that the complexities of the observable world could ultimately be analysed into a variety of regular logical relationships, the abundant everyday illustrations of such regularity, which impress us today, were not so overwhelmingly clear at that time. Nor had the concept of organic evolution been formulated in a credible form. In succeeding years, vast areas of precise understanding have been revealed—physics, on the largest and smallest scales imaginable, chemistry, genetics, microbiology, physiology, pharmacology, and molecular biology, to name but a few. In all these areas important principles have been established which allow a proportion of hitherto unpredictable events in the world to be predicted, and sometimes to be controlled. The growth of science has thus made it widely credible that nature obeys systematic causal principles.

However, science does not, and cannot, prove that the world is free from caprice. Indeed it would be quite naïve to think we lived in a world that was basically predictable in all its aspects. Where a large number of interdependent variables are involved the extent to which predictions can be made is highly circumscribed. Examples of disciplines in which such constraints on prediction apply are: meteorology, ecology, psychology, and especially those disciplines (whose inclusion amongst the sciences is questionable), where large numbers of human beings are in interaction with one another—such as economics, geography, history, politics. Amongst the latter we must also class Darwin's theory of evolution. This is without doubt an underlying context to most of biology, and holds together an enormous range of otherwise disconnected facts in a form which compels widespread belief. However this theory could never be tested in its entirety, and its predictive power is very limited. We could no more predict the course of evolution in the next 100 000 years than we could have predicted the rise of Alexander the Great or Genghis Khan. The concept of causality—of the regularity of the natural world—seems of little practical use in such cases.

Despite the advance of science, the world we inhabit, and in which we evolve, is therefore, as always, in part predictable, in part capricious. Though unquestionable prediction of distant events is seldom possible, there are enough regularities in the world for it to be an evolutionary advantage to be able to detect them. This presumably is the 'environmental pressure' which has led to the evolution of mechanisms for inductive inference. An organism which has been endowed with such mechanisms, but yet is constrained to avoid making a decision about the likely course of events, until such a time as his prediction amounts to virtual certainty, would be overtaken by events. Such is the fate of the sceptic, in whom the 'set point' is at one extreme. An organism which makes decisions, on the basis of hunches which are very far from certain, may well be the first to recognize the shape of things to come, but will make so many mistakes as well that he also will be at considerable risk. Such is the fate of the credulous, in whom the 'set point' is at the opposite extreme. Thus, the 'set point' is not arbitrary but has evolved by compromise, or 'trade-off' between two different types of risk attendant upon inductive inference.

There is no certain way in which we can specify what should be the balance point in any situation. To do so, we would need to have a complete understanding of our environment already, so that we know which of all its aspects were regular, which were capricious, which had threatening implications for us, and to what degree they were threatening. Nevertheless we do seem to have some ability to assess where the 'set point' should be in different circumstances. In some situations we are happy to be credulous, in others we think it more appropriate to be sceptical. Such judgements cannot, however, be strictly formalized, but are another interesting facet of our capacity to believe, in the face of uncertainty. Those animals and humans, who by chance happen to have the right balance between scepticism and credulity in any particular circumstance, cannot be proved right on logical grounds, though evolution may prove them right in the end.

Let any modern-day sceptic, who is still doubtful about the usefulness of inductive inference as a method, consider the following two questions. (i) Is it not highly credible that there are regular principles governing the behaviour of at least some aspects of nature? (ii) Is not the theory of origin of species by natural selection also highly credible? If these two premises by chance are granted, then it may be concluded that a capacity for inductive inference would be an evolutionary advantage for any species that possessed it.

The scientific laws which describe the regularities in our environment may be divided into two types—'categorical' and 'statistical' laws. The former have arisen because it has been possible to isolate entities which, in themselves, are so simple that their interactions are predictable. In the case of the latter, we are dealing with large numbers of entities together, and though we can predict with considerable accuracy how they may interact individually, we are quite unable to predict how an individual entity will behave over a period of time in interaction with all the other entities which may influence it. It may, however, be possible to make predictions about measurable properties of the whole collection of these entities (e.g. the temperature of a cloud of gas). These properties are generalizations of the statistical properties of the vast number of interacting entities.

'Categorical laws', such as those which govern the behaviour of colliding billiard balls, allow reversal of cause and effect: if a set of moving billiard balls were to be stopped, then set in motion again with equal and opposite velocities and spins, then, in due course, these balls should retrace, in reverse sequence, the events which led to the situation at the moment of reversal. On the other hand, no such reversibility is possible with statistical laws. Schrödinger (1959) gives, as an analogy of a statistical process, the act of shuffling a pack of cards: this may be predicted to disorganize the pack after it has been arranged, numerically and in suits, but it would hardly be predicted that one could also reverse the process, 'unshuffle' the cards, and restore the original ordered state. It is thus the statistical laws, not the categorical ones, which determine the fact that time has a direction of flow, an arrow (see Schrödinger 1959), as clearly embodied in the law of increasing entropy (a statistical law). In organisms that possess mechanisms for inductive inference, we see a means whereby constant features of the world (regularities, particularly those which determine categorical laws), are retained as memories, whereas the fluctuating episodes governed by chance are disregarded. If we have any innate *a priori* knowledge, in the Kantian sense, it is knowledge that there *are* regularities in the world. What these regularities may be is not specified *a priori*. That is for us to discover. The capacity for inductive inference is, in a sense, the ultimate in biological negative feedback: in a world ultimately doomed to the cold death of total disorder, we, as conscious beings have a mechanism for preserving records of those regular and constant associations, which are not subject to caprice, and the continual erosion of time. The Designer of Brains seems also to have been a reader of hymn books:

> Change and decay in all around I see;
> O Thou that changeth not, Abide with me.

Was Hume really as sceptical as is often made out? Concerning the Cartesians his sarcasm is thinly veiled:

> There is a species of scepticism, antecedent to all study and philosophy, which is much inculcated by Descartes and others as a sovereign preservative against error and precipitate judgement. It recommends an universal doubt, not only of all our former opinions and principles, but also of our faculties; of whose veracity, say they, we must assure ourselves, by a chain of reasoning deduced from some original principle which cannot possibly be fallacious or deceitful. But neither is there any such original principle, which has a prerogative above others, that are self-evident and convincing: or, if there were, could we advance a step beyond it, but by the use of those very faculties of which we are supposed to be already diffident. The Cartesian doubt, therefore were it ever possible to be attained by any human creature (as it plainly is not), would be entirely incurable; and no reasoning could ever bring us to a state of assurance and conviction upon any subject.

Concerning Custom and Habit, he writes without pejorative implications (see p. 8), and he even uses the word 'contiguity' in much the same way as have learning theorists in the present century. He was obviously curious about the inner working of the mind which could so exemplify his philosophical ideas:

> The thinking on any object readily transports the mind to what is contiguous, but it is only the actual presence of an object that transports it with a superior vivacity. When I am a few miles from home, whatever relates to it touches me more nearly than when I am two hundred leagues distant; though even at that distance the reflecting on any thing in the neighbourhood of my friends or family naturally produces an idea of them.

Although he had no difficulty accepting that there were inner happenings in the mind, he could not accept that these gave access to any *a priori* knowledge:

> All belief of matter of fact or real existence is derived merely from some object, present to the memory or senses, and a customary conjunction between that and some other object.

Had Hume lived in the post-Darwinian era, he might have accepted more easily that we had, as individuals, some *a priori* knowledge of the nature of the world (as explained above), though, as members of an evolving species this knowledge was initially acquired empirically by our interaction with the environment. We had best accept Hume's own description of his philosophical position—that of mitigated scepticism (see *An Enquiry Concerning Human Understanding*, from which the above quotations were also taken).

8.3. Psychophysical parallelism—a reappraisal

In Chapter 1, the philosophical position which was expounded rested fundamentally upon a desire to give an important status to acts of introspection, and at the same time to allow observational science to proceed without the logical possibility that the internal reality revealed by such acts can interfere with the systems we are observing. It was claimed that this philosophical position—psychophysical parallelism—was of particular use for the purposes of this book, namely, in analysis and resynthesis of the biological mechanisms which might underlie conscious processes. In support of this claim it is now appropriate to review some of the ways in which psychophysical parallelism *has* been useful, or, to put it another way, to review points in the argument which were made more easily on account of our faculty for introspection. Amongst these points we may include.

(i) The all-embracing idea that conscious processes are an integrated whole.

(ii) The notion that 'meaning' corresponds to 'abstract structure' which we can to some extent analyse in our minds.

(iii) The idea that some aspects of our learning depend on positive and negative reinforcement, which correspond to inner experiences of reward and punishment.

(iv) The feeling we have of freedom with regard to initiation of actions, i.e. that acts in our behavioural repertoire need not be tied to a particular stimulus, but can be initiated at times we feel to be appropriate.

(v) The feeling we have that certain classes of goals or motives should have predominance at a particular time, as guides for our behaviour (e.g. feelings of hunger, thirst, etc.).

(vi) The feeling we have of differences between the process of acquisition of memory and that of searching our memory for what we have already learned (this being an apparently paradoxical notion, which led us towards a revision of the simpler theory presented in the early part of the book).

(vii) Our perception of novelty and familiarity in our environment.

(viii) The feeling that we can selectively direct our attention upon certain aspects of our experience, with the partial exclusion of others.

(ix) Our awareness of our own thought processes, and our guess that they consist of internalized combinatorial operations (when anyone observing us while we were thinking would merely record a delay before we spoke or responded).

(x) Our ability to envisage in our minds the consequences of events which have not yet been brought to pass.

(xi) Our experience of insight—that a certain problem can be solved in a certain way, even though we have never yet attempted to actually solve it in practice.

(xii) Our sense of the passage of time.

The list could easily be extended.

None of these items are observations, but depend on acts of introspection, of self-awareness of some internal process. In the first instance they derive from my own acts of introspection, as indeed they should, since I have direct experience only of the workings of my own mind. In using such items I have, however, been helped and guided by a large variety of chance phrases I have come across, in speech and writing, and by a number of well-worn phrases in the English language, all used to identify experiences common to the user. This has lead me to the belief that many of the experiences of which I have first hand awareness, are experienced and reported in a broadly similar form by others who care to exercise their introspective powers. I therefore trust that, in using such ideas as those listed above, I am not being totally solipsistic. Nevertheless, I do recognize that introspection is a fickle source of information, and that there can be quite radical disagreement between different subjects about the description of internal occurrences in similar external conditions. An attempt has therefore been made to limit the use of ideas based on introspection mainly to cases which are fairly fundamental and where some consensus between subjects appears to exist. Given this proviso, the claim that introspection provides insight into brain function, available from no other source, receives some support. Likewise the fruitfulness and usefulness of the philosophy of psychophysical parallelism, if not its ultimate veracity, has been upheld, especially since many aspects of the theory constructed with the help of this philosophy can be tested experimentally, regardless of the philosophical beliefs of the experimenter.

In Section 7.3 brief consideration was given to the suggestion that introspection may be an objectively investigable phenomenon. In this, the experimental approach is to identify those internal states which an animal or human could use as cues for initiation of behaviour. Experimental evidence clearly shows that at least some internal states fall within this category, in animals as well as in man. Although no specific explanation of the evidence can at present be given there is no clear reason to think that this evidence, and the instances of introspection listed above, require radical restructuring of the theoretical constructs presented here. Suppose, that at some future time, we actually had an empirically based explanation of all those processes, then it could be argued that we would have abolished the need for a dualist philosophy. Introspection would no longer be the mystical unanalysed process by means of which the parallelism between subjective and objective information in the brain could be established. All acts of introspection could be expressed in terms of objective observations of behaviour and brain state, and could be explained as relationships between observables. If, in the present state of knowledge, we can look forward with confidence in the belief that all these matters have a potential scientific explanation, should we not here and now abandon the dualist philosophy in favour of some form of materialism?

In my view this would not be justified. Dualist philosophies, including psychophysical parallelism, will still have a legitimate claim for allegiance from philosophically minded people, including both non-scientists and specialists in brain research. I believe this for three reasons.

(i) Although some acts of introspection may be given a good scientific explanation, I find it inconceivable that all aspects of human introspection could ever come within the direct grasp of observational science. (I may be proved wrong here if there is a real breakthrough in parapsychological investigations.) No matter what colossal expenditures we go to, I do not believe we could ever establish objectively the crucial internal states which constitute all types of inner awareness in the living human brain. It is likely, therefore, that we must carry on, as before, trusting to acts of introspection (with some reservations) as being the only source (though not an infallible source) of certain types of information. The ultimate nature of that of which we are spectators in these acts of introspection must remain, as before, an unanalysable *a priori*.

(ii) It is easy, when amongst specialists in neuroscience, to imagine that everyone has similar interests. In fact, of course, the vast majority of mankind has far more pressing concerns than the explanation in objective terms of acts of introspection. Their interests are as valid as ours. In many walks of life the philosophy of psychophysical parallelism, or perhaps some other dualist philosophy, is of more use than is a materialist philosophy in its pure and rigorous form. Consider some of the following professions: lawyer, doctor, nurse, priest, psychiatrist, poet, novelist, composer. We may think we can do without the services of some of these, but not without that of all of them. For all of these professions, and many more, a fundamental assumption is made that either the professionals themselves, or their clients, have knowledge of inner feelings within their own minds. Many of the roles of doctors even depend upon this, rather than on the laboratory measurements of scientific medicine. Communal recognition of our capacity for introspection is thus an essential part of the fabric of any human society, and as such, is a far more fundamental aspect of our existence than the specialized ideas and philosophies of neuroscientists. If it is at all possible to carry out neuroscientific research using the same basic context of ideas as the rest of our fellow human beings find useful, it is, for pragmatic reasons, important that we should try to do so.

(iii) If we think, that by explaining acts of introspection, we are 'explaining them away', that is, dispensing with the need for further acts of introspection, we are cutting ourselves off from the vital creative drive upon which science, amongst other human endeavours, depends. We are thus abandoning part of our scientific heritage. When Dalton put forward his theory of atoms, or Kekulé his concept of the structure of aromatic carbon compounds, or Van t'Hoff his notions about asymmetrical carbon atoms, these suggestions existed in the first place as mental constructs, rather than as publically demonstrable or measurable facts. It is of course true that the widespread acceptance of these scientists' ideas came about by rigorous experimentation. Ultimately, such objective demonstrations depend on acts of measurement—a method of assessment which is operationally defined and therefore does not depend on major idiosyncracies of subjective judgements. The success of science is amply illustrated by the large number of parameters which we are now able to measure, in a way which demands no participation of the human mind other than the appreciation of the concept of number. However all of these measurable parameters existed initially as mental constructs. Dalton's atoms existed for a century in this form before their discrete nature could be demonstrated by direct experiment. Wegener's theory of continental drift was despatched to a scientific limbo for half a century, until methods were found for measuring the relevant geomorphological variables. Was Wegener's mistake that he was right at the wrong time? Even such a simple variable as temperature existed, from time immemorial, as a mental construct—the subjective awareness of degrees of cold and heat—long before it was even thought of measuring it.

In short, we cannot dispense with acts of introspection in the future, we cannot do so now, and it is a misreading of the history of science to think they did not occur in the past.

In Western science Galileo has the reputation of being the first to emphasize observation, quantitative measurement, and mathematical relationships between variables. It is easy to idealize Galileo as the formulator of a foolproof method for scientific study. In fact, Galileo was not consistent in application of a method. On occasion, he would infer conclusions which observation would not have confirmed, without performing the relevant experiment, and he sometimes explained observable facts from premises which were subsequently abandoned (see Shea 1972). Presumably he used the faculties he had been endowed with to the best of his ability. Who could do more? In so far as he advanced a method for scientific study it was not demonstrably the correct method in his day. Galileo's enormous significance lies not so much in that be formulated *the* correct scientific method, but rather that a great deal of his approach has stood the test of time. Galileo's achievement was an important step in evolution of a scientific method, and that process of evolution is, of course, still in progress.

It has not escaped the author that many of the arguments used in this chapter and elsewhere in this book are relevant not only to matters of scientific fact and theory, but also to matters of value. The theories we have about human nature may be used to justify the way we behave towards one another. If we have unduly simple ideas we will tend to degrade human nature. Arguments about learning theory conducted in purely psychological terms can easily have such an effect. As a purely theoretical exercise amongst academics, such debates can of course be very instructive. However, they have not always been confined in this way, but are used to formulate descriptions of how humans can or should behave in actual practice. There is, however, likely to be such a large gap between theory and practice that dangerously unrealistic expectations of human behaviour may result. For instance, positive and negative reinforcers certainly influence human behaviour; but it is quite naïve to think that they can be used with this intent, without the human concerned becoming aware of the intentions, and showing resistance.

Behaviour of man and animals is a complex universe. We cannot describe behaviour without initial theoretical constructs, and any observations, described in terms of these constructs, naturally tend to support the theories rather than refute them. In such a subject, arguments become similar to the disputations of medieval schoolmen. They are essentially circular, which in itself is not objectionable, except that they purport not to be. The only way in which such disputations can be anchored to more secure ground is by framing them in biological terms, because biological observations do not depend upon psychological theory.

A purely biological approach to human nature leads to equally dangerous simplifications. If we were to think that there was nothing worth saying about human beings, other than could be expressed in terms of the unambiguous observations of the neuroanatomists, electrophysiologists or neurochemists, we would be denying the existence of fundamental aspects of human nature, including of course the active curiosity of the experimenter who makes the observations. Despite the importance of strictly biological observations, they allow no understanding of the functioning of the whole brain and the consciousness it embodies. To keep biological observations segregated away from psychological ideas is part of the regrettable process, to which C. P. Snow has drawn attention, by which our culture is divided into two mutually isolated factions (Snow 1960).

The notion of determinism, as applied to human behaviour, is easily misconstrued, again with dangerous implications. Determinism is not a scientific fact, nor yet a testable scientific hypothesis. It is of the same status as the causality principle itself, or the theory of evolution. It determines the way we think. In fact, as argued in Section 8.2., it is the way we have evolved to think.

It is thus the philosophy which underlies the scientific approach to the nervous system. In none of these three examples—causal regularity in the physical world, determinism in the central nervous system, and organic evolution—is the philosophy testable, because of the complexity of the real world compared to the simplified situations which the scientist deliberately chooses for his study. Thus, though we may believe in determinism as a philosophical principle, logically necessary to us as scientists, nevertheless, in practice we cannot predict individual human behaviour. Any understanding we can have of the intact human must be of a different type altogether.

The concept of free-will has not arisen from scientific observation of any kind. It arises in the first instance, *from the universal human experience of involvement in the decisions we take*. Such an experience is of an entirely different category from scientific observations that might be made about human beings. It is also of a different category from the philosophy of determinism which arises from the scientific way of thinking. It is not valid, therefore, to counterpose the philosophy of determinism with the experience of freewill, as though the latter necessarily implied that mind could override the constraints of physical laws. The experience of 'free exercise of one's will' is valid, as an experience, whatever the nature of the processes occurring in our brains. There need be no conflict between ideas of 'free-will' and 'determinism'. They arise from entirely different ground rules of assumptions, concerning different forms of reality. The objective counterpart of free-will (the *experience* of volition) would seem to be the enormous *opportunity* or *potentiality* for using a wide range of sensorimotor relationships in highly flexible fashion, rather than a frank evasion of physical laws.

Both the words 'consciousness' and 'voluntary' action, when used loosely, contain hidden within themselves the false assumption that both are all or none phenomena. The present analysis of these two suggests, in contrast, that they are both matters of degree. It has been stressed repeatedly that integration of the cognitive aspects of consciousness is relative rather than absolute. Similarly 'voluntariness' may be defined as the *degree* to which the total strategy of response of an organism is matched to the total sensory situation the organism is placed in. Again this is not an all or none property, and there can be many levels of 'voluntariness', even amongst 'healthy' and 'well integrated' persons. If, however, we wish to preserve the assumption that consciousness and freewill are all or none phenomena, we can only do so by concluding that they are philosophical abstractions, or ideals, which are never to be met with in practice. In much the same way the physicist uses the concept of a frictionless surface to aid clarity of thought, though he never encounters such a surface in practice.

At various points in this book the word 'holism' or 'holistic' has been used. Its use was connected entirely with theoretical scientific issues. However these words, in etymological origin, have a quite definite evaluative component to their meaning—and have the same derivation as the words healthy and holy. Why should these two components of meaning become linked together in the same word? From all that has been said in earlier chapters, we can form some kind of answer to this question, and suggest ways in which holistic function of the brain constitutes health, and departures from this are more or less unhealthy. If there are barriers which prevent different aspects of our experience from interacting with one another, and combining to create new syntheses in our minds, we cannot really say that we learn from experience. If there are such barriers we cannot adequately reckon with reality, and we will not be able to adapt flexibly to aspects of reality which challenge and disturb hitherto accepted assumptions. This applies certainly to disturbances coming from without, and, with some qualifications, also to those coming from within. In the brain sciences in particular, we are not adequately reckoning with reality unless we acknowledge both the inner and the outer realities of human nature. When it is said that consciousness is an idealized property of the brain to which individuals approximate to greater or lesser extent, this is not just a scientific statement. The degree to which we approximate that ideal is an indication of health, at least in some of its aspects.

One specific aspect of this health, in my view, lies in how we approach the business of understanding. We should be interested in more than binary decisions between the absolute truth and absolute falsehood of a statement. In some shape, we should be prepared to accept induced conclusions when they are delivered to our consciousness. Along with this, we have to accept that there is a valid category of understanding called *belief*. We should try to establish in our minds a carefully constructed hierarchy of degrees of belief. We cannot accomplish this unless we acknowledge the existence of, and take interest in the operations of the internal realities lying secret within each of us. Knowledge having the appearance of certainty may then emerge from our beliefs, provided we have sufficient confidence in our capacity to believe, and in the strength of specific beliefs, to state them and let them be tested. If we set out only interested in certain knowledge, and reject subjective intuitions on the grounds of their fallibility, we will end up with neither beliefs nor knowledge.

References

Ades, H. W. and Raab, D. H. (1949). Effects of pre-occipital and temporal decortication on learned visual discrimination in monkeys. *J. Neurophysiol.* **12**, 101–8.

Adey, W. R., Segundo, J. P., and Livingston, R. B. (1957). Corticofugal influences on intrinsic brainstem conduction in cat and monkey. *J. Neurophysiol.* **20**, 1–16.

Agid, Y., Javoy, F., and Glowinski, J. (1973). Hyperactivity of remaining dopaminergic neurons after partial destruction of the nigro–striatal dopaminergic system in the rat. *Nature: New Biology* **245**, 150–1.

Ahlenius, S. and Engel, J. (1971). Behavioural and biochemical effects of L-DOPA after inhibition of dopamine β hydroxylase in reserpine pretreated rats. *Naunyn-Schmiedebergs Arch. exp. Path. Pharmak.* **270**, 349–60.

Airapetyants, E. SH. and Sotnichenko, T. S. (1967). The limbic cortex, its connectivity and visceral analysers. *Prog. Brain Res.* **27**, 293–304.

Akert, K. and Andersson, B. (1951). Experimenteller Beitrag zur Physiologie des Nucleus caudatus. *Acta physiol. scand.* **22**, 281–98. [In German]

Amaral, D. G. and Foss, J. A. (1975). Locus coeruleus lesions and learning. *Science, N.Y.* **188**, 377–8.

—— Routtenberg, A. (1975). Locus coeruleus and intracranial self-stimulation: a cautionary note. *Behav. Biol.* **13**, 331–8.

Andén, N-E., Dahlström, A., Fuxe, K., and Larsson, K. (1966). Functional role of the nigro–neostriatal dopamine neurons. *Acta pharmac. tox.* **24**, 263–74.

Andersen, P. (1975). Organization of hippocampal neurons and their interconnections. In *The hippocampus*, Vol. I (ed. R. L. Isaacson and K. L. Pribram) pp. 155–75. Plenum Press, New York, London

—— Andersson, S. A. (1968). *Physiological basis of the alpha rhythm.* Appleton-Century Crofts, New York.

—— Sundberg, S. H., Sveen, O., and Wigström, H. (1978). Specific long-lasting potentiation of synaptic transmission in hippocampal slices. *Nature, Lond.* **266**, 736–7.

Anlezark, G. M., Crow, T. J., and Greenway, A. P. (1973). Impaired learning and decreased cortical norepinephrine after bilateral locus coeruleus lesions. *Science, N.Y.* **181**, 682–4.

Arluison, M., Agid, Y., and Javoy, F. (1978). Dopaminergic nerve endings in the neostriatum of the rat. *Neuroscience* **3**, 657–83.

Balsara, J. J., Jadhav, J. H., and Chandorkar, A. G. (1979). Effect of drugs influencing central serotonergic mechanisms on haloperidol-induced catalepsy. *Psychopharmacology* **62**, 67–9.

Banerjee, U. (1971). Acquisition of conditioned avoidance response in rats under the influence of addicting drugs. *Psychopharmacologia* **22**, 133–43.

Baranyi, A. and Fehér, O. (1978). Conditioned changes of synaptic transmission in motor cortex of the cat. *Exp. Brain Res.* **33**, 283–98.

Barasi, S. (1979). Response of substantia nigra neurones to noxious stimulation. *Brain Res.* **171**, 121–30.

Barker, J. L. (1976). Peptides: roles in neural excitability. *Physiol. Rev.* **56**, 435–52.

Baudry, M. and Lynch, G. (1979). Regulation of glutamate receptors by cations. *Nature, Lond.* **282**, 748–50.

Bawin, S. M., Gavalas-Medici, R. J., and Adey, W. R. (1973). Effects of modulated very high frequency fields on specific brain rhythms in cats. *Brain Res.* **58**, 365–84.

Beckstead, R. M. (1979). An autoradiographic examination of corticocortical and subcortical projections of the mediodorsal-projection (prefrontal) cortex in the rat. *J. comp. Neurol.* **184**, 43–62.

—— Domesick, V. B., and Nauta, W. J. H. (1979). Efferent connections of the substantia nigra and ventral tegmental area in the rat. *Brain Res.* **175**, 191–218.

Bedard, P., Parkes, J. D., and Marsden, C. D. (1977). Nomifensine in Parkinson's disease. *Br. J. clin. Pharmac.* **4**, 187–90.

Bennett, T. L. (1975). The electrical activity of the hippocampus and processes of attention. In *The hippocampus*, Vol. II (ed. R. L. Isaacson and K. L. Pribram) pp. 71–99. Plenum Press, New York.

—— Hébert, P. N., and Moss, D. E. (1973). Hippocampal theta activity and the attention component of discrimination learning. *Behav. Biol.* **8**, 173–81.

Berger, B., Thierry, A. M., Tassin, J. P., and Moyne, M. A. (1976). Dopaminergic innervation of the rat prefrontal cortex: a fluorescence histochemical study. *Brain Res.* **106**, 133–45.

Bernheimer, H., Birkmayer, W., Hornykiewicz, O., Jellinger, K., and Seitelberger, F. (1973). Brain dopamine and the syndromes of Parkinson and Huntington: clinical, morphological and neurochemical correlations. *J. Neurol. Sci.* **20**, 415–55.

Beurle, R. L. (1956). On the properties of a mass of cells capable of regenerating pulses. *Phil. Trans. R. Soc. B* **240**, 55–94.

Beyerchen, A. D. (1977). *Scientists under Hitler*. Yale University Press, New Haven.

Bird, E. D., MacKay, A. V. P., Rayner, C. N., and Iversen, L. L. (1973). Reduced glutamic-acid-decarboxylase activity of post-mortem brain in Huntington's chorea. *Lancet* **i**, 1090–2.

Birkmayer, W. (1978). Long term treatment with L-Deprenyl. *J. Neural Transm.* **43**, 239–44.

Björklund, A. and Lindvall, O. (1975). Dopamine in dendrites of substantia nigra neurons: suggestions for a role in dendritic terminals. *Brain Res.* **83**, 531–7.

Black, A. H. (1975). Hippocampal electrical activity and behaviour. In *The hippocampus, Vol. II* (ed. R. L. Isaacson and K. L. Pribram) pp. 129–68. Plenum Press, New York.

Blake, D. (1974). Electrophysiological mapping of cortico–caudate projections of the cat. *Fedn Proc. Fedn Am. Socs exp. Biol.* **33**, 342.

—— Zarzecki, P., and Somjen, G. G. (1976). Electrophysiological study of corticocaudate projections in cats. *J. Neurobiol.* **7**, 143–56.

Blakemore, C. and Mitchell, D. E. (1973). Environmental modification of the visual cortex and the neural basis of learning and memory. *Nature, Lond.* **241**, 467–8.

Bliss, T. V. P., Burns, B. D., and Uttley, A. M. (1968). Factors affecting the conductivity of pathways in the cerebral cortex. *J. Physiol., Lond.* **195**, 339–67.

Blodgett, H. C. (1929). The effect of introduction of reward upon the maze performance of rats. *Univ. Calif. Publs Psychol.* **4**, 113–34.

Blum, K. and Geller, I. (1969). Facilitation of brain stimulation with para-chlorophenylalanine. *Fedn Proc. Fedn Am. Socs exp. Biol.* **28**, 794.

Blumenthal, A. L. (1977). *The process of cognition*. Prentice-Hall, Englewood Cliffs, New Jersey.

Botwinick, C. Y., Quartermain, D., Freedman, L. S., and Hallock, M. F. (1977). Some characteristics of behaviour induced by FLA-63, an inhibitor of dopamine beta hydroxylase. *Pharmacol. Biochem. Behav.* **6**, 487–91.

Brady, J. V. and Conrad, D. G. (1960). Some effects of limbic system self-stimulation upon conditioned emotional behaviour. *J. comp. physiol. Psychol.* **53**, 128–37.

Brain, W. R. (1957). Hughlings Jackson's ideas of consciousness in the light of today. In *The Brain and its functions: a symposium*, pp. 83–91. Blackwell, Oxford.

Braitenberg, V. (1978). Cortical architectonics: general and areal. In *Architectonics of the cerebral cortex* (ed. M. A. B. Brazier and H. Petsche) pp. 443–65. Raven Press, New York.

Brindley, G. S. (1969). Nerve net models of plausible size that perform many simple learning tasks. *Proc. R. Soc. B.* **174**, 173–91.

—— (1973). Sensory effects of electrical stimulation of the visual and paravisual cortex in man. In *Handbook of sensory physiology*, Vol VII/3 Part B (ed. R. Jung) pp. 583–94. Springer, Berlin.

Broadbent, D. E. (1958). *Perception and communication*. Pergamon Press, Oxford.

Brodal, A. (1969). *Neurological anatomy in relation to clinical medicine*, 2nd edn. Oxford University Press, New York.

Broekkamp, C. L. E. and Van Rossum, J. M. (1974). Effects of apomorphine on self-stimulation behaviour. *Psychopharmacologia* **34**, 71–80.

Brooks, B. and Jung, R. (1973). Neuronal physiology of the visual cortex. In *Handbook of sensory physiology*, Vol. VII/3 Part B (ed. R. Jung) pp. 325–440. Springer, Berlin.

Brown, A. G. and Gordon, G. (1977). Subcortical mechanisms concerned in somatic sensation. *Br. med. Bull.* **33**, 121–8.

Brown, M. W. and Horn, G. (1978). Context dependent neuronal responses recorded from hippocampal region of trained monkeys. *J. Physiol, Lond.* (proceedings) **282**, 15P–16P.

Browning, M., Dunwiddie, T., Bennett, W., Gispen, W., and Lynch, G. (1979). Synaptic phosphoproteins: specific changes after repetitive stimulation of the hippocampal slice. *Science, N.Y.* **203**, 60–2.

Brozovski, T. J., Brown, R. M., Rosvold, H. E., and Goldman, P. S. (1979). Cognitive deficit caused by regional depletion of dopamine in prefrontal cortex of rhesus monkey. *Science, N.Y.* **205**, 931–3.

Buchwald, N. A., Wyers, E. J., Lauprecht, C. W., and Heuser, G. (1961). The 'caudate spindle': IV. A behavioural index of caudate-induced inhibition. *Electroenceph. clin. Neurophysiol.* **13**, 531–7.

Bucy, P. C. and Case, T. J. (1937). Athetosis. II. Surgical treatment of unilateral athetosis. *Archs Neurol. Psychiat., Chicago* **37**, 983–1020.

Bunge, M. (1977). Emergence and the mind. *Neuroscience* **2**, 501–9.

Bureš, J. and Burešova, O. (1960*a*). The use of Leão's spreading cortical depression in research on conditioned reflexes. *Electroenceph. clin. Neurophysiol. Suppl.* **13**, 359–76.

—— —— (1960*b*). The use of Leão's spreading depression in the study of interhemispheric transfer of memory traces. *J. comp. physiol. Psychol.* **53**, 558–63.

—— —— (1963). Cortical spreading depression as a memory disturbing factor. *J. Comp. physiol. Psychol.* **56**, 268–72.

—— —— and Fifkova, E. (1964). Interhemispheric transfer of a passive avoidance reaction. *J. comp. physiol. Psychol.* **57**, 326–30.

Burns, B. D. (1968). *The uncertain nervous system*. Edward Arnold, London.

Cajal, S. Ramon Y. (1911). *Histologie du système nerveux de l'homme et des vertébrés*, Vol. II, p. 590. A. Maloine, Paris. [In French.]

Calas, A., Besson, M. J., Gaughy, C., Alonso, G., Glowinski, J., and Chéramy, A. (1976). Radioautographic study of in vivo incorporation of ^{3}H monoamines in cat caudate nucleus: identification of serotoninergic fibres. *Brain Res.* **118**, 1–13.

Carman, J. B., Cowan, W. M., and Powell, T. P. S. (1963). The organization of the cortico–striate connexions in the rabbit. *Brain* **86**, 525–62.

Chomsky, N. (1971). *Chomsky: selected readings* (ed. J. P. B. Allen and P. Van Buren). Oxford University Press, New York.

Chronister, R. B. and White, L. E. (1975). Fiberarchitecture of the hippocampal formation: anatomy, projections, and structural significance. In *The hippocampus*,

Vol. I (ed. R. L. Isaacson and K. L. Pribram), pp. 9–39. Plenum Press, New York.

Collier, T. J., Kurtzman, S., and Routtenberg, A. (1977). Intracranial self-stimulation derived from entorhinal cortex. *Brain Res.* **137**, 188–96.

Colonnier, M. and Sas, E. (1978). An anterograde degeneration study of the tangential spread of axons in cortical areas 17 and 18 of the squirrel monkey (*Saimiri sciurus*). *J. comp. Neurol.* **179**, 245–62.

Constantinidis, J., Bartholini, G., Tissot, R., and Pletscher, A. (1968). Accumulation of dopamine in the parenchyma after decarboxylase inhibition in the capillaries of the brain. *Experientia* **24**, 130–1.

Corbett, D. and Wise, R. A. (1979). Intracranial self-stimulation in relation to the ascending noradrenergic fibre systems of the pontine tegmentum and caudal midbrain: a moveable electrode mapping study. *Brain Res.* **177**, 423–36.

—— Skelton, R. W., and Wise, R. A. (1977). Dorsal noradrenergic bundle lesions fail to disrupt self-stimulation from the region of locus coeruleus. *Brain Res.* **133**, 37–44.

Corrodi, H., Fuxe, K., and Ungerstedt, U. (1971). Evidence for a new type of dopamine receptor stimulating agent. *J. Pharm. Pharmac.* **23**. 989–91.

—— —— Ljungdahl, A., and Ögren, S.-O. (1970). Studies on the action of some psychoactive drugs on central noradrenaline neurones after inhibition of dopamine-β-hydroxylase. *Brain Res.* **24**, 451–70.

Costa, E. and Meek, J. L. (1974). Regulation of biosynthesis of catecholamines and serotonin in the CNS. *A. Rev. Pharmac.* **14**, 491–511.

Costall, B. and Naylor, R. J. (1974*a*). Stereotyped and circling behaviour induced by dopaminergic agonists after lesions of midbrain raphe nuclei. *Eur. J. Pharmacol.* **29**, 206–22.

—— —— (1974*b*). Specific asymmetric behaviour induced by the direct chemical stimulation of neostriatal dopaminergic mechanisms. *Naunyn-Schmiedebergs Arch. exp. Path. Pharmak.* **285**, 83–98.

—— —— Neumeyer, J. L. (1975). Differences in the nature of stereotyped behaviour induced by apomorphine derivatives in rat, and their actions in extrapyramidal and meso-limbic brain areas. *Eur. J. Pharmacol.* **31**, 1–16.

—— —— Marsden, C. D., and Pycock, C. (1976). Serotonergic modulation of the dopamine response from the nucleus accumbens. *J. Pharm. Pharmac.* **28**, 523–6.

Cotzias, G. C., Mena, I., Papavasiliou, P. S., and Mendes, J. (1974). Unexpected findings with apomorphine and their possible consequences. *Adv. Neurol.* **5**, 295–300.

Creese, I. and Iversen, S. D. (1972). Amphetamine response in rat after dopamine neurone destruction. *Nature: New Biology* **238**, 247–8.

Creutzfeldt, O. D. (1978). The neocortical link: thoughts on the generality of structure and function on the neocortex. In *Architectonics of the cerebral cortex* (ed. M. A. B. Brazier and H. Petsche) pp. 357–83. Raven Press, New York.

Crossman, A. R., Sambrook, M. A., Gergies, S. W., and Slater, P. (1977). The neurological basis of motor asymmetry following unilateral 6-hydroxydopamine brain lesions in the rat: the effect of motor decortication. *J. Neurol. Sci.* **34**, 407–14.

Crow, T. J. (1968). Cortical synapses and reinforcement—a hypothesis. *Nature, Lond.* **219**, 736–7.

—— (1972*a*). Catecholamine-containing neurones and electrical self-stimulation: I. A review of some data. *Psychol. Med.* **2**, 414–21.

—— (1972*b*). Catecholamine-containing neurones and electrical self-stimulation: a theoretical interpretation and some psychiatric implications. *Psychol. Med.* **3**, 66–73.

—— (1978). An evaluation of the dopamine hypothesis of schizophrenia. In *The biological basis of schizophrenia* (ed. G. Hemmings and W. A. Hemmings) pp. 63–78. MTP Press, Lancaster.

—— (1979). What is wrong with dopaminergic transmission in schizophrenia? *Trends Neurosci.* **1**, 53–5.

—— Wendlandt, S. (1976). Impaired acquisition of a passive avoidance response after lesions induced in the locus coeruleus by 6-hydroxydopamine. *Nature, Lond.* **259**, 42–4.

—— Spear, P. J., and Arbuthnott, G. W. (1972). Intracranial self-stimulation with electrodes in the region of locus coeruleus. *Brain Res.* **36**, 275–83.

Crowne, D. P. and Radcliffe, D. D. (1975). Some characteristics and functional relations of the electrical activity of the primate hippocampus and hypotheses of hippocampal function. In *The hippocampus*, Vol. II (ed. R. L. Isaacson and K. L. Pribram) pp. 185–206. Plenum Press, New York.

Cummings, J. P. and Felten, D. L. (1979). A raphe dendrite bundle in the rabbit medulla. *J. comp. Neurol.* **183**, 1–24.

Davies, J. A., Jackson, B., and Redfern, P. H. (1974). The effect of amantadine, L-DOPA, (+)-amphetamine and apomorphine on the acquisition of the conditioned avoidance response. *Neuropharmacology* **13**, 199–204.

Deadwyler, S. A., West, J. R., Cotman, C. W., and Lynch, G. (1975). Physiological studies of the reciprocal connections between the hippocampus and the entorhinal cortex. *Expl Neurol.* **49**, 35–57.

de Caro, G., Massi, M., and Micossi, L. G. (1978). Antidipsogenic effect of intracranial injections of substance P in rats. *J. Physiol., Lond.* **279**, 133–40.

Dennis, M. and Whitaker, H. A. (1976). Language acquisition following hemidecortication: linguistic superiority of the left over the right hemisphere. *Brain Lang.* **3**, 404–33.

Descarries, L., Watkins, K. C., and Lapierre, Y. (1977). Noradrenergic axon terminals in the cerebral cortex of rat: III Topometric ultrastructural analysis. *Brain Res.* **133**, 197–222.

Descartes, R. (1964) (first published 1937). Discours de la méthode. In *Descartes: philosophical writings*. (Translated from French and edited by E. Anscombe and P. T. Geach). Nelson, Sidney.

Deutsch, J. A. (1963). Learning and electrical self-stimulation of the brain. *J. theor. Biol.* **4**, 193–214.

—— (1979) Drive—another point of view. *Trends Neurosci.* **2**, 242–3.

—— Di Cara, L. (1967). Hunger and extinction in intracranial self-stimulation. *J. comp. physiol. Psychol.* **63**, 344–7.

Dismukes, K. (1977). New look at the aminergic nervous system. *Nature, Lond.* **269**, 557–8.

Di Chiara, G., Camba, R., and Spano, P. F. (1971). Evidence for inhibition by brain serotonin of mouse killing behaviour in rats. *Nature, Lond.* **233**, 272–3.

Dru, D. and Walker, J. B. (1976). CNS recovery of function: serial lesion effects. *Adv. Psychobiol.* **3**, 193–218.

Duvoisin, R. C. (1974). Variations in the 'on–off' phenomenon. *Adv. Neurol.* **5**, 339–40.

—— Heikkila, R. E., and Manzine, L. (1978). Circling induced by dopamine uptake inhibitors. *J. Pharm. Pharmac.* **30**, 714–16.

Edelman, G. M. (1978). Group selection and phasic reentrant signaling: a theory of higher brain function. In *The mindful brain*. MIT Press, Cambridge, Mass.

Ehrlich, Y. H., Rabjohns, A., and Routtenberg, A. (1977). Experimental input alters the phosphorylation of specific proteins in brain membrane. *Pharmacol. biochem. Behav.* **6**, 169–74.

Eimas, P. D., Siqueland, E. R., Jusczyk, P., and Vigorito, J. (1971). Speech perception in infants. *Science, N.Y.* **171**, 303–6.

Elazar, Z. and Adey, W. R. (1967). Spectral analysis of low frequency components in the electrical activity of the hippocampus during learning. *Electroenceph. clin. Neurophysiol.* **23**, 225–40.

Ernst, A. M. (1967). Mode of action of apomorphine and dexamphetamine on gnawing compulsion in rats. *Psychopharmacologia* **10**, 316–23.

Evans, W. O. (1967). The dimensional bases of stimulus generalization. In *Foundations of conditioning and learning* (ed. G. A. Kimble) pp. 320–36. Appleton-Century Crofts, New York.

Evarts, E. V. (1973). Motor cortex reflexes associated with learned movement. *Science, N.Y.* **179**, 501–3.

Faull, R. L. M. and Mehler, W. R. (1978). The cells of origin of nigrotectal, nigrothalamic and nigrostriatal projections in the rat. *Neuroscience* **3**, 989–1002.

Fetz, E. E. (1969). Operant conditioning of cortical unit activity. *Science, N.Y.* **163**, 955–7.

Fibiger, H. C., Fibiger, H. P., and Zis, A. P. (1973). Attenuation of amphetamine-induced motor stimulation and sterotypy by 6-hydroxydopamine in the rat. *Br. J. Pharmacol.* **47**, 683–92.

Flemenbaum, A. (1979). Failure of apomorphine to induce dopamine receptor hypersensitivity. *Psychopharmacology* **62**, 175–80.

Forman, D. and Ward, J. W. (1957). Response to electrical stimulation of caudate nucleus in cats in chronic experiments. *J. Neurophysiol.* **20**, 230–44.

Fowler, H. (1965). *Curiosity and exploratory behaviour*. Macmillan, New York.

Fulginiti, S., Molina, V. A., and Orsingher, O. A. (1976). Inhibition of catecholamine biosynthesis and memory processes. *Psychopharmacology* **51**, 65–9.

Fuxe, K. and Jonsson, G. (1974). Further mapping of central 5-hydroxytryptamine neurons: studies with the neurotoxic dihydroxytryptamines. *Adv. biochem. Psychopharmacol.* **10**, 1–13.

Gallistel, C. R. (1973). Self-stimulation: the neurophysiology of reward and motivation. In *The Physiological basis of memory* (ed. J. A. Deutsch) pp. 176–267. Academic Press, New York.

Garcia-Rill, E., Hull, C. D., Levine, M. S., and Buchwald, N. A. (1978). The spontaneous firing patterns of forebrain neurones: IV. Effects of bilateral frontal cortical ablations on firing of caudate, globus pallidus and thalamic neurones. *Brain Res.* **165**, 23–36.

Gastaut, H. (1958). Some aspects of the neurophysiological basis of conditioned reflexes and behaviour. In *Neurological basis of behaviour* (ed. G. E. W. Wolstenholme and C. M. O'Connor) pp. 255–72. Ciba Foundation Symposium, 1958. Churchill, London.

Gavalas, R. J., Walter, D. O., Hamer, J., and Adey, W. R. (1970). Effect of low-level, low-frequency electric fields on EEG and behaviour in *Macaca nemestrina*. *Brain Res.* **18**, 491–501.

Gazzaniga, M. S. (1978). Is seeing believing: notes on clinical recovery. In *Recovery from brain damage* (ed. S. Finger) pp. 409–14. Plenum Press, New York.

Geffen, L. B., Jessell, T. M., Cuello, A. C., and Iversen, L. L. (1976). Release of dopamine from dendrites in rat substantia nigra. *Nature, Lond.* **260**, 258–60.

German, D. C. and Bowden, D. M. (1974). Catecholamine systems as the neural substrate for intracranial self-stimulation: a hypothesis. *Brain Res.* **73**, 381–419.

Geschwind, N. (1965*a*). Disconnexion syndromes in animals and man. Part 1, *Brain* **88**, 237–94.

—— (1965*b*) Disconnexion syndromes in animals and man. Part 2, *Brain* **88**, 585–644.

Gibson, S., McGeer, E. G., and McGeer, P. L. (1970). Effect of selective inhibition of tyrosine and tryptophan hydroxylases on self-stimulation in the rat. *Expl Neurol.* **27**, 283–90.

Graeff, F. G. (1974). Tryptamine antagonists and punished behaviour. *J. Pharmac. exp. Ther.* **189**, 344–50.

Goldman, P. S. and Nauta, W. J. H. (1977). Columnar distribution of cortico–cortical fibres in the frontal association, limbic, and motor cortex of the developing rhesus monkey. *Brain Res.* **122**, 393–413.

Grahame-Smith, D. G. (1971). Studies *in vivo* on the relationship between brain tryptophan, brain 5-HT synthesis and hyperactivity in rats treated with a monoamine oxidase inhibitor and L-tryptophan. *J. Neurochem.* **18**, 1053–66.

Grantyn, R., Margnelli, M., Mancia, M., and Grantyn, A. (1973). Post-synaptic potentials in the mesencephalic and pontomedullary reticular regions, underlying descending limbic influences. *Brain Res.* **56**, 107–21.

Grastyán, E., Lissák, K., Mádarász, I., and Donhoffer, H. (1959). Hippocampal electrical activity during the development of conditioned reflexes. *Electroenceph. clin. Neurophysiol.* **11**, 409–30.

Graybiel, A. M. and Ragsdale, C. W. (1978). Histochemically distinct compartments in the striatum of human, monkey, and cat demonstrated by acetyl-thiocholinesterase staining. *Proc. natn. Acad. Sci., U.S.A.* **75**, 5723–6.

Green, A. R. and Grahame-Smith, D. G. (1974). The role of brain dopamine in the hyperactivity syndrome produced by increased 5-hydroxytryptamine synthesis in rats. *Neuropharmacology* **13**, 949–59.

Green, J. D. (1964). The hippocampus. *Physiol. Rev.* **44**, 561–608.

Green, T. K. and Harvey, J. A. (1974). Enhancement of amphetamine action after interruption of ascending serotonergic pathways. *J. Pharmac. exp. Ther.* **190**, 109–17.

Gross, C. G., Rocha-Miranda, C. E., and Bender, D. B. (1972). Visual properties of neurons in inferotemporal cortex of the macaque. *J. Neurophysiol.* **35**, 96–111.

Haigler, H. J. and Aghajanian, G. K. (1977). Serotonin receptors in the brain. *Fedn Proc. Fedn Am. Socs exp. Biol.* **36**, 2159–64.

Hamburg, M. D. and Kerr, A. (1976). DDC-induced retrograde amnesias prevented by injections of dl-DOPS. *Pharmacol. Biochem. Behav.* **5**, 499–501.

Harper, R. M. (1971) Frequency changes in hippocampal electrical activity during movement and tonic immobility. *Physiol. Behav.* **7**, 55–8.

Harris, R. T. and Balster, R. L. (1971). An analysis of the function of drugs in the stimulus control of operant behaviour. In *Stimulus properties of drugs* (ed. T. Thompson and R. Pickens) pp. 111–32. Appleton-Century Crofts, New York.

Harter, M. R. (1967). Excitability cycles and cortical scanning: a review of two hypotheses of central intermittency in perception. *Psychol. Bull.* **68**, 47–58.

Hattori, T., Fibiger, H. C., McGeer, P. L., and Maler, L. (1973). Analysis of the fine structure of dopaminergic nigrostriatal projection by electron microscopic autoradiography. *Expl Neurol.* **41**, 599–611.

Hayward, J. N. (1977). Functional and morphological aspects of hypothalamic neurones. *Physiol. Rev.* **57**, 574–658.

Heath, C. J. (1978). The somatic sensory neurons of pericentral cortex. In *International review of physiology. Neurophysiology III, Vol. 17* (ed. R. Porter) pp. 193–237. University Park Press, Baltimore.

Hebb, D. O. (1949). *The organization of behaviour.* John Wiley, New York.

—— (1958). *A textbook of psychology.* W. B. Saunders, Philadelphia.

Hilgard, E. R. and Marquis, D. G. (1964) *Conditioning and learning.* Methuen, London.

Hillarp, N.-A., Fuxe, K., and Dahlström, A. (1966). Demonstration and mapping of central neurons containing dopamine, noradrenaline and 5-hydroxytryptamine and their reactions to psychopharmaca. *Pharmac. Rev.* **18**, 727–41.

Hirsch, H. V. and Spinelli, D. N. (1970). Visual experience modifies distribution of horizontally and vertically oriented receptive fields in cats. *Science, N.Y.* **168**, 869–71.

Hjorth-Simonsen, A. (1972). Projection of the lateral part of the entorhinal area to the hippocampus and fascia dentata. *J. comp. Neurol.* **146**, 219–32.

—— Jeune, B. (1972). Origin and termination of the hippocampal perforant path in the rat, studied by silver impregnation. *J. comp. Neurol.* **144**, 215–32.

Hobson, J. A., McCarley, R. W., and Wyzinski, P. W. (1975). Sleep cycle oscillation: reciprocal discharge by two brainstem neuronal groups. *Science, N.Y.* **189**, 55–8.

Hockman, C. H., Lloyd, K. G., Farley, I. J., and Hornykiewicz, O. (1971). Experimental midbrain lesions: neurochemical comparison between the animal model and Parkinson's Disease. *Brain Res.* **35**, 613–18.

Hoebel, B. G. and Teitelbaum, P. (1962). Hypothalamic control of feeding and self-stimulation. *Science, N.Y.* **135**, 375–7.

Hoffer, B. J., Siggins, G. R., Oliver, A. P., and Bloom, F. E. (1971). Cyclic AMP mediation of norepinephrine inhibition in rat cerebellar cortex: a unique class of synaptic responses. *Ann. N.Y. Acad. Sci.* **185**, 531–49.

Hökfelt, T., Ljungdahl, A., Fuxe, K., and Johansson, O. (1974). Dopamine nerve terminals in the rat limbic cortex: aspects of the dopamine hypothesis of schizophrenia. *Science, N.Y.* **184**, 177–9.

Hole, K., Fuxe, K., and Jonsson, G. (1976). Behavioural effects of 5,7-dihydroxytryptamine lesions of ascending 5-HT pathways. *Brain Res.* **107**, 385–99.

Howarth, C. I. and Deutsch, J. A. (1962). Drive decay: the cause of fast 'extinction' of habits learned for brain stimulation. *Science, N.Y.* **137**, 35–6.

Hubel, D. H. and Wiesel, T. N. (1962). Receptive fields, binocular interaction and functional architecture in the cat's visual cortex. *J. Physiol., Lond.* **160**, 106–54.

Hull, C. D., Levine, M. S., Buchwald, N. A., Heller, A., and Browning, R. A. (1974). The spontaneous firing pattern of forebrain neurones: I. The effects of dopamine and non-dopamine depleting lesions on caudate unit firing patterns. *Brain Res.* **73**, 241–62.

Hull, C. L. (1932). The goal-gradient hypothesis and maze learning. *Psychol. Rev.* **39**, 25–43.

Hume, D. (1965, first published 1740). *An abstract of a treatise of human nature* (ed. J. M. Keynes and P. Sraffa). Archon Books, Hamden, Conn.

—— (1977, first published 1748). *An enquiry concerning human understanding* (ed. E. Steinberg). Hackett, Indianapolis.

Hydén, H. (1959). Biochemical changes in glial cells and nerve cells. In *Fourth International Congress of Biochemistry*, Vol. 3 (ed. F. Brache) pp. 64–89. Pergamon Press, Oxford.

—— (1960). The neuron. In *The cell: biochemistry, physiology, morphology*, Vol. IV (ed. J. Brachet and A. E. Mirsky) pp. 215–323. Academic Press, New York.

Hyvärinen, J. (1966). Analysis of spontaneous spike potentials activity in developing rabbit diencephalon. *Acta. physiol. scand. Suppl.* **278**, 8–67.

—— Poranen, A. (1974). Function of the parietal associative area 7 as revealed from cellular discharges in alert monkeys. *Brain* **97**, 673–92.

Imig, T. J. and Adrian, H. O. (1977). Binaural columns in the primary field (A1) of the cat auditory cortex. *Brain Res.* **138**, 241–52.

Innocenti, G. M. and Frost, D. O. (1979). Effects of visual experience on the maturation of the efferent system to the corpus callosum. *Nature, Lond.* **280**, 231–4.

Isaacson, R. L. (1974). *The limbic system*, p. 61. Plenum Press, New York.

Jacobs, B. L. and Cohen, A. (1976). Differential behavioural effects of lesions of the median or dorsal raphe nuclei in rats: open field and pain-elicited aggression. *J. comp. physiol. Psychol.* **90**, 102–8.

—— Simon, S. M., Ruimy, D. D., and Trulson, M. E. (1977). A quantitative rotational model for studying serotonergic function in the rat. *Brain Res.* **124**, 271–81.

Jahns, R. (1976). Different projections of cutaneous thermal inputs to single units of the midbrain raphe nuclei. *Brain Res.* **101**, 355–61.

Jalfre, M. and Haefely, W. (1971). Effects of some centrally acting agents in rats after intraventricular injections of 6-hydroxydopamine. In *6-Hydroxydopamine and catecholamine neurons* (ed. T. Malmfors and H. Thoenen) pp. 333–46. North Holland, Amsterdam.

James, W. (1890). *The principles of psychology*. Henry Holt, New York.

John, E. R. (1967). *Mechanisms of memory*. Academic Press, New York.

—— Shimokocki, M., and Bartlett, F. (1969). Neural readout from memory during generalization. *Science, N.Y.* **164**, 1534–6.

Jones, E. G. and Powell, T. P. S. (1969). Connexions of the somatic sensory cortex of the rhesus monkey. I. Ipsilateral cortical connexions. *Brain* **92**, 477–502.

—— Coulter, J. D., and Hendry, S. H. C. (1978). Intracortical connectivity of architectonic fields in the somatic sensory, motor and parietal cortex of monkeys. *J. comp. neurol.* **181**, 291–348.

—— —— Burton, H., and Porter, R. (1977). Cells of origin and terminal distribution of corticostriatal fibers arising in the sensory-motor cortex of monkeys. *J. comp. Neurol.* **173**, 53–80.

Jouvet, M. (1972). The role of monoamine- and acetylcholine-containing neurones in the regulation of the sleep-waking cycle. *Ergebn. Physiol.* **64**, 166–307.

Jung, R. and Hassler, R. (1960). The extrapyramidal motor system. In *Handbook of physiology*; Section I (Neurophysiology) Vol. II (ed. H. W. Magoun) pp. 863–927. Williams and Wilkins, Baltimore.

Justesen, D. R., Sharp, J. C., and Porter, P. B. (1963). Self-stimulation of the caudate nucleus by instrumentally naïve cats. *J. comp. physiol. Psychol.* **56**, 371–4.

Kaas, J. H., Lin, C. S., and Wagor, E. (1977). Cortical projections of posterior parietal cortex in owl monkeys. *J. comp. Neurol.* **171**, 387–408.

Kant, I. (1934, first published in 1781). *Critique of pure reason* (translated by J. M. D. Meiklejohn). Dent, London.

Kasamatsu, T. and Pettigrew, J. D. (1976). Depletion of brain catecholamines: failure of ocular dominance shift. *Science, N.Y.* **194**, 206–9.

Kawamura, K. (1973). Corticocortical fibre connections of the cat cerebrum. *Brain Res.* **51**, 41–60.

Keene, J. J. (1975). Reward-associated excitation and pain-associated inhibition lasting seconds, in rat medial pallidal units. *Expl Neurol.* **49**, 97–114.

—— (1978). Affect-related unit activity in forebrain. *Fedn Proc. Fedn Am Socs exp. Biol.* **37**, 2246–50.

Kelemen, K. and Bovet, D. (1961). Effect of drugs upon the defensive behaviour of rats. (Effect of strychnine, compound 1757 I.S., amphetamine and chlorpromazine.) *Acta physiol. hung.* **19**, 143–54.

Kelly, J. S. (1975). Microiontophoretic application of drugs onto single neurons. In *Handbook of psychopharmacology*, Vol. 2 (ed. L. L. Iversen, S. D. Iversen, and S. H. Snyder) pp. 29–67. Plenum Press, New York.

Kemp, J. M. (1968). An electronmicroscopic study of the termination of afferent fibres in the caudate nucleus. *Brain Res.* **11**, 464–7.

—— Powell, T. P. S. (1970). The cortico–striate projection in the monkey. *Brain* **93**, 525–46.

Kendler, H. H. (1946). The influence of simultaneous hunger and thirst drives upon learning of two opposed spatial responses of the white rat. *J. exp. Psychol.* **36**, 212–20.

Kennard, M. A. (1944). Experimental analysis of the functions of the basal ganglia in monkeys and chimpanzees. *J. Neurophysiol.* **7**, 127–48.

Kent, E. and Grossman, S. P. (1969). Evidence for a conflict interpretation of anomalous effects of rewarding brain stimulation. *J. comp. physiol. Psychol.* **69**, 381–90.

Kimble, D. P. (1969). Possible inhibitory functions of the hippocampus. *Neuropsychologia* **7**, 235–44.

Klawans, H. L., Goetz, C., Volkman, P., Nauseida, P. A., and Weiner, W. J. (1978). Lergotrile in the treatment of Parkinsonism. *Neurology, Minneap.* **28**, 699–702.

Klemm, W. R. (1971). EEG and multi-unit activity in limbic and motor systems during movement and immobility. *Physiol. Behav.* **7**, 337–43.

—— (1976). Hippocampal EEG and information processing: a special role for the theta rhythm. *Prog. Neurobiol.* **7**, 197–214.

Köhler, W. (1927). *The mentality of apes.* Harcourt Brace, New York. [Translated from German by E. Winter.]

—— (1938). In *A source book of Gestalt psychology* (ed. W. D. Ellis). Routledge and Kegan Paul, London.

Konorski, J. (1967). *Integrative activity of the brain: An interdisciplinary approach.* University of Chicago Press.

Kostowski, W., Giacalone, E., Garattini, S., and Valzelli, L. (1968). Studies on behavioural and biochemical changes in rats after lesion of midbrain raphe. *Eur. J. Pharmacol.* **4**, 371–6.

Kramis, R. C., Vanderwolf, C. H., and Bland, B. H. (1975). Two types of hippocampal rhythmic slow activity in both the rabbit and the rat: relations to behaviour and effects of atropine, diethylester urethane and pentobarbital. *Expl Neurol.* **49**, 58–85.

Künzle, H. and Akert, K. (1977). Efferent connections of cortical area 8 (frontal eye field) in *Macaca fascicularis.* A reinvestigation using the autoradiographic technique. *J. comp. Neurol.* **173**, 147–64.

Lashley, K. S. (1950). In search of the engram. *Symp. Soc. exp. Biol.* **4**, 454–82.

Laursen, A. M. (1963). Corpus striatum. *Acta. physiol. scand.* Suppl. **211**, 1–106.

Laverty, R. (1974). On the roles of dopamine and noradrenaline in animal behaviour. *Prog. Neurobiol.* **3**, 31–70.

Legendy, C. R. (1978). Cortical columns and the tendency of neighbouring neurons to act similarly. *Brain Res.* **158**, 89–105.

Lemon, R. N. and Porter, R. (1976). Afferent input to movement-related precentral neurones in conscious monkeys. *Proc. R. Soc. B* **194**, 313–39.

LeVay, S., Stryker, M. P., and Shatz, C. J. (1978). Ocular dominance columns and their development in layer IV of the cat's visual cortex: a quantitative study. *J. comp. Neurol.* **179**, 223–44.

Levick, W. R. (1972). Receptive fields of retinal ganglion cells. In *Handbook of sensory physiology*, Vol. VII/2 (ed. M. G. F. Fuortes) pp. 531–66. Springer, Berlin.

Leviel, V., Chéramy, A., and Glowinski, J. (1979). Role of the dendritic release of dopamine in the reciprocal control of the two nigro-striatal dopaminergic pathways. *Nature, Lond.* **280**, 236–9.

Levine, M. S., Hull, C. D., and Buchwald, N. A. (1974). Pallidal and entopeduncular intracellular response to striatal, cortical, thalamic and sensory inputs. *Expl Neurol.* **44**, 448–60.

Lewis, M. S., Molliver, M. E., Morrison, J. H., and Lidov, H. G. W. (1979). Complementarity of dopaminergic and noradrenergic innervation in cingulate cortex of the rat. *Brain Res.* **164**, 328–33.

Libet, B. (1973). Electrical stimulation of cortex in human subjects, and conscious sensory aspects. In *Handbook of sensory physiology*, Vol. II (ed. A. Iggo) pp. 743–90. Springer, Heidelberg.

—— Kobayashi, H., and Tanaka, T. (1975). Synaptic coupling into the production and storage of a neuronal memory trace. *Nature, Lond.* **258**, 155–7.

Liddell, E. G. T. and Phillips, C. G. (1940). Experimental lesions in the basal ganglia of the cat. *Brain* **63**, 264–74.

Lieb, J. P., Walsh, G. O., Babb, T. L., Walter, R. D., and Crandall, P. H. (1976). A comparison of EEG seizure patterns recorded with surface and depth electrodes in patients with temporal lobe epilepsy. *Epilepsia* **17**, 137–60.

Llinás, R. (1970). Neuronal operations in cerebellar transactions. In *The neurosciences: second study program* (ed. F. O. Schmitt) pp. 409–26. Rockefeller University Press, New York.

Lloyd, K. G., Davison, L., and Hornykiewicz, O. (1975). The neurochemistry of Parkinson's disease: effect of L-DOPA therapy. *J. Pharmac. exp. Ther.* **195**, 453–64.

Lorens, S. A. and Guldberg, H. C. (1974). Regional 5-hydroxytryptamine following selective midbrain raphe lesions in the rat. *Brain Res.* **78**, 45–56.

—— —— Hole, K., Köhler, C., and Srebro, B. (1976). Activity, avoidance learning, and regional 5-hydroxytryptamine following intra-brainstem 5,7-dihydroxytryptamine and electrolytic midbrain raphe lesions in the rat. *Brain Res.* **108**, 97–113.

Lucki, I. and Harvey, J. A. (1979). Increased sensitivity to d- and l-amphetamine action after midbrain raphe lesions, as measured by locomotor activity. *Neuropharmacology* **18**, 24–50.

Lund, R. D., Mitchell, D. E., and Henry, G. H. (1978). Squint-induced modification of callosal connections in cats. *Brain Res.* **144**, 169–72.

Luria, A. R. (1973). *The working brain*. Penguin, London.

Lynch, G. S., Dunwiddie, T., and Gribkoff, V. (1978). Heterosynaptic depression: a post-synaptic correlate of long-term potentiation. *Nature, Lond.* **266**, 737–9.

McEntee, W. J. and Mair, R. G. (1978). Memory impairment in Korsakoff's psychosis: a correlation with brain noradrenergic activity. *Science, N.Y.* **202**, 905–7.

McGonigle, B. O. and Chalmers, M. (1977). Are monkeys logical? *Nature, Lond.* **267**, 694–6.

MacKay, D. M. (1978). Selves and brains. *Neuroscience* **3**, 599–606.

MacMurray, J. (1935). *Reason and emotion*. Faber and Faber, London.

McNaughton, B. L., Douglas, R. M., and Goddard, G. V. (1978). Synaptic enhancement in fascia dentata: cooperativity among coactive afferents. *Brain. Res.* **157**, 272–93.

Maddison, S. (1977). Intraperitoneal and intracranial cholecystokinin depress operant responding for food. *Physiol. Behav.* **19**, 819–24.

Maillis, A. G. (1974). Interneuronal activity as a factor interfering with the interpretation of results from microiontophoretic studies. *Neuropharmacology* **13**, 487–94.

Malliani, A. and Purpura, D. P. (1967). Intracellular studies of the corpus striatum. II Patterns of synaptic activities in lenticular and entopenduncular neurons. *Brain Res.* **6**, 341–54.

Margules, D. L. and Olds, J. (1962). Identical 'feeding' and 'rewarding' systems in the lateral hypothalamus of rats. *Science, N.Y.* **135**, 374–5.

Mark, R. (1974). *Memory and nerve cell connections*. Oxford University Press, London.

Marks, P. C., O'Brien, M., and Paxinos, G. (1977). 5,7-DHT-induced muricide: inhibition as a result of preoperative exposure of rats to mice. *Brain Res.* **135**, 383–8.

Marr, D. (1970). A theory of cerebral neocortex. *Proc. R. Soc. B* **176**, 161–234.

Marsden, C. D., Merton, P. A., Morton, H. B., and Adam, J. (1977). The effect of lesions of the sensorimotor cortex and the capsular pathways on servo responses from human long thumb flexor. *Brain* **100**, 503–26.

Mason, S. T. (1978). Parameters of the dorsal bundle extinction effect: previous extinction experience. *Pharmacol. Biochem. Behav.* **8**, 655–9.

—— Fibiger, H. C. (1978). Noradrenaline and partial reinforcement in rats. *J. comp. physiol. Psychol.* **92**, 1110–18.

—— Iversen, S. D. (1974). Learning impairment in rats after 6-hydroxydopamine-induced depletion of brain catecholamines. *Nature, Lond.* **248**, 697–8.

—— —— (1975). Learning in the absence of forebrain noradrenaline. *Nature, Lond.* **258**, 422–4.

—— —— (1977). An investigation of the role of cortical and cerebellar noradrenaline in associative motor learning in the rat. *Brain Res.* **134**, 513–27.

—— —— (1979). Theories of the dorsal bundle extinction effect. *Brain Res.* **180**, 107–37.

Mason, W. A. and Harlow, H. F. (1959). Initial responses of infant rhesus monkeys to solid foods. In *Explorations in exploration: stimulation seeking* (ed. D. Lester) pp. 97–101. Van Nostrand, New York.

Mesulam, M. M., Van Hoesen, G. W., Pandya, D. N., and Geschwind, N. (1977). Limbic and sensory connections of the inferior parietal lobule (area PG) in the rhesus monkey: a study with a new method for horseradish peroxidase histochemistry. *Brain Res.* **136**, 393–414.

Mettler, F. A. and Mettler, C. C. (1942). The effects of striatal injury. *Brain* **65**, 242–55.

Meyers, R. (1951). Surgical experiments in the therapy of certain extrapyramidal diseases: a current evaluation. *Acta psychiat. neurol. scand. Suppl.* **67**, 9–42.

—— Sweeney, D. B. and Schwidde, J. T. (1950). Hemiballismus: aetiology and surgical treatment. *J. Neurol. Neurosurg. Psychiat.* **13**, 115–26.

Miliaressis, E., Bouchard, A., and Jacobowitz, D. M. (1975). Strong positive reward in median raphe: specific inhibition by para-chlorophenylalanine. *Brain Res.* **98**, 194–201.

Miller, J. J., Richardson, T. L., Fibiger, H. C., and McLennan, H. (1975). Anatomical and electrophysiological identification of a projection from the mesencephalic raphe to the caudate-putamen in the rat. *Brain Res.* **97**, 133–6.

Miller, R. (1975). Distribution and properties of commissural and other neurons in cat sensorimotor cortex. *J. comp. Neurol.* **164**, 361–74.

—— (1976). Schizophrenic psychology, associative learning and the role of forebrain dopamine. *Med. Hypotheses* **2**, 203–11.

Mogenson, G. J. and Stevenson, J. A. F. (1966). Drinking and self-stimulation with electrical stimulation of the lateral hypothalamus. *Exp. Brain Res.* **3**, 111–16.

Mora, F., Phillips, A. G., Koolhaas, J. M., and Rolls, E. T. (1976). Prefrontal cortex and neostriatum self-stimulation in rat: differential effects produced by apomorphine. *Brain Res. Bull.* **1**, 421–4.

Morgan, J. M. and Routtenberg, A. (1977). Angiotensin injected into the neostriatum after learning disrupts retention performance. *Science, N.Y.* **196**, 87–9.

Morgan, M. J. (1979). The concept of drive. *Trends Neurosci.* **2**, 240–1.

Morrell, F. and Jasper, H. H. (1956). Electrographic studies of the formation of temporary connections in the brain. *Electroenceph. clin. Neurophysiol.* **8**, 201–15.

Moskowitz, B. A. (1978). The acquisition of language. *Scient. Am.* **239**, 82–92.

Mountcastle, V. B. (1978). An organizing principle for cerebral function: the unit module and the distributed system. In *The mindful brain.* MIT Press, Cambridge, Mass.

—— Lynch, J. C., Georgopoulos, A., Sakata, H., and Acuna, C. (1975). Posterior parietal association cortex of the monkey: command functions for operations within extrapersonal space. *J. Neurophysiol.* **38**, 871–908.

Murray, H. G. and Heath, C. J. (1978). The spread of connections within cat primary somatic sensory cortex. *Brain Res.* **141**, 160–4.

Naito, H., Miyakawa, F., and Ito, N. (1971). Diameters of callosal fibers interconnecting cat sensorimotor cortex. *Brain Res.* **27**, 369–72.

Nakai, Y. and Takaori, S. (1974). Influence of norepinephrine-containing neurons derived from the locus coeruleus on lateral geniculate neuronal activities of cats. *Brain Res.* **71**, 47–60.

Nakamura, S. and Iwama, K. (1975). Antidromic activation of the rat locus coeruleus neurons from hippocampus, cerebral and cerebellar cortices. *Brain Res.* **99**, 372–6.

Nathanson, J. A. (1977). Cyclic nucleotides and nervous system function. *Physiol. Rev.* **57**, 127–256.

Nauta, W. J. H., Smith, G. P., Faull, R. L. M., and Domesick, V. B. (1978). Efferent connections and nigral afferents of the nucleus accumbens septi in the rat. *Neuroscience* **3**, 385–401.
Neill, D. B. and Grossman, S. P. (1970). Behavioural effects of lesions or cholinergic blockade of the dorsal and ventral caudate of rats. *J. comp. physiol. Psychol.* **71**, 311–17.
—— Herndon, J. G. (1978). Anatomical specificity within the rat striatum for the dopaminergic modulation of DRL responding and activity. *Brain Res.* **153**, 529–38.
Niki, H., Sakai, M., and Kubota, K. (1972). Delayed alternation performance and unit activity of the caudate and medial orbitofrontal gyrus in monkey. *Brain Res.* **38**, 343–53.
Nybäck, H. (1972). Effect of brain lesions and chlorpromazine on accumulation and disappearance of catecholamines formed *in vivo* from ^{14}C-tyrosine. *Acta physiol. scand.* **84**, 54–64.
Oakley, D. A. (1979*a*). Neocortex and learning. *Trends Neurosci.* **2**, 149–52.
—— (1979*b*). Learning with food reward and shock avoidance in neodecorticate rats. *Expl Neurol.* **63**, 627–42.
—— (1980). Improved instrumental learning in neodecorticate rats. *Physiol. Behav.* **24**, 357–66.
—— Russell, I. S. (1979). Instrumental learning on fixed ratio and GO–NOGO schedules in neodecorticate rats. *Brain Res.* **161**, 356–60.
Oei, T. P. and Ng, C. P. (1978). 6-Hydroxydopamine induced catecholamine depletion and passive avoidance learning in rats. *Pharmacol. Biochem. Behav.* **8**, 533–6.
Oke, A., Keller, R., Mefford, I., and Adams, R. N. (1978). Lateralization of norepinephrine in human thalamus. *Science, N.Y.* **200**, 1410–12.
O'Keefe, J. and Nadel, L. (1978). *The hippocampus as a cognitive map*. Clarendon Press, Oxford.
Olds, J. (1958). Self-stimulation of the brain. *Science, N.Y.* **127**, 315–24.
—— (1963). Mechanisms of instrumental conditioning. In *The physiological basis of mental activity* (ed. R. Hernández Peón) (*Electroenceph. clin. Neurophysiol.*, Suppl. **24**, 219–34).
—— (1965). Operant conditioning of single unit responses. In *XXIII International Congress of Physiological Sciences (Lectures and Symposia)*, Tokyo, September 1965, pp. 372–80. Excerpta Medica, Amsterdam.
—— (1977). *Drives and reinforcement*. Raven Press, New York.
—— Milner, P. (1954). Positive reinforcement produced by electrical stimulation of septal area and other regions of rat brain. *J. comp. physiol. Psychol.* **47**, 419–27.
Olds, M. E. (1975). Effects of intraventricular 6-hydroxydopamine and replacement therapy with norepinephrine, dopamine and serotonin on self-stimulation in diencephalic and mesencephalic regions in the rat. *Brain Res.* **98**, 327–42.
—— Olds, J. (1963). Approach-avoidance analysis of rat diencephalon. *J. comp. Neurol.* **120**, 259–95.
Olpe, H.-R. and Koella, W. P. (1978). The effect of some neuroleptics on the interaction of cortically and nigrally evoked potentials in the rat striatum. *Naunyn-Schmiedebergs Arch. exp. Path. Pharmak.* **303**, 165–70.
Olson, L. and Fuxe, K. (1971). On the projections from the locus coeruleus noradrenaline neurons: the cerebellar innervation. *Brain Res.* **28**, 165–71.
—— Seiger, A., and Fuxe, K. (1972). Heterogeneity of striatal and limbic dopamine innervation: highly fluorescent islands in developing and adult rats. *Brain Res.* **44**, 283–8.
Orbach, J. and Fantz, R. L. (1958). Differential effects of temporal neocortical resection on overtrained and non-overtrained visual habits in monkeys. *J. comp. physiol. Psychol.* **51**, 126–9.

Overton, D. A. (1971). Discriminative control of behaviour by drug states. In *Stimulus properties of drugs* (ed. T. Thompson and R. Pickens) pp. 87–110. Appleton-Century Crofts, New York.

—— (1978). Major theories of state dependent learning. In *Drug discrimination and state dependent learning* (ed. B. T. Ho, D. W. Richards, and D. L. Chute) pp. 283–318. Academic Press, New York.

—— Ercole, M. A., and Dutta, P. (1976). Discriminability of the postictal state produced by electroconvulsive shock in rats. *Physiol. Psychol.* **4**, 207–12.

Owen, F., Cross, A. J., Crow, T. J., Longden, A., Poulter, M., and Riley, G. J. (1978). Increased dopamine-receptor sensitivity in schizophrenia. *Lancet* **ii**, 223–6.

Pandya, D. N. and Kuypers, H. G. J. M. (1969). Corticocortical connections in the rhesus monkey. *Brain Res.* **13**, 13–26.

Park, D. M., Findley, L. J., and Teychenne, P. F. (1977). Nomifensine in Parkinsonism. *Br. J. clin. Pharmac.* **4**, 185–6.

Parton, D. A. (1976). Learning to imitate in infancy. *Child Dev.* **47**, 14–31.

Pavlov, I. P. (1927). *Conditioned reflexes: an investigation of the physiological activity of the cerebral cortex* (translated and edited by G. V. Anrep). Oxford University Press, London.

Pearlman, C. A. (1966). Similar retrograde amnesic effects of ether and spreading cortical depression. *J. comp. physiol. Psychol.* **61**, 306–8.

Pellionisz, A. and Llinás, R. (1979). Brain modelling by tensor network theory and computer simulation. The cerebellum: distributed processor for predictive coordination. *Neuroscience* **4**, 323–48.

Penfield, W. G. (1958). *The excitable cortex in conscious man.* Liverpool University Press.

—— Perot, P. (1963). The brain's record of auditory and visual experience. *Brain* **86**, 595–696.

Pettigrew, J. D. and Kasamatsu, T. (1978). Local perfusion of noradrenaline maintains visual cortical plasticity. *Nature, Lond.* **271**, 761–2.

Phillips, A. G., Mora, F., and Rolls, E. T. (1979). Intracranial self-stimulation in orbitofrontal cortex and caudate nucleus of rhesus monkey: effects of apomorphine, pimozide and spiroperidol. *Psychopharmacology* **62**, 79–82.

Phillips, C. G. (1973). Cortical localization and sensorimotor processes at the middle level in primates. *Proc. R. Soc. Med.* **66**, 987–1002.

Phillips, M. I. (1978). Angiotensin in the brain. *Neuroendocrinology* **25**, 354–77.

Phillipson, O. T. (1979). Afferent projections to the ventral tegmental area of Tsai and the interfascicular nucleus: a horseradish peroxidase study in the rat. *J. comp. Neurol.* **187**, 117–44.

Piaget, J. and Inhelder, B. (1969). *The psychology of the child.* Routledge and Kegan Paul, London. [Translated from French by H. Weaver.]

Pickel, V. M., Joh, T. H., and Reis, D. J. (1976). Monoamine synthesizing enzymes in central dopaminergic, noradrenergic and serotonergic neurons. Immunocytochemical localization by light and electron microscopy. *J. Histochem. Cytochem.* **24**, 792–806.

Piercy, M. F. (1977). Experimental studies of the organic amnesic syndrome. In *Amnesia*, 2nd edn (ed. C. W. M. Whitty and O. L. Zangwill) pp. 1–51. Butterworths, London.

Poirier, L., Filion, M., Langelier, P., and Larochelle, L. (1975). Brain nervous mechanisms involved in the so-called extrapyramidal and psychomotor disturbances. *Prog. Neurobiol.* **3**, 31–70.

Polanyi, M. (1958). *Personal knowledge.* Routledge and Kegan Paul, London.

Poletti, C., Kinnard, M., and McLean, P. (1973). Hippocampal influence on unit activity of hypothalamus, preoptic region, and basal forebrain in awake sitting squirrel monkeys. *J. Neurophysiol.* **36**, 308–24.

Popper, K. R. and Eccles, J. C. (1977). *The self and its brain: an argument for interactionism*. Springer, Berlin.

Poschel, B. P. H. and Ninteman, F. W. (1971). Intracranial reward and the forebrain's serotonergic mechanism: studies employing *para*-chlorophenylalanine and *para*-chloramphetamine. *Physiol. Behav.* **7**, 39–46.

—— —— McLean, J. R., and Potoczak, D. (1974). Intracranial reward after 5, 6-dihydroxtryptamine: further evidence for serotonin's inhibitory role. *Life Sci.* **15**, 1515–22.

Powell, D. A. and Joseph, J. A. (1974). Autonomic-somatic interaction and hippocampal theta activity. *J. comp. physiol. Psychol.* **87**, 978–86.

Powell, E. W., Akagi, K., and Hatton, J. B. (1974). Subcortical projections of the cingulate gyrus. *J. Hirnforsch.* **15**, 269–78.

Prado-Alcalá, R. A., and Cobos-Zapiaín, G. G. (1979). Interference with caudate nucleus by potassium chloride. Evidence for a 'moving' engram. *Brain Res.* **172**, 577–83.

Pujol, J. F., Keane, P., McRae, A., Lewis, B. D., and Renaud, B. (1978). Biochemical evidence for serotonergic control of the locus ceruleus. In: *Interactions between putative neurotransmitters in the brain* (ed. S. Garattini, J. F. Pujol, and R. Samanin) pp. 401–10. Raven Press, New York.

Putnam, T. J. (1940). Treatment of unilateral paralysis agitans by section of the lateral pyramidal tract. *Archs Neurol. Psychiat., Chicago* **44**, 950–76.

Raisman, G., Cowan, W. M., and Powell, T. P. S. (1966). An experimental analysis of the efferent projections of the hippocampus. *Brain* **89**, 83–108.

Ramos, A., Schwartz, E. L., and John, E. R. (1976). Stable and plastic unit discharge patterns during behavioural generalization. *Science, N.Y.* **192**, 393–6.

Ranck, J. B. (1975). Behavioural correlates and firing repertoires of neurons in the dorsal hippocampal formation and septum of unrestrained rats. In *The hippocampus*, Vol. II (ed. R. L. Isaacson and K. L. Pribram) pp. 207–46. Plenum Press, New York.

Ranje, C. and Ungerstedt, U. (1977). Lack of acquisition in dopamine denervated animals tested in an underwater Y-maze. *Brain Res.* **134**, 95–111.

Randrup, A. and Munkvad, I. (1967). Stereotyped activities produced by amphetamine in several animal species and man. *Psychopharmacologia* **11**, 300–10.

—— —— Fog, R., and Ayhan, I. H. (1975). Catecholamines in activation, stereotypy, and level of mood. In *Catecholamines and behaviour*, Vol. I (ed. A. J. Friedhoff) pp. 89–107. Plenum Press, New York.

Randt, C. T., Quartermain, D., Goldstein, M., and Anagnoste, B. (1971). Norepinephrine biosynthesis inhibition: effects on memory in mice. *Science, N.Y.* **172**, 498–9.

Rauschecker, J. P. and Singer, W. (1979). Changes in the circuitry of the kitten visual cortex are gated by post-synaptic activity. *Nature, Lond.* **280**, 656–60.

Reddington, M., Rodnight, R., and Williams, M. (1973). Turnover of protein-bound serine phosphate in respiring slices of guinea-pig cerebral cortex. Effects of putative transmitters, tetrodotoxin and other agents. *Biochem. J.* **132**, 475–82.

Rensch, B. and Rahmann, H. (1960). Einfluss des Pervitins auf das Gedächtnis von Goldhamstern. *Pflügers Arch. ges. Physiol.* **271**, 693–704. [In German, English summary.]

Revusky, S. H. and Garcia, J. (1970). Learned associations over long delays. In *The psychology of learning and motivations*, Vol. 4 (ed. G. H. Bower) pp. 1–84. Academic Press, New York.

Richardson, T. L., Miller, J. J., and McLennan, H. (1977). Mechanisms of excitation and inhibition in the nigrostriatal system. *Brain Res.* **127**, 219–34.

Rinne, V. K., Siirtola, T., and Sonninen, V. (1978). L-deprenyl treatment of on-off phenomena in Parkinson's disease. *J. Neural Transm.* **43**, 253–62.

Ritter, S. and Stein, L. (1973). Self-stimulation of noradrenergic cell group (A6) in locus coeruleus of rats. *J. comp. physiol. Psychol.* **85**, 443–52.

Roberts, D. C. S., Price, M. T. C., and Fibiger, H. C. (1976). The dorsal tegmental noradrenergic projection: an analysis of its role in maze learning. *J. comp. physiol. Psychol.* **90**, 363–72.

Robinson, T. E. and Vanderwolf, C. H. (1978). Electrical stimulation of the brainstem in freely moving rats: II. Effects on hippocampal and neocortical electrical activity and relations to behaviour. *Expl Neurol.* **61**, 485–515.

—— Kramis, R. C., and Vanderwolf, C. H. (1977). Two types of cerebral activation during active sleep: relations to behaviour. *Brain Res.* **124**, 544–9.

—— Vanderwolf, C. H., and Pappas, B. A. (1977). Are the dorsal noradrenergic bundle projections from the locus coeruleus important for neocortical or hippocampal activation? *Brain Res.* **138**, 75–98.

Rolls, E. T. (1975). *The brain and reward.* Pergamon Press, Oxford.

—— Perrett, D., Thorpe, S. J., Puerto, A., Roper-Hall, A., and Maddison, S. (1979). Response of neurons in area 7 of the parietal cortex to objects of different significance. *Brain Res.* **169**, 194–8.

Rosene, D. L. and Van Hoesen, G. W. (1977). Hippocampal efferents reach widespread areas of cerebral cortex and amygdala in the rhesus monkey. *Science, N.Y.* **198**, 315–17.

Ross, R. B. and Russell, I. S. (1964). Lateralization and one-trial interhemispheric transfer of avoidance conditioning. *Nature, Lond.* **204**, 909–10.

—— —— (1967). Subcortical storage of classical conditioning. *Nature, Lond.* **214**, 210–11.

Routtenberg, A. and Huang, Y. H. (1968). Reticular formation and brainstem unitary activity: effects of posterior hypothalamic and septal-limbic stimulation at reward loci. *Physiol. Behav.* **3**, 611–17.

Royce, G. J. (1978). Autoradiographic evidence for a discontinuous projection to the caudate nucleus from the centromedian nucleus in the cat. *Brain Res.* **146**, 145–50.

Russell, B. (1946). *History of Western Philosophy.* George Allen and Unwin, London.

Russell, I. S. and Ochs, S. (1963). Localization of a memory trace in one cortical hemisphere and transfer to the other hemisphere. *Brain* **86**, 37–54.

Sacks, O. (1974). *Awakenings.* Doubleday, New York.

Sakai, K., Touret, M., Salvert, D., and Jouvet, M. (1978). Afferents to the cat locus coeruleus and rostral raphe nuclei as visualized by the horseradish peroxidase technique. In *Interactions between putative neurotransmitters in the brain* (ed. S. Garattini, J. F. Pujol, and R. Samanin) pp. 319–42. Raven Press, New York.

Sakata, H., Takaoka, Y., Kawarasaki, A., and Shibutani, H. (1973). Somatosensory properties of neurons in the superior parietal cortex (area 5) of the rhesus monkey. *Brain Res.* **64**, 85–102.

Sasa, M. and Takaori, S. (1973). Influence of the locus coeruleus on transmission in the spinal trigeminal nucleus neurons. *Brain Res.* **55**, 203–8.

Schallert, T., Whishaw, I. Q., Ramirez, V. D., and Teitelbaum, P. (1978). Compulsive abnormal walking caused by anticholinergics in akinetic 6-hydroxydopamine-treated rats. *Science, N.Y.* **199**, 1461–3.

Schmidt, E. M., Bak, M. J., McIntosh, J. S., and Thomas, J. S. (1977). Operant conditioning of firing patterns in monkey cortical neurons. *Expl Neurol.* **54**, 467–77.

Schoenfield, R. I. (1976). Lysergic acid diethylamide- and mescaline-induced attenuation of the effect of punishment in the rat. *Science, N.Y.* **192**, 801–3.

Schrödinger, E. (1959). *Mind and matter.* Cambridge University Press.

Schultz, W. and Ungerstedt, U. (1978). Short-term increase and long-term reversion of striatal cell activity after degeneration of the nigro–striatal dopamine system. *Exp. Brain Res.* **33**, 159–71.

Segal, D. (1975). Behavioural and neurochemical correlates of repeated d-amphetamine administration. *Adv. biochem. Psychopharmacol.* **13**, 247–62.

Seggie, J. and Berry, M. (1972). Ontogeny of interhemispheric evoked potentials in the rat: significance of myelination of the corpus callosum. *Expl Neurol.* **35**, 215–32.

Seiden, L. S. and Peterson, D. D. (1968). Reversal of the reserpine-induced suppression of the conditioned avoidance response by L-DOPA: correlation of behavioural and biochemical differences in two strains of mice. *J. Pharmac. exp. Ther.* **159**, 422–8.

Sessions, G. R., Kant, G. J., and Koob, G. F. (1976). Locus coeruleus lesions and learning in the rat. *Physiol. Behav.* **17**, 853–9.

Seward, J. P. (1947). A theoretical derivation of latent learning. *Psychol. Rev.* **54**, 83–98.

Shaw, K. M., Lees, A. J., and Stern, G. M. (1978). Bromocriptine in Parkinson's disease. *Lancet* **i**, 1255.

Shaw, S. G. and Rolls, E. T. (1976). Is the release of noradrenaline necessary for self-stimulation of the brain? *Pharmacol. Biochem. Behav.* **4**, 375–9.

Shea, W. R. (1972). *Galilleo's intellectual revolution.* McMillan, London.

Sherrington, C. S. (1940). *Man on his nature – The Gifford Lectures, 1937–8.* Cambridge University Press.

Shinkman, P. G., Bruce, C. J., and Pfingst, B. E. (1974). Operant conditioning of single-unit response patterns in visual cortex. *Science, N.Y.* **184**, 1194–6.

Siegel, A. and Tassoni, J. P. (1971). Differential efferent projections from the ventral and dorsal hippocampus of the cat. *Brain Behav. Evol.* **4**, 185–200.

Simon, H., Le Moal, M., and Cardo, B. (1975). Self-stimulation in the dorsal pontine tegmentum in the rat. *Behav. Biol.* **13**, 339–47.

—— —— Stinus, L., and Calas, A. (1979). Anatomical relationships between the ventral mesencephalic tegmentum – A 10 region and the locus coeruleus as demonstrated by anterograde and retrograde tracing techniques. *J. Neural Transm.* **44**, 77–86.

Sloper, J. J. and Powell, T. P. S. (1978). Dendro-dendritic and reciprocal synapses in the primate motor cortex. *Proc. R. Soc. B* **203**, 23–38.

—— Hiorns, R. W., and Powell, T. P. S. (1979). A qualitative and quantitative electron microscopic study of the neurons in the primate motor and somatic sensory cortices. *Phil. Trans. R. Soc. B* **285**, 173–97.

Snow, C. P. (1960). *The two cultures and the scientific revolution. (Rede Lecture 1959).* Cambridge University Press.

Soltysik, S., Hull, C. D., Buchwald, N. A., and Fekete, T. (1975). Single unit activity in basal ganglia of monkeys during performance of a delayed response task. *Electroenceph. clin. Neurophysiol.* **39**, 65–78.

Somekh, D. E. (1976). The effect of embedded words in a brief visual display. *Br. J. Psychol.* **67**, 529–35.

Spanis, C. W., Haycock, J. W., Handwerker, M. J., Rose, R. P., and McGaugh, J. L. (1977). Impairment of retention of avoidance responses in rats by post-training diethyldithiocarbamate. *Psychopharmacology* **53**, 213–15.

Spinelli, D. N. and Jensen, F. E. (1979). Plasticity: the mirror of experience. *Science, N.Y.* **203**, 75–7.

Srebro, B. and Lorens, S. A. (1975). Behavioural effects of selective midbrain raphe lesions in the rat. *Brain Res.* **89**, 303–25.

Stafekhina, V. S. and Vinogradova, O. S. (1978). Characteristics of the hippocampal cortical input. Functional differences between lateral and medial entorhinal areas. *Neurosci. behav. Physiol.* **9**, 8–14.

St Laurent, J., Leclerc, R. R., Mitchell, M. L., and Miliaressis, T. E. (1973). Effects of apomorphine on self-stimulation. *Pharmacol. Biochem. Behav.* **1**, 581–5.

Stein, L., and Beluzzi, J. D. (1979). Brain endorphins: possible role in reward and memory formation. *Fedn Proc. Fedn Am. Socs exp. Biol.* **38**, 2468–72.

—— —— and Wise, C. D. (1975). Memory enhancement by central administration of norepinephrine. *Brain Res.* **84**, 329–35.

Stephan, H., Bauchot, R., and Andy, O. J. (1970). Data on size of the brain and of various brain parts in insectivores and primates. In *Advances in primatology*, Vol. 1. *The primate brain* (ed. C. R. Noback and W. Montagna) pp. 289–97. Appleton-Century Crofts, New York.

Steranka, L. R. and Barrett, R. J. (1974). Facilitation of avoidance acquisition by lesions of the median raphe nucleus: evidence for serotonin as a mediator of shock-induced suppression. *Behav. Biol.* **11**, 205–13.

Stern, W. C., Johnson, A., Bronzino, J. D., and Morgane, P. J. (1979). Influence of electrical stimulation of the substantia nigra on spontaneous activity of raphe neurons in the anaesthetized rat. *Brain Res. Bull.* **4**, 561–5.

Stevens, D. A. and Fechter, L. D. (1969). The effects of *para*-chlorophenylalanine, a depletor of brain serotonin on behaviour: (ii) Retardation of passive avoidance learning. *Life Sci.*, **8**, 379–85.

Struble, R. G., Desmond, N. L., and Levy, W. B. (1978). Anatomical evidence for interlamellar inhibition in the fascia dentata. *Brain Res.* **152**, 580–5.

Studdert-Kennedy, M. and Shankweiler, D. (1969). Hemispheric specialization for speech perception. *J. acoust. Soc. Am.* **48**, 579–94.

Stutz, R. M., Butcher, R. E., and Rossi, R. (1969). Stimulus properties of reinforcing brain shock. *Science, N.Y.* **163**, 1081–2.

Sutherland, N. S. and MacKintosh, N. J. (1971). *Mechanisms of animal discrimination learning*. Academic Press, New York.

Swadlow, H. A., Geschwind, N., and Waxman, S. G. (1979). Commissural transmission in humans. *Science, N.Y.* **204**, 530–1.

Sweet, R. D. and McDowell, F. H. (1974). The 'on–off' response to chronic L-DOPA treatment of Parkinsonism. *Adv. Neurol.* **5**, 331–8.

Szabadi, E. and Bradshaw, C. M. (1974). The role of physical and biological factors in determining the time course of neuronal responses. *Neuropharmacology* **13**, 537–46.

Szentágothai, J. (1978*a*). The Ferrier lecture, 1977. The neuron network of the cerebral cortex: a functional interpretation. *Proc. R. Soc. B* **201**, 219–48.

—— (1978*b*). Specificity versus (Quasi-) randomness in cortical connectivity. In *Architectonics of the cerebral cortex* (ed. M. A. B. Brazier and H. Petsche) pp. 77–98. Raven Press, New York.

Taylor, C. A. (1969). *Physics and music*. *Proc. R. Instn Gt Br.* **42**, 237–52.

Tenen, S. S. (1967). The effects of p-chlorophenylalanine, a serotonin depletor on avoidance acquisition, pain sensitivity and related behaviour in the rat. *Psychopharmacologia* **10**, 204–19.

Tennyson, V. M., Heikkila, R., Mytilineou, C., Côté, L., and Cohen, G. (1974). 5-Hydroxydopamine tagged boutons in rabbit neostriatum: interrelationship between vesicles and axonal membrane. *Brain Res.* **82**, 341–8.

Thatcher, R. W. and John, E. R. (1977). *Foundations of cognitive processes*. Lawrence Erlbaum, Hillsdale, N.J.

Thistlethwaite, D. (1951). A critical review of latent learning and related experiments. *Psychol. Bull.* **48**, 97–129.

Thompson, R. W. (1964). Transfer of avoidance learning between normal and functionally decorticate states. *J. comp. physiol. Psychol.* **57**, 321–5.

Tolman, E. C. (1932). *Purposive behaviour in animals and men*. Century Co., New York and London.

—— Honzik, C. H. (1930). Introduction and removal of reward and maze performance in rats. *Univ. Calif. Publs Psychol.* **4**, 257–75.

Towe, A. L. and Harding, G. W. (1970). Extracellular microelectrode sampling bias. *Expl Neurol.* **29**, 366–81.

Travis, R. P. and Sparks, D. L. (1963). The influence of unilateral and bilateral spreading depression during learning upon subsequent relearning. *J. comp. physiol. Psychol.* **56**, 56–9.

Tye, N. C., Everitt, B. J., and Iversen, S. D. (1977). 5-Hydroxytryptamine and punishment. *Nature, Lond.* **268**, 741–3.

Ungar, G. (1968). Molecular mechanisms in learning. *Perspect. Biol. Med.* **11**, 217–32.

Ungerstedt, U. (1971*a*). Stereotaxic mapping of the monoamine pathways in the rat brain. *Acta physiol. scand. Suppl.* **367**, 1–48.

—— (1971*b*). Striatal dopamine release after amphetamine or nerve degeneration revealed by rotational behaviour. *Acta physiol. scand. Suppl.* **367**, 49–68.

—— (1971*c*). Postsynaptic supersensitivity after 6-hydroxydopamine induced degeneration of the nigro–striatal dopamine system. *Acta physiol. scand. Suppl.* **367**, 69–93.

Valenstein, E. S. and Nauta, W. J. H. (1959). A comparison of the distribution of the fornix system in the rat, guinea-pig and monkey. *J. comp. Neurol.* **113**, 337–63.

Vanderwolf, C. H., Kramis, R., Gillespie, L. A., and Bland, B. H. (1975). Hippocampal rhythmic slow activity and neocortical low voltage fast activity: relations to behaviour. In *The hippocampus*, Vol. II (ed. R. L. Isaacson and K. L. Pribram) pp. 101–28. Plenum Press, New York.

Van Hoesen, G. W. and Pandya, D. N. (1975). Some connections of the entorhinal (area 28) and perirhinal (area 35) cortices of the rhesus monkey. I Temporal lobe afferents. *Brain Res.* **95**, 1–24.

—— Pandya, D. N. and Butters, N. (1972). Cortical afferents to the entorhinal cortex of the rhesus monkey. *Science, N.Y.* **175**, 1471–3.

—— —— —— (1975). Some connections of the entorhinal (area 28) and perirhinal (area 35) cortices of the rhesus monkey. II Frontal lobe afferents. *Brain Res.* **95**, 25–38.

Vinogradova, O. S. (1975). Functional organization of the limbic system in the process of registration of information: facts and hypotheses. In *The hippocampus*, Vol. II (ed. R. L. Isaacson and K. L. Pribram) pp. 3–69. Plenum Press, New York.

Von Voigtlander, P. F. and Moore, K. E. (1973). Involvement of nigro–striatal neurons in the *in vivo* release of dopamine by amphetamine, amantadine and tyramine. *J. Pharmac. exp. Ther.* **184**, 542–52.

Waldbillig, R. L. (1979). The role of dorsal and median raphe in the inhibition of muricide. *Brain Res.* **160**, 341–6.

Wall, P. D. (1977). The presence of ineffective synapses and the circumstances which unmask them. *Phil. Trans. R. Soc. B* **278**, 361–72.

Walshe, F. (1965). *Further critical studies in neurology and other essays and addresses*, pp. 115–42. E. and S. Livingstone, Edinburgh.

Wauquier, A. and Niemegeers, C. J. E. (1973). Intracranial self-stimulation in rats as a function of various stimulus parameters. III Influence of apomorphine on medial forebrain bundle stimulation with monopolar electrodes. *Psychopharmacologia* **30**, 163–72.

Webster, K. C. (1965). The cortico–striatal projection in the cat. *J. Anat.* **99**, 329–37.

Werner, G. and Whitsel, H. L. (1973). Functional organization of the somatosensory cortex. In *Handbook of sensory physiology*, Vol. II (ed. A. Iggo) pp. 621–700. Springer, Berlin.

Whishaw, I. Q. (1972). Hippocampal electroencephalograph activity in the Mongolian gerbil during natural behaviours and wheel running, and in the rat during wheel running and conditioned immobility. *Can. J. Psychol.* **26**, 219–39.

—— Robinson, T. E., Schallert, T., de Ryck, M., and Ramirez, V. D. (1978). Electrical activity of the hippocampus and neocortex in rats depleted of brain dopamine and norepinephine: relation to behaviour and effects of atropine. *Expl Neurol.* **62**, 748–67.

Whitaker, P. M. and Seeman, P. (1977). Hallucinogen binding to dopamine/neuroleptic receptors. *J. Pharm. Pharmac.* **29**, 506–7.

Whitfield, I. C. (1967). *The auditory pathway*. Edward Arnold, London.

Williams, M. and Rodnight, R. (1976). Protein phosphorylation in respiring slices of guinea pig cerebral cortex. *Biochem. J.* **154**, 163–70.

Wise, C. D. and Stein, L. (1969). Facilitation of brain self-stimulation by central administration of norepinephrine. *Science, N.Y.* **163**, 299–301.

Wise, R. A. (1978). Catecholamine theories of reward: a critical review. *Brain Res.* **152**, 215–47.

Witelson, S. F. (1977). Anatomic asymmetry in the temporal lobes: its documentation, phylogenesis and relationship to functional asymmetry. *Ann. N.Y. Acad. Sci.* **299**, 328–54.

Woody, C. D. and Black-Cleworth, P. (1973). Differences in excitability of cortical neurones as a function of motor projections in conditioned cats. *J. Neurophysiol.* **36**, 1104–15.

Woolsey, R. M. and Nelson, J. S. (1975). Asymptomatic destruction of the fornix in man. *Arch. Neurol.* **32**, 566–8.

Wyler, A. R. and Burchiel, K. J. (1978). Factors influencing accuracy of operant control of pyramidal tract neurons in monkey. *Brain Res.* **152**, 418–21.

Yahr, M. D. (1978). Overview of present day treatment of Parkinson's disease. *J. Neural Transm.* **43**, 227–38.

Yamamoto, T., Watanabe, S., Oishi, R., and Ueki, S. (1979). Effects of midbrain raphe stimulation and lesions on EEG activity in rats. *Brain Res. Bull.* **4**, 491–5.

Yoshida, M. and Precht, W. (1971). Monosynaptic inhibition of neurons of the substantia nigra by caudato–nigral fibres. *Brain Res.* **32**, 225–8.

—— Rabin, A., and Anderson, M. (1972). Monosynaptic inhibition of pallidal neurones by axon collaterals of caudato-nigral fibres. *Exp. Brain Res.* **15**, 333–47.

Yoshii, N. and Hockaday, W. J. (1958). Conditioning of frequency-characteristic repetitive electroencephalographic response with intermittent photic stimulation. *Electroenceph. clin. Neurophysiol.* **10**, 487–502.

Young, R. M. (1970). *Mind, brain, and adaption in the nineteenth century*, pp. 58–80. Clarendon Press, Oxford.

Zarzecki, P., Blake, D. J., and Somjen, G. G. (1977). Neurological disturbances, nigro–striate synapses and iontophoretic dopamine and apomorphine after haloperidol. *Expl Neurol.* **57**, 956–70.

Zis, A. P., Fibiger, H. C., and Phillips, A. G. (1974). Reversal by L-DOPA of impaired learning due to destruction of the dopaminergic striatal projection. *Science, N.Y.* **185**, 960–2.

Author index

Subject index